jackiestyle

jackiestyle

Introduction by
VALENTINO

Pamela Clarke Keogh

HarperCollins*Publishers*

HarperCollins books may be purchased for educational, business, or sales promotional use. For information, please write: Special Markets Department, HarperCollins Publishers Inc., 10 East 53rd Street, New York, NY 10022.

Grateful acknowledgment is made for permission to reprint "Memory of Cape Cod" by Edna St. Vincent Millay. From *Collected Poems*, HarperCollins Publishers, copyright 1923, 1951 by Edna St. Vincent Millay and Norma Millay Ellis. All rights reserved. Reprinted by permission of Elizabeth Barnett, Literary Executor.

An extension of this copyright page appears on page 254.

Designed by Lindgren/Fuller Design

Printed on Japanese Matt Art

Library of Congress Cataloging-in-Publication Data
Keogh, Pamela Clarke.
    Jackie style / Pamela Clarke Keogh. — 1st ed.
        p. cm.
    ISBN 0-06-019952-0
    1. Onassis, Jacqueline Kennedy, 1929–1994 —
    Clothing.
    2. Celebrities — United States — Biography.
    3. Presidents' spouses — United States — Biography.
    4. Fashion — United States — History — 20th
    century. I. Title.
    CT275.O552 K46 2001
    973.922'092 — dc21
    [B]   00-054031

07 /SC 10 9 8 7 6 5 4

For my sisters and best friends,
Patricia Keogh
Deirdre Keogh-Anderson
Terri Austin Keogh—
always first ladies in my book.

contents

I FIRST MET JACKIE KENNEDY in New York in 1964, only months after the president had been killed. Since her early days in the White House, everyone had perceived Jackie as the epitome of young motherhood and as an enchanting first lady who charmed not only the heads of state at home and abroad but also the citizens of the world. She was admired widely for her wit and her beauty.

But after her husband's death, people began to recognize through her unwavering dignity the breadth of her character. Few women in history have captured the imagination the way she did, and it was Jackie's courage and grace that have made her image an enduring one. She was an original, an icon. When she became my customer, I was thrilled. When she became my darling friend, I was honored. Her sense of elegance inspires me to this day.

Much has been said about Jackie's style. Her look was feminine and simple with a legendary ease. Through her example she taught American women about modern fashion. And she was imitated by everyone, something that I have seen firsthand. Whenever she wore one of my coats, or more spectacularly, when she married Aristotle Onassis wearing an ivory skirt and lace-covered sweater that I designed, we immediately had countless orders from women who wanted to emulate her. So modern in her own time, Jackie's influence over fashion is far from diminished. It has transcended time.

Quite simply, Jackie's power was to fascinate. Her manner crossed the populist with the regal, and it captivated the people who knew her well and those who felt that they had come to know her through her photographs. Once, I remember, while on a visit to Capri, Jackie said that she'd like to see my home. "Why don't we run?" she asked, slipping off her sandals. We dashed through the streets to my house, and the next day pictures of our sprint were printed in newspapers around the world.

Although she attracted so much attention, Jackie was an intensely private person. I often recall the quiet times we spent together at lunch or at tea. We'd talk about a thousand things — fashion, the people we knew, books and paintings. Of course, many people have special memories of Jacqueline Kennedy Onassis, as I think this book will illustrate. She affected those close to her and those she never knew in ways both personal and profound. She was a dynamic, extraordinary woman, and though I miss her, my memories of her make such beautiful souvenirs.

Valentino

introduction

Jackie may have been an
angel many times,
but she wasn't a saint.

— HUGH D. 'YUSHA'
AUCHINCLOSS III

prelude

S HE STANDS STRAIGHT AS A SOLDIER in the soft March sun in britches and boots, the uniform of her childhood, elegant even in riding clothes originally designed for men. Her hacking jacket fits flawlessly, perfectly cupping her shoulders. Hands in her pockets like a bemused little boy, she is at ease in the country with the horses she loves.

Her dark, smooth cap of hair is uncovered. Sunlight falls across her brow. Whatever her thoughts, they amuse her — and she keeps them to herself. She stands calmly at the center of her world, unconcerned that people are looking at her, certain that they are. In the great cities of Europe, crowds stood in the streets and cheered as she passed by.

She is the first lady of the United States, but more than that, she is an American woman: vibrant, athletic, optimistic. Her children are healthy, her husband strong. She welcomes the future. At thirty-two, standing in a Virginia field smiling peacefully to herself, she seems to have everything anyone could ever want. Like a great actress, she takes our dreams and reflects them back to us with more clarity than we could ever hope to articulate.

Jacqueline Bouvier Kennedy Onassis was known by many names, but to us she is Jackie. And although her life can be seen as one continuous act of courage, more than anything else, Jackie is associated with style.

Style as it is manifested not just in the clothes she wore (which went far to define who she was and how she wanted to be perceived), but in her homes, the people she loved, the books she read, how she responded to events and

challenges in her life, and even the causes she supported. Jackie's style is so articulated, so well thought out that it is as defined as a snapshot, as unique as a fingerprint. With her particular kind of intelligence, she resides fully in each era — from her childhood to the White House, from marriage to Aristotle Onassis to her work as a book editor — but never fails to imbue it with her own personality, her own self.

We think of her as a young mother in khakis and a white shirt, water up to her knees, twirling her daughter in Nantucket Sound. On Inauguration Day, seated beside her husband, John F. Kennedy, in an open car in a fawn-colored coat and fur muff, buoyant at the adventure they are about to embark on. And much later, dressed in black linen trousers, a silk blouse, and black ballet flats, sitting in Central Park eating an ice-cream cone, sharing secrets with her eldest granddaughter, Rose.

And what is the Jackie look? For Italian designer Valentino, it is "a mix of naturalness and sophistication, an outdoorsy kind of beauty." Bill Blass says, "No one could touch her peculiar kind of glamour. She was always appropriately dressed, never glitzy." Jackie's clothing choices mirrored the life she led, which is why her style was so authentic and why it subtly changed and developed as a reflection of where she was in the world.

Jackie's stylistic influences came from her life — East Hampton, the sea, and the beautiful homes she lived in; horses; Audrey Hepburn; the exquisite French tailoring of Hubert de Givenchy and Chanel; her love of family and books. Even when she wore the most expensive European designers, Jackie's look was never precious — it was athletic, American. As designer Cynthia Rowley observed, "Even when she was dressed for a state dinner, she had a sportiness, a casualness about her."

The intriguing thing about Jackie's style, and why it is still so present today — in fashion, in design, in culture — is that it was never static. It evolved over the years. After developing a basic style that worked for her, Jackie always moved forward as the society she lived in changed. As designer Kate Spade notes, "There were several looks that she had, and they didn't really overlap. There was definitely the sixties, the seventies, and her later years. And none of them was really much like the one before it. It was really her own look. The sixties look she had in the White House was not the same look she had when she was walking around New York in her white jeans and black t-shirt and that big hairdo, hanging out on the yacht with Aristotle Onassis; it was a different look."

Another element of style is being able to read the societal barometer; otherwise you can get stuck in the past, and that was a place Jackie never wanted to be. As a teenager she loved to waltz, rumba, and foxtrot with her stepbrother Hugh D. "Yusha" Auchincloss III. In the White House, she had her personal couturier, Oleg Cassini, teach her the twist. After a childhood spent reading Chekhov and Shaw (much of which, she admitted, was too old for her), she moved on to Shakespeare, W. B. Yeats, Jack Kerouac, Sartre, and even Deepak Chopra. Her mind, the main contributor to style, was always searching, active. Jackie would never be left behind; she knew the precise moment to put away her perfect suits and little white gloves.

Like Audrey Hepburn and Grace Kelly, fellow "Depression babies" who were also born in 1929, Jackie came along during the postwar years when Americans had the time and the wherewithal to even consider style. At first, the Kennedy political apparatus kept her in the background. With her whispery voice, faraway gaze, and love of all things French, the Boston pols considered her "exotic." She was.

They were afraid she might turn off voters. She never did.

Thirty-one years old when her husband was elected president, decades younger than her two immediate predecessors in the White House, Bess Truman and Mamie Eisenhower, Jackie was a breath of fresh air. But she was more than that, and the impact of her style reached far beyond her youth or her wardrobe choices. As the creator of Camelot ("She's the one who had the time, the desire, the taste," says Oleg Cassini), the mythical time that came to represent the glamour and grace of the Kennedy years, Jackie did something few presidents and no other first lady had ever done. She elevated America in the eyes of Europe and, more important, to ourselves. Realizing the power of symbols, she did it through style.

According to Hugh Sidey, who covered the Kennedys for *Time* magazine, "I would say that in some ways, Jackie was about as influential a woman in terms of culture as we've had in this century—intelligent, cultured, and with an eye and a sense of what needed to be done."

In addition to lifting America's profile abroad and showing the necessity of having a cultural life, Jackie made a subtler but even further-reaching impact by raising the sights not only of American women, but of women around the world. She did this by example. As we learned of her knowledge of history, her love of family, her joy in dressing well, her work on the White House restoration, we saw that Jackie tried. In making the attempt, no matter what the outcome, she encouraged others to raise their expectations and consider the art of what is possible, whatever their current situation in life.

June Weir, fashion editor at *W* and *Women's Wear Daily* when Jackie was in the White House, says, "The Kennedys truly encouraged people to try their best. This is something that has been totally lost today. Whether it was the Peace Corps, or the events they had at the White House, or the kinds of menus

that they had, or the ballet, or the people that they invited. There was always something that was trying to bring people up!"

Through the country's breathless interest in her every move, Jackie lifted the curtain on the rituals of upper-class America and disseminated them throughout all echelons of society more readily than any government social program. Through the clothing she wore, she loosened social distinctions since her style was simple and accessible to anyone. In addition to popularizing the sleeveless shift, bouffant hairdo, and pearl necklace, Jackie provided Americans with their own finishing school, exposing them to Pablo Casals, French couture, the ballet, Robert Frost, and fine cuisine.

But style is not just about choosing an outfit or decorating a room; it is also seen in the way you conduct your life. Raised in the last gasp of East Coast aristocracy, Jackie had a Puritan's sense of duty—of what one should and should not do—that Cotton Mather would appreciate. She knew what had to be done, did it, and got on with it. She didn't complain. She never lost sight of her responsibilities, which were those closest to her: her family, and after her husband died, her children. "She was a big example for her children," recalls her friend C. Z. Guest, "and no one ever talks about that. And she did it very well. I don't know anybody who did it better!"

With few exceptions, Jackie behaved impeccably. For someone forced to live more than half her life under the harsh glare of celebrity, there was little scandal associated with her—apart from a few shopping sprees in the early 1960s and 1970s (when, after all, she had every designer in the world throwing things at her). She did not pose for *Playboy*. She never wrote her memoirs. She kept her thoughts to herself, recognizing the power of discretion. "I have often regretted my speech, never my silence," said Publilius Syrus, a first-century philosopher. A sentiment Jackie surely would have agreed with.

Another facet of style is freedom; without it, there is no individuality. With her marriage to Aristotle Onassis she became Jackie O., the most famous woman in the world, and still a style leader. Society joked that she married him "for the island," but Ari gave Jackie her freedom and, for a time, she turned her back to us. Hounded by photographers, she tried to escape, as both her sunglasses and her jewelry got bigger.

During the Onassis years, Jackie showed that she was a rebel, a free spirit. She would do as she pleased, and this is what kept her from being a bore. This is also what kept the world endlessly entertained, wondering what she would do next. Jackie lived her life as much as possible below the radar screen. "One's real life," she confided, "is lived on another private level."

Once she felt that she could trust you, Jackie was a wonderful confidante. According to her lifelong friend Vivian Crespi, "You never knew when

Jackie would pop up. There were always funny phone calls. She was very unpredictable, which I loved — you never knew what was going to happen. She was always sending funny little notes on her paper."

In the last third of her life, Jackie found emotional and intellectual equilibrium in her children, close friendships, and in work. She had been a daughter, a sister, a wife, a mother, and finally, her own person. If her life were different, Jackie might have been a writer. She thought artists and writers were, as Hemingway put it, the "true Gen." "Like a lot of people," she once said, "I dreamed of writing the Great American Novel." Instead, she worked as a book editor in New York City. Although her three years in the White House and eight years as the wife of Aristotle Onassis received most of the attention in the world's psyche, she worked for close to twenty years in the publishing industry.

As a working woman, Jackie wore trousers and favored Valentino's softly draped Italian designs. She was the best-dressed woman in the world — but this was a meager compliment after what she had accomplished. For those who knew her, this emphasis on appearances overshadowed her true worth. As Vivian Crespi observes, "Frankly, I think Jackie would be horrified if she was remembered as a clotheshorse; she would have hated it!" Jackie knew that many people thought of her that way, and it rankled her. Reading a draft of Carl Sferrazza Anthony's book *First Ladies*, Jackie came upon the sentence, "If there was one sphere where Jacqueline had great influence, it was fashion." "Much to her annoyance," she scribbled in the margin.

Jackie preferred to be remembered for her work in historic preservation. Through her efforts, and by galvanizing others to join her, she restored the White House from the shabby department store it resembled in the 1940s and 1950s to its current glory. She saved Grand Central Station in New York City from the wrecking ball and, in the process, persuaded cities across the country to value their own monuments as worth saving. With a series of letters and phone calls, she saw to it that the Temple of Dendur was given to the Metropolitan Museum of Art. Through her efforts, she taught us that with single-minded focus, charm, and ingenuity, one woman can make a difference.

Today, just as she did in the White House and afterward, Jackie still influences us. In fashion, her style from the 1960s, 1970s, and beyond still resonates on the runway as classic American style. Ralph Lauren, Tom Ford, Carolina Herrera, Michael Kors, Craig Natiello for Halston, and Susan Dell all draw inspiration from the clean lines that she favored. Although most of the young designers were born years after Camelot ended and have no actual memory of her tenure in the White House, Jackie's image remains a compelling symbol of what an American woman can and should be.

June Weir thinks Jackie retains such strong influence on fashion because "we have no one today to look up to! I think the thing is that Mrs. Kennedy really and truly conducted herself with such dignity." Cynthia Rowley says, "It's interesting that her style is still so timeless — it's sort of like Jackie and Babe Paley and C. Z. Guest. No matter what happens in fashion, it's always right, it still works. What is extraordinary, particularly in fashion where every thing is change, change, change, is that Jackie is *still* held up as a great way of looking, that people still feel her influence."

In studying Jacqueline Kennedy Onassis's life, we see that fashion is just one facet of what defines Jackie Style. Like the most authentic people her style comes from her life, her history, the choices she made, and those she loved. She died young, but lived a long life — could anyone have experienced more? And there are still a great many lessons to be learned from her life.

As we shall see, Jackie Style is about courage and grace. Cherishing those closest to you. Playing hooky, taking chances, buying a Schlumberger bracelet if you feel like it. Saying no, making the best of a situation. And always, always moving forward.

Jackie was a great fan of history, recognizing that the past provides a map to our current lives. There will never be another Jackie nor, perhaps, should there be. And it does us no good to thoughtlessly mime her forty years after Camelot. But knowing her situation, her history, and the elements of her style can help us make decisions in our own lives — to make the best of our own situation, no matter what it may be. And isn't this, really, what true style is all about?

She was very dazzling,
and she made them watch.
She was like an Olympic athlete.

— PAT SUZUKI

maison blanche

On November 9, 1960, Senator John F. Kennedy of Massachusetts was elected the thirty-fifth president of the United States by 115,000 votes, the slimmest margin since Benjamin Harrison defeated Grover Cleveland in 1888. Kennedy was a fatalist by nature, if not experience, and when he went to bed at 4:30 that morning ("There's nothing more that can be done," he told Bobby), he did not know how the contest would turn out. He had done his best. Now it was up to the American people, or his father's friends in Cook County, or whoever decided these things.

Hours later, his two-and-a-half-year-old daughter, Caroline, prompted by her English nanny, Maud Shaw, marched into her parents' bedroom and woke them with a phrase she could repeat but not fully comprehend: "Good morning, Mr. President."

He was in.

That morning, Jackie did not join in the unabashed optimism at Bobby's house. Wishes came true readily for the children of Joseph P. Kennedy with none of the weight of struggle. They imagined things they could only inchoately express, and their father saw to it that their dreams, as long as they coincided with his, became reality. He was the architect of their lives. Out of the entire clan, Jackie was the first to have some dawning realization of the cost that the presidency would have on her and her little family—that there even *was* a cost. But Jackie knew, as the worldly Joseph P. did, that every success, even more than failure, had a price.

Her first instinct was to go outside, away from the Kennedys and their cockeyed sense of entitlement, to turn her back, just for now, on what was expected of her. First lady! She was barely thirty-one years old. It overwhelmed her. She threw on an old raincoat and headed out the door. Photographer Jacques Lowe looked out the window and saw her go for a walk by the sea. It had just begun to drizzle.

Lowe recalls that "although, like every family and staff member, Jackie had anticipated this moment for a long time, she seemed stunned by the realization that she was now the first lady." Lowe was the only one inside the house to notice Jackie was missing. As he watched, fascinated, a reporter rushed up to her with his hand outstretched in congratulation. "She took the hand but instantly walked on. Nobody else noticed or paid any attention to her. Everyone was too preoccupied and overwhelmed by this triumph after the three long years of reaching for it."

Jackie took a deep breath and walked along the sand, turning her back on what was expected of her. It was good to get away from the furor of the Kennedy Compound. She did not have the obvious bravado of her sisters-in-law, the "rah rah girls," she called them. At Vassar, girls like that played field hockey or ran student council. Jackie had never been a joiner, had never needed the approval of her peers. She had the quiet confidence of her intelligence and an innate sense that she could accomplish anything she set out to. With her hands deep in her coat pockets as the wind whipped at her hair, she had the passing thought that her entire life had led to this moment: walking alone on the beach at Hyannisport in her favorite raincoat, knowing her life was about to change.

Mrs. Kennedy, her mother-in-law, was fond of quoting St. Luke: "Those to whom much is given, much is expected." As she steeled herself for the days and months ahead, and the baby she was soon expecting, Jackie had her own thought: *There are no accidents.*

She knew she would have to fight for a space for herself, her children, and her husband. If she didn't, it would be impossible to maintain any kind of a normal life in the White House, with the Secret Service and all those sycophants hovering around. And the women reporters — harpies, the worst! — wanting to know what she ate, how she exercised, whose clothes she wore. Regardless of what Jack said, she would give the public what she had to and not a scintilla more. Jackie was not handing her life over to anyone for a vote or the price of a five-cent newspaper.

Since her marriage to Jack, she had seen what living in the public eye could do to you. If you were not careful, it could transform you into a caricature, a reflection of what people read in magazines. Her children, she feared, would become column fodder, written about by some hack on deadline.

"We love Jack!" She had read the signs in the towns they passed and the placards waved at the Democratic convention in Los Angeles, where he was nominated. But Americans were fickle, Jackie knew. They tore down those they admired. She didn't even like politics; she was just in it because of her husband. Winning meant so much to the Kennedys. Like so much else, it came from their father.

On the eve of World War II, Joseph P. Kennedy had had a disastrous run as American ambassador to the Court of St. James. Nevertheless, the title stuck. Back in the library at the ambassador's big house, Jacques Lowe was trying to corral the adult Kennedys and their spouses for a photo. They were all there: Jack, now called "Mr. President" ("I like the sound of that," he said, smiling. "I could get used to it."); Bobby, who had run the campaign; the ambassador and his wife, Rose, of course; and the girls.

Basking in the success of their brother, who stood in front of the fireplace, his hands characteristically half in and half out of his blazer pockets, they were an uncommonly vibrant group. Peter Lawford, the actor, was off to the side, smiling handsomely. "If there's anybody I'd hate worse than an actor as a son-in-law, it's a *British* actor," Joe had said when Pat married Lawford. But all seemed forgiven for now. The Kennedy siblings orbited Jack, the new prince, with their spouses on the periphery. All seven of the women wore pearl necklaces. The posture of those who were seated mirrored Rose: their legs crossed daintily at the ankles like the proper Manhattanville girls (well, except for Jackie, who went to that Protestant school) they were.

Within the family, everyone had their place. Bobby was the tough guy and the moral touchstone — everyone knew he would do anything for Jack; Ethel, the most athletic; Jackie, the smart one and the outsider; Joan, the pretty one. Teddy, the youngest, had none of his brothers' mettle; he did not need it — their parents' favorite, he was forgiven everything. Stephen Smith, Jean's husband, kept the secrets and, other than old Joe, was the only one who could handle money. Eunice prided herself on being most like Jack. "If that girl had been born with balls she would have been a hell of a politician," her father said admiringly. This was meant, and accepted, as a compliment.

The president-elect noticed Jackie was missing and asked for her. Told that she had gone for a walk on the beach, he went to get her. A few minutes later, he returned to the library alone. Jackie was upstairs dressing. Sipping champagne and joking about who would get to be ambassador to the French Riviera or Palm Beach, they waited.

As Lowe remembers, Jackie finally appeared, "looking radiant and quite beautiful. And whatever it was that drove her down to the beach to commune with the sea had been resolved. JFK walked over to the door and took her by the arm, and the entire family applauded her. It was a magnificent moment."

They took their places and settled down, everyone together, with the years stretched out before them. What a father they had to make all this possible! Jackie looked directly into the camera, young and proud, imagining her future, as Jacques Lowe clicked the shutter for posterity.

Jackie turned her attention to the White House. Now that she knew she would be first lady (a ridiculous title that she thought made her sound like a saddle horse), she had two concerns — making sure the White House was livable, and deciding her wardrobe.

Before the inauguration, Mrs. Eisenhower had given her a tour of the residence and Jackie could not believe the shape it was in. Richard Nelson, who was decorator Sister Parish's assistant and worked with Jackie on her Georgetown house, says the White House "was furnished by B. Altman after the 1948–49 restoration of the building by the Trumans and it was *terrible!* I mean, it looked like a hotel." He laughs at the memory of how awful the place was. "Even in the wildest dreams of Mrs. Kennedy, it would never work!" Jackie thought the White House looked ridiculous, says Oleg Cassini. "The food, the whole atmosphere was very, very middle class."

While resting in Palm Beach after the birth of her son, John Jr., on November 25, 1960, Jackie had a conversation with J. B. West, the head White

House usher (a concierge, of sorts, of the residence), and asked him to send her any current photographs he had of the rooms so that she could make preliminary plans. West was happy to comply. He sent her a brown leatherette binder with THE WHITE HOUSE centered on its cover, and in small white lettering on the bottom, THE USHERS OFFICE.

Inside, in protective plastic sleeves, were eight-by-ten-inch color shots of every room in the house. Jackie went through the book with her usual rigor and tucked into the corner of most of the pages notes to herself on slips of unlined white paper.

If there is one word that best captures the overall feeling of the White House before Jackie moved in, it is "brown." Or, on the third floor, "scuffed linoleum." (Okay, that's two.) Clearly, home decorating was not high on the Eisenhowers' list of priorities. The two portals for the "his and her" side-by-side television sets come to mind. Ike was an army man and to him, 1600 Pennsylvania Avenue was probably just another posting.

Of the West Hall, Jackie wondered, "Where are the bookcases? Don't any presidents ever read?" Of Room 222 she commented, "This used to be a sitting room where no one sits." The Lincoln Bedroom is the only room she liked — "We can't change it," she wrote, and did not.

The woman Jackie originally chose to plump the pillows was the establishment decorator of the time, Mrs. Henry Parish II, better known by her nickname, "Sister," which *really* confused people. "Kennedys Pick Nun to Decorate White House!" trumpeted the *Daily News*. If America was concerned about a Catholic president's fealty to Rome, wait until they learned of this.

At first, Sister was not sure she even wanted the job. Although it would bring her tremendous publicity (which she did not really need or want), Parish was reluctant to accept because she did not work in restoration or preservation. "I just do pretty houses," she said with Yankee understatement — for families like the Paleys, the Whitneys, and the Rockefellers.

Jackie did not like change and her first thought for the family's quarters on the second floor was simply to use the same fabrics they had used in Georgetown. Even with her lack of training, Sister knew that would not do — Georgetown was formal, but it was also simple, cozy, and warm. The White House, on the other hand, was full of grand rooms with daunting ceilings and great spaces to fill. Finally, Sister told Jackie she would help, but the bright cottons she had used for her first home would not work.

Jackie was so concerned about the amount of work to be done that she cooked up a plan to get Sister Parish and Richard Nelson into the White House before they were really supposed to be there. Come down to Washington, Jackie suggested, and she would sneak them into the White House as her aunt and nephew. Sister Parish talked her out of it. "The most dangerous thing would be for you to get off on the wrong foot," she advised Jackie. "We have plenty of time to go about it in the proper way."

Sister Parish and her husband, Henry, were invited to the inauguration, so Richard and Sister packed up her black Humber with red canvas T. Anthony bags full of fabric samples for Mrs. Kennedy and drove to Washington, D.C. There was a terrible snowstorm that day and Sister was concerned they would not make it to the White House for her meeting with Jackie, never mind the inaugural festivities. She had barely made it to the outskirts of Washington when they got stuck in a snowdrift. Fortunately, Sister made it to a phone and called the White House in desperation. Jackie dispatched some civil servants to pull them out of the snow.

The next day, practically at dawn, Sister and Richard were in the Oval Room of the Family Quarters waiting for Mrs. Kennedy when Richard noticed a handwritten note from the president on a side table: "Jackie, let's declare war on toilet paper — where the hell is it?" Kennedy's first official memo. Richard thought briefly about nicking it for posterity, but was afraid that the guards (or, worse, Sister Parish) would find out and ask him to leave.

Shortly thereafter, there was a minor decorating situation in the Kennedy White House that could have had international repercussions. Sister had sent down a group of samples for Caroline's bedroom that Jackie went through and left in the Oval Room. They were perfect for a little girl — there was one lovely pink linen toile in particular, with cherubs flying all around it and baskets of flowers and garlands, that everyone liked a lot. Richard thought it might be the tiniest bit adult for Caroline, but it was charming.

The president happened to wander by and went through the samples on the desk. He couldn't help it — he was interested in pretty much everything that went on in the White House. Moments later, one of the White House operators got Richard on the phone. Kennedy told him, "I love this sample, I want it for my bedroom!" and read him the lot number off the tag.

Richard scribbled down the order number. It turned out that it came from Brunschwig and he ordered a piece of it. That afternoon it arrived at Parish's office.

Kennedy had chosen the pink intended for Caroline's room. "Mrs. Parish," Nelson cried, "this is a *disaster*! This is material for Caroline's room, and the president wants pink fabric in his bedroom.... It's got flowers and ribbons and bows and baskets and cherubs — it's just not going to work!"

Kennedy didn't care. He was determined to get that material. He was president of the United States, a World War II vet — what the hell did he care what people thought of him? For some reason, he really liked those angels. Finally, Richard and Sister convinced him that pink was not right for him, that it should be *blue*.

The president got his angels, but the material was blue-and-cream toile, and Mrs. Kennedy picked a lovely Cowton and Tout little rosebud in organdy for under curtains and a chintz for the bed. It stayed there the entire time that he was in the White House.

"It was funny," says Nelson. "He obviously had an opinion about things, but 'Mrs. Parish,' I said, 'the country will go crazy if they learn that the president has a pink bedroom with cherubs and flowers and garlands — they'll think he's Liberace, or something! Can you imagine if Castro found out?'"

At thirty-one, Jackie was third youngest first lady in the nation's history. When she arrived at the White House, she was overwhelmed and mildly depressed at the amount of work to be done — none of the windows opened, the fireplaces did not draw properly, the second floor reeked of drying paint. At first, she did not like being there, complaining to Hugh Sidey about all the people standing around in the halls, watching her. But then, realizing what had to be done, acknowledging the extraordinary opportunity she had been given, and most of all, wanting to do a good job for her husband, she rallied.

"She was the idea girl," recalls J. B. West, "and I enjoyed trying to carry out things." Some of the changes Jackie brought to the White House had to do with entertaining, like the time she decided to host a state dinner at Mount Vernon, the home of George Washington, for the president of Pakistan. In addition to figuring out how to transport 132 high-powered guests by boat down the Potomac to a place that had no electricity, she also wanted the menu to be reminiscent of what Martha Washington would have served. And it had to take place in four weeks. West's job was not to ask why. His job was to make it happen. And he did.

Some of Jackie's changes in the White House were more personal, affecting the day-to-day interaction between the first family and the staff. The first time she and her husband walked down the hall, the housekeepers stopped and turned to face the wall until they passed by. "What was wrong with them?" Jackie asked Mr. West. He explained that the Eisenhowers had a less enlightened view of the help and did not want to see them. Jackie immediately asked him for photos and a listing of all the staff so she and Jack could learn them by name.

Jackie and Mr. West communicated mostly by memo or telephone, although she also came down to his office quite a bit — something Mrs. Eisenhower never did. "She'd get off the elevator on the first floor, and she and I would sit on the marble steps and talk. We sat on the ground-floor corridor with papers spread out. And whenever she might be going out for a walk or returning from one, if I had something to ask her, I knew what was the best time to reach her."

Jackie was a big list maker. "She always had a list for me. She had a tablet, a big yellow pad. Each person that had any authority over anything, she had their name, and under it there would be all the things that she wanted to discuss with them," says West.

At night, when she thought of things and no one else was around, Jackie would jot them down on a large pad she kept at her bedside. The next day she would call up the various people involved and go down the list and scratch the items off. Very little escaped her notice.

While her whispery voice and faraway gaze gave outsiders the impression that Jackie's role in the White House was merely decorative, nothing was further from the truth. Although her instinct was to be charming, Jackie knew what she wanted to accomplish and went after it methodically and relentlessly. And while she always presented her requests with a well-bred "please" and "thank you," J. B. West and those who worked for her knew a request from her was a polite command.

When Jackie wanted something, she was as skilled as any politician in getting it. On the night of June 8, 1962, Jackie turned off her record player, sat at her desk in the Family Quarters on the second floor of the White House, and wrote a remarkable, handwritten, twelve-page letter to her friend the painter and journalist Bill Walton, trying to persuade him to head up the Fine Arts Committee she had formed to assist in the restoration of the White House public rooms.

The letter is a fascinating revelation of style, because it shows the essentially political cast of Jackie's mind. In discussing the Fine Arts Committee, Jackie argued that if David Finley resigned, Walton was the best choice for chairman, "because on that scattered committee the only person who has any influence is the chairman — and he should be one who knows Washington — and one who knows the uses of power — all the more important when you really don't have any." Jackie knew Walton was having second thoughts about taking on the project — after all, he was an artist, not a bureaucrat. And he would have hated to have anything ruin their friendship. But Jackie had also had to overcome her doubts about becoming first lady and becoming involved in public life. She passed on what she had learned thus far to Walton.

She advised him about the importance of having good help, a secretary or assistant he could rely on, so that he could paint and step in only when absolutely necessary. Jackie admitted to Walton that she, too, liked to live freely. "But I spent about 1 week organizing things as well as Field Marshal Rommel ever did — And now my life is the way I want it." She encouraged him, as only she could, to take the position, hinting that JFK could work for *him* someday, "Jack can be your deputy in 1964 (or 8???????????)."

Walton accepted the position.

Along with getting the White House up and running, Jackie was concerned about her official wardrobe. With the whole world watching and scrutinizing her every move, she knew she would feel more confident if she at least looked the part. As the first and probably only first lady to read both French *Vogue* and *Mademoiselle* in her private dressing room at "Maison Blanche," as she had taken to calling her new home, she tracked what was going on in fashion as astutely as her friend Diana Vreeland, the larger-than-life editor at *Harper's Bazaar*.

First, the question of what she should wear had to be resolved. Down in Palm Beach prior to the inauguration, as JFK interviewed cabinet appointments, Ambassador Kennedy got involved in the conversation. In between stints on Wall Street, he had run a minor Hollywood studio called FBO, and he was vitally aware of the connection between appearance and success. Once, after he had taken a rare hit in the stock market selling short, he hired a limousine and had himself driven around the city, making sure he was noticed on Wall Street.

Kennedy knew that much of his son's appeal was dependent on Jackie and on her style. Women loved her. They wanted to *be* her. She was everything they imagined American aristocracy to be — Vassar educated, fluent in French, skilled in foxhunting. She was even in the *Social Register*. The ambassador was the first to admit she had more class then the Kennedys, which is why he had pushed Jack to marry her: she was the perfect political wife.

At first, he suggested that Jackie wear a different American designer every season, but Jackie demurred because this would make her seem like a fitting model. After Jackie made a brief pass at Mainbocher (C. Z. Guest recalls that "Jackie had asked Main to do the clothes but he didn't want to because he had a lot of clients") and Bergdorf Goodman, the ambassador narrowed her options down to one man.

With the canny political acumen he was known for, Kennedy Sr. quickly decided the first lady's couturier had to be an American, in the same way Kennedys drove only American cars — for the president's wife to wear anything else would be a public relations disaster. Although he did not let on to Jackie, he had been giving the matter some thought. The Kennedys placed a premium on friendship and family loyalty: Who did they know? Who could be trusted? Who would best serve the family's interests?

Since he would be footing the bills (at only 25 to 50 percent above cost as it turned out), Kennedy decided that the family's friend Oleg Cassini, a former costume designer at Paramount — well-born, urbane, discreet, and briefly engaged to Grace Kelly — would be responsible for producing Jackie's clothes while she was in the White House. And that was that.

While Oleg Cassini was Jackie's official designer when she was in the White House (her personal secretary Mary Gallagher says that "for the most part, he was"), Jackie "simply could not resist getting things from her favorite couturiers abroad, too, using her dress scouts to order, so it would not be known the gown was for her. Sometimes the gown was supposed to be for her sister, Lee."

Like many wealthy, clothes-conscious women of the day, Jackie had used "clothes scouts" (as they were known) when she was a senator's wife in Georgetown. Before jet travel made it simple to go to Europe, and before fashion was covered extensively on television or in dozens of glossy magazines, these women attended the couture shows and reserved special outfits for their clients. Letizia Mowinckel kept an eye on what was going on in Paris, while Princess Irene Galitzine staked out Rome. Among the several scouts Jackie used in New York, there was the wonderfully monikered Mrs. Tackaberry McAdoo, Molly, who owned Chez Ninon, the New York specialty shop on Park Avenue that Jackie favored. Mrs. Mowinckel also kept her younger sister, Lee, apprised of what the French designers were up to, but Jackie warned her not to show anything to her sister until Jackie had passed on it first.

In addition to these scouts, Gallagher notes that "Jackie herself kept track of what the couturiers in Paris and London were featuring and would get in touch with her scouts to order the items she wanted without anyone's knowing they were for her. She would sometimes fall in love with the material a famous designer had used and order something in the same fabric to be made for her by another designer."

Once Jackie got to the White House, with Joe Kennedy picking up the tab, the fun really began. Endless amounts of clothes arrived from Bergdorf Goodman, from Cassini, and, although she promised to wear American, from Givenchy and Chanel, too. In July 1961, there was a four-thousand-dollar bill from Givenchy—which covered one three-month time period. To put this in perspective, Mary Gallagher worked full time for an entire year (and weekends, too) for forty-eight hundred dollars.

Jack called in Carmine Bellino, the Kennedy accountant who helped Bobby unravel the Mafia's creative accounting, to review Jackie's expenses, but Jackie was adamant—as the first lady, she had no other choice. "I have to dress well, Jack," she countered, "so I won't embarrass you. As a public figure you'd be humiliated if I was photographed in some saggy old housedress. Everyone would say your wife is a slob and refuse to vote for you."

As first lady, Jackie tried very hard to wear American, but, as Gallagher said, she "was not above checking on what Balenciaga and Givenchy and others were doing and drawing, and bringing particular sketches to Cassini's attention and suggesting how he could incorporate certain points in what he was planning for her." After Mark Shaw shot Dior's collection in Paris for *Life*, he wanted to send Jackie copies of the proofs so she could preview the latest fashion. Mary Gallagher called Cassini and asked him to call Shaw about it, but only at home, to keep Shaw out of trouble with his editors.

Jackie's tendency was to do what she wanted. In this instance, she wore what she wanted, from wherever she wanted—Bergdorf, Chanel, Gustave Tassell, Chez Ninon. In one hilarious instance that, thankfully, the public never found out about, the official White House photographer, Army Captain Cecil Stoughton, was dispatched to New York City to shoot a fashion show at Chez Ninon for Jackie.

Stoughton remembers that in September 1962, the first lady's social secretary, Letitia Baldrige, called him to her office. "Cecil, I have a great job for you. How would you like to go to New York and shoot a fashion show?" It wasn't the usual grip-and-grin in the Oval, but it sounded okay to him. He went up to New York with a 35-millimeter camera and sat in the front row of Chez Ninon. There was a mirror and Stoughton made sure he got the front of each dress while the mirror reflected the back. "I thought that was pretty clever of me," he recalls.

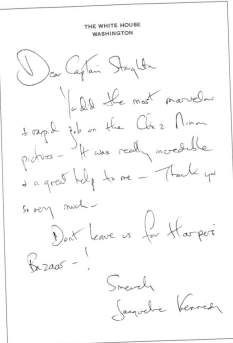

Fashion shows were fairly staid affairs in those days (no music, no scrum of photographers, no Madonna in the front row), but Stoughton got into it. For starters, he was the only man in the room. "All the ladies were sitting there in their gold chairs, and then there's this *guy* and I'm there clicking these pictures!"

After the show, Stoughton went backstage and got swatches of material and the prices. When he returned to Washington, he made an album with all the information and gave it to Tish to give to Jackie. Neophyte fashionista Stoughton must have done a job to make Diana Vreeland proud. A few days later he got a handwritten note from Jackie thanking him for the pictures. "Don't leave us for *Harper's Bazaar*," she asked.

Although Jackie wore a slew of classic designers during the White House years, the one she loved above all else was Hubert de Givenchy. He was *it* for her. Jackie and her sister, Lee, were introduced to Givenchy's work by their friend Hélène Arpels, who brought back some Givenchys from Paris after his first collection in 1952. They visited her suite at the St. Regis Hotel in Manhattan and attempted to try on a few of his gowns. "They were schoolgirls, young girls," she recalled. "And both of them so big they could not get into them!" Hélène laughs at the memory. "When I saw them a few years later, they were *skinny*, but not then!"

Givenchy, for his part, was a master couturier whose clean design, modern silhouettes, and use of luxurious, yet unadorned, material dovetailed with Jackie's style. He said, "I persist in not understanding flashy elaborations whose sole purpose, in my opinion, is to shock." What Givenchy understood was line and form, which in turn produced the timeless elegance of his style.

Givenchy was, and still is, an absolute gentleman. He never failed to acknowledge his indebtedness to fashion visionary Cristóbal Balenciaga, who took his client American Listerine heiress Bunny Mellon (née Rachel Lambert) across the street to Givenchy's atelier after he closed his doors. Hubert was everything Jackie wanted in a designer — discreet, wildly talented, generous, disciplined, an artist. In short, he was *the* French master.

Seemingly overnight Jackie became a style leader. Cassini recalls that they strove to create the first American style that was not beholden to Europe. But really, if one looks at what was going on in Paris in those years, particularly at Dior, Givenchy, and Balenciaga, what Cassini created for Jackie was exceedingly French, which was not surprising, considering what a Francophile the first lady was.

History bears this out. Fashion illustrator Joe Eula accompanied Eugenia Sheppard — whose influential column "Inside Fashion" was syndicated in Chicago's *Herald Tribune* — to Paris to sketch the designs featured in Sheppard's coverage of the shows. If one studies the sketches Eula did of the Fall 1960 collections (which were shown the previous spring, well before the election), there are several design trends that show up in Jackie's official wardrobe the following year. The neat suit with fitted shoulders and three-quarter bracelet sleeves was everywhere; rich, vibrant wools were the material of choice; even the pillbox hat first seen at Dior around 1956 was in.

This fashion copying was not unique to Jackie. She just brought it to a higher level by telling Cassini precisely what she wanted. In fact, it was the way Seventh Avenue worked at the time. Then, as now, there was no stigma in America in producing line-for-line copies of couture dresses that had been shown in Paris six weeks earlier. In 1960, Bergdorf's representative Ethel Frankau (with help from her young assistant, Roy Halston Frowick, later known as Halston) bought two hundred suits in Paris to be reproduced in the store's workrooms. Altman's, Ohrbach's, Macy's, even Saks Fifth Avenue were all known for their knockoffs. Representatives of their stores traveled to Paris to buy the outfits they liked and rushed back to the States, often displaying the original alongside their version of it. When *Breakfast at Tiffany's* was released, Ohrbach's sold hundreds of affordable versions of the softly shaped red coat with stand-up collar that Givenchy had created for Audrey Hepburn.

Chez Ninon was known for bringing French couture to New York City from Paris (when air travel was much rarer than it is today), and for making high-quality copies. For stylish women of a certain age (and Cecil Stoughton, too), Chez Ninon holds glowing memories. Jackie's White House social secretary, Letitia Baldrige, *adored* it. "It was on Park at about Sixty-first, on the corner. Mrs. McAdoo ran it, a great lady of society. I couldn't afford to shop there, it was all very expensive, but lovely, lovely clothes." Vivian Crespi remembers Chez Ninon as "a place where my mother and Jackie's mother went. It was sort of a Henri Bendel of the old days and had a made-to-order department. Jackie and I were the same age, so this was sort of our treat, to get one or two things a year at Chez Ninon, which even in the 1950s was very expensive for us."

All of this is not to say Oleg Cassini consciously copied the French (although that claim was leveled against him at the time). It's just that the look he and Jackie favored was in the air. In Paris. Simply put, fashionable women of Jackie's class took their cues from the Paris runway. Even Gustave Tassell, an American designer whose fashions Jackie wore in the White House, admitted, "We were all influenced by Balenciaga."

For some reason, the garment industry of New York City, better known as Seventh Avenue, and Oleg Cassini have never really gotten along. Was it because he was too successful? Too closely linked to the woman they all dreamed of dressing, Jackie Kennedy? Cassini not only designed clothing for Jackie, he taught her the twist. He discussed the *Kama Sutra* with Jack Kennedy. He was the first designer invited upstairs to the White House, not with pins in his mouth but as a welcome guest in a dinner jacket. Speaking with Oleg Cassini today, he immediately launches into an unprovoked diatribe against Seventh Avenue. "It's a lousy world, this fashion," says Cassini with the practiced air of a man in his mid-eighties who has squired legends like Grace Kelly, Gene Tierney, and Marilyn Monroe. Relaxing in the sitting room of his Oyster Bay country house, the former Louis Comfort Tiffany estate on forty-eight manicured acres overlooking the Long Island Sound, he heatedly observes, "It's a beautiful world, but it's lousy!"

Seventh Avenue is *still* ruthless. One story is that it was not Cassini who designed Jackie's clothes, but Givenchy. A well-known fashion photographer swears they were made in a workroom in New York City under Givenchy's supervision and that Cassini stitched his label on them because Jackie could not wear French clothes. Another stunning rumor has it that Cassini was not responsible for the extraordinary gown Jackie wore to the inaugural gala, but Givenchy.

"She wore Cassini," recalls decorator Keith Irvine, who spent a lot of time in the Georgetown drawing rooms of the day, "but the things she *really* liked were Givenchys, so she wore him, too." Vivian Crespi agrees, "When Jackie was 'on,' as we used to say, she used to wear Hubert or Oleg, because she had to wear an American designer. I think Hubert was her favorite, but she was very patriotic and Oleg was a good friend."

There is no doubt that Oleg Cassini did an extraordinary job translating the "Jackie Look" to the world. Jackie had so many other things on her mind before she and her family moved into the White House that Cassini's appearance was a godsend. "ARE YOU SURE YOU ARE UP TO IT, OLEG? Please say yes —" she wrote Cassini on December 13, 1960, from Palm Beach.

To take care of Jackie's needs, Cassini immediately formed a separate atelier, hiring a *première,* an assistant to research fabrics and colors, a draper, a cutter, and sample hands to produce the clothes. In the almost three years the Kennedys resided in the White House, Cassini produced nearly three hundred one-of-a-kind outfits for Jackie, both evening and day wear, in addition to running his own design firm.

Mary Gallagher is the closest unbiased witness we have to Jackie and Cassini's working relationship, since she was in the room taking notes to ensure Jackie's wishes were carried out. Gallagher recalls that Jackie and Oleg worked closely together to create a look she was comfortable with, one that properly suited her role as first lady. It appears they were decidedly collaborative, with Jackie keeping tabs on what Cassini was up to and letting her preferences be known.

Jackie approached her wardrobe with the same rigor and attention to detail that she brought to restoring the public rooms of the White House, state dinners, or planning menus for her children. "Soon after the election," recounts Gallagher, who was with her in Palm Beach, "Mrs. Kennedy dictated a long letter to Oleg Cassini in New York, outlining her specific needs with her usual precision — types of ensembles, fabrics, colors. She requested that Cassini send her some sketches, but her preference was for materials used by Balenciaga and Givenchy. She was so meticulous about the fabric used that she was willing to wait for the sketches until Cassini had seen the new material."

Gallagher also noted that "before Cassini cut the precious material for outfits made specifically for her, he would have Jackie's complete instructions. First he would send Jackie swatches and sketches beautifully rendered, and Jackie would study them carefully as she dictated her comments on them to me. She liked sketches A or B but wanted the shoulder changed, or the neckline a bit higher. He also sent her swatches of gorgeous materials in the color in which he thought each dress would look best on her."

"She had an eye," concedes Cassini, "but she had no means. She never had any money! She *had* nothing, she *wanted* everything. And then she had this extraordinary joy of having everything and she could do what she wanted." In other words, Jackie had the background, the training, and finally, with her ally Joseph P. Kennedy footing the bills, the wherewithal to be truly well dressed.

You say Cassini, I say Givenchy. In the end, does it matter? For his part, Givenchy remains unperturbed, as befits a man who has dressed everyone from Audrey Hepburn and Babe Paley to the duchess of Windsor, Marlene Dietrich, Lauren Bacall, Gloria Guinness, and Bunny Mellon. "I designed clothes for Mrs. Kennedy before, during, and after the White House — well before Oleg Cassini's arrival."

Cassini, on the other hand, claims full credit for developing Jackie's style. "She changed herself from a *housefrau* of a senator to first lady — and how did she do it? From picking people who knew their job very well! She was a Francophile and I was the best possible choice. Why? Because I was born in France myself."

Fashion historians — or anyone with a good eye, for that matter — can study the seams and tell precisely where a dress originated; the inner workmanship of couture doesn't lie. But regardless of who claims authorship of a design (and really, in fashion, isn't practically everything derivative?), Jackie was not a woman who was ever overpowered by what she chose to wear on a particular day, or at a certain event. Jackie knew what she wanted, and in looking at the clothing she wore during this time, it is obvious she chose what suited her best. "She picked a lot of brains," said a friend. But in the end, *she* wore the clothing, which is the hallmark of fashion consciousness.

With Oleg Cassini being invited to private dinner parties with the first family, style was a very big deal in the Kennedy White House. It came from the president and the first lady down. Style was not just fashion, but a kind of shorthand to see if you were on the team, whether you got the jokes. Good manners, staying cool under pressure, and who your father or uncle was went a long way. The whole bunch of them were, to use that awful Harvard phrase, "clubbable." To a great degree (years later this faith in appearances is almost touching), the JFKs linked style with substance.

For the women who worked there, what passed for chic in the Kennedy White House came right from Jackie, and had all the exactness of a West Point uniform: copies of good French suits with three-quarter bracelet sleeves, low heels, nothing too flashy or showy. For daytime officewear, the "nice girl" look ruled: nude stockings, a discreet pearl necklace (no more than three strands), hair neatly styled.

For all of the Kennedys, but particularly John F. Kennedy and his wife, style was a prism through which to view the world. Like being a Kennedy or Roman Catholic, having style — an ingrained habit of responding to the world — set you apart from others; it made you special and held you up. For both Jackie and her husband, style served another purpose: to gloss over the fact that in their lives, things were not precisely as they appeared.

For an administration so associated with youth, high spirits, physical fitness, and (as JFK put it) "vigah," it is alarming how unwell the young president actually was. Few people aside from Jackie and the family knew that before the age of forty Kennedy had received last rites three times. He was obsessed with death and convinced he would die young. In excruciating pain much of the time, Kennedy's response was to turn his back on the proper, rule-laden way his mother ordered her world. Disregarding what was "expected" of him morally, socially, and intellectually, JFK lived each day to the fullest.

Lauded as the first Irish Catholic American president, JFK was, in reality, more English than Irish, more Protestant than Catholic, more Brahmin than Boston. He gave the impression of being cool, of distrusting deep emotion. If anything, his friend Lord Harlech believed the opposite was true. "I think he had very deep emotions. He very much disliked the display of them. . . . He had deep emotions and strong passions underneath and when his friends were hurt or a tragedy occurred or his child died, I think he felt it very deeply. But somehow public display was anathema to him."

Although he defined cool, Kennedy was affectionate and playful, even sentimental, traits he kept well hidden from everyone but Jackie. As a senator, he would sometimes drive over to Merrywood, his in-laws' home in Virginia, in the afternoon. Alone and unannounced, he would play with his golden retriever, Tippy, who stayed in the country after they moved to Georgetown. One of the gardeners once saw a young man in a tie playing with the dog and told Mrs. Auchincloss a friend of her son's was visiting.

But there was something about Jack. Of all the Kennedys, he was the one people fell in love with. "Unlike other members of his family, he had the ability to laugh at himself, and enjoyed doing so — so did Jackie," recalls Yusha Auchincloss. "That's what gave him his special charm, and, like Jackie, I think his innate shyness gave him his special grace."

For the Kennedys, appearances clearly mattered. And prosperous postwar America, with the time and inclination to pay attention to style, was ravenous for someone to show them "how it was done." Jackie took the lead in this by lifting the curtain on the rituals, idiosyncrasies, and jargon of the American upper class.

Thanks to endless (Republicans would say excessive) coverage of the Kennedys in *Time, Life, Look,* and *Newsweek* (many of whose reporters came straight from the Harvard *Crimson* and were the social equals of JFK), average Americans were given entrée into a world they had only glimpsed in Katharine Hepburn movies. Now, by following Jackie's example — and she was always, much to her chagrin, Jackie, never "Jacqueline" or the more proper and distancing "Mrs. Kennedy" — they could incorporate some of that rarefied world into their own.

There was such extraordinary, almost obsessive, interest in All Things Kennedy that, as first lady, Jackie's personal interests, her *taste*, was passed on to the American public — and the world — in a way that has not happened before or since. Not only was Jackie's style accessible, but the things that captured her attention ran the gamut — they were both high and low, rarefied and easily reproduced.

Under Jackie's aegis, ballet became the next big thing. Manners were back. Good stationery (with a monogram or family crest), along with the loopy backhanded scrawl favored by Farmington graduates and *Vogue* editors of a certain era, was acquired. Horses were very much in. Thanks to Jackie, the average American became conversant in the arcane, particular language of the upper class: foxhunting, couture, Oleg Cassini, spindly eighteenth-century French furniture, Scalamandré, Diana (pronounced "Dee-a-nah" among the cognoscenti) Vreeland.

Jackie's interests, while she was first lady, became the country's interests. Her *style* became ours. French wine, daiquiris, capri pants, smoking and all its accoutrements, got it. Locust Valley lockjaw? Back in. Country clubs, sailing, well-behaved children, religious and racial tolerance, the Ivy League, dogs on the couch, the Army-Navy game, big big big. The Peace Corps. The twist. All were given equal attention.

American women of every income, class, and race connected with Jackie Kennedy and her style. For enraptured Kennedy watchers, the first lady's inter-

ests were both broad *and* deep, ranging from the sacred to the not-so-serious — that is what made Jackie so endlessly entertaining. If you looked silly in pillbox hats or had no interest in Paris fashion, you could still mime Kennedy style by playing touch football (or, as Jackie chose, not playing) or by smoking Jackie's favorite brand of cigarettes, Newports.

The Kennedys and their friends roared into Washington in January 1961 and for the first time in a long time politics was fun, it was personal. People *cared*. As designer Kate Spade recalls, "My family is Irish Catholic, so my mother, in particular, had a lot of things around the house about the Kennedys — books, pictures, I mean, it was kind of a big deal. The Kennedys were like a member of your family — you read about them in the papers and always wanted to know what they were up to."

People connected with the Kennedys, and particularly Jackie. They must have seen themselves in her — she lived in a larger house, but she was a young mother with small children, like many of them. So many teenagers wrote offering to "help out" in case Caroline needed a baby-sitter that a form response letter had to be written. Interest in Jackie was unprecedented — nine thousand letters, gifts, and requests poured into the White House every week. At one point Tish Baldrige implored the president's special assistant Kenny O'Donnell and press secretary, Pierre Salinger, to take the avalanche of requests seriously: "A lot of organizations that appear harmless from their letterhead are either inferior or social climbing.... We say no thirty thousand times a day."

Taking their cue from the first lady, the secretaries' responses to quasi-official correspondence in the East Wing soon fell into two categories: the Effusive Thank You or the Polite Brush Off.

Given that Jackie preferred foxhunting in Middleburg to her official duties but did not want to tick off her husband and his constituents, the PBO — curt, occasionally frosty, and always typewritten — got a lot of play during Jackie's White House years. For additional impact, it was both drafted *and* signed by a secretary while she was in Palm Beach for the weekend.

In contrast to her PBOs, Jackie's ETYs were more girlish in nature. They tended to be handwritten, on good stationery, and covered a range of situations from "thanks for dinner last night," to gratitude for donating a rare, original copy of the Declaration of Independence (as Walter Annenberg of Philadelphia did) to the White House.

Of course, there were a few missteps in the beginning as the enthusiastic administration got off the ground. Sometimes it seemed they were having too much fun. At an early press conference, fellow Vassarite Tish Baldrige described Jackie as "the girl who has everything — including the president of the United States." Shortly thereafter, Pierre Salinger informed the Washington press corps that Miss Baldrige would no longer be giving briefings on behalf of the first lady.

During her White House years, there were many facets to Jackie's style, from the way she dressed to the stage she set for the Kennedy myth to play itself out on. One thinks of Jackie looking impossibly glamorous in a Newport blue strapless evening gown with a diamond pendant on the front; "Moon River" wafting out of the Family Quarters as the president and first lady take their afternoon nap with orders not to be disturbed; Caroline leading her horse "Macaroni" through the French doors of the Oval Office; Peter Lawford padding down the hall in black tie, shoeless, wearing red socks; a maid delivering a bottle of beer on a silver tray to the Lincoln Bedroom where Jackie's sister, Princess Radziwill, stayed — so that she could rinse her hair with it.

Jackie restored an elevated manner to the White House, and by example, to this country. As first lady, she understood that beauty, brilliance, and having the best in the White House resonated with the American people. Designer Kate Spade also noticed this. "Jackie's look in the sixties was representing America as the wife of the president. Those perfect French suits that she wore were almost like state wear; they were colorful and made to stand out in the

lineup of men in dark suits. She wasn't really revealing very much of herself but she was representing our country—what it means to be an American—in a way that hasn't been done before or since, I think. You were proud of her."

Jackie loved history, something she shared with her husband. "She loved the kings and queens of Ireland. She wanted to make Washington magical, central to the life of this country," recalls Yusha Auchincloss. A romantic, she understood people's need for heroes. If they did not have them, they would create them. Having been raised Catholic, Jackie also understood the need for pageantry. She raised state dinners to an art form. Understanding the importance of history, Jackie facilitated people's need for heroes by creating symbols—the newly elegant White House, the Nobel Dinner, even Air Force One—with which to remember them by. "You have the opportunity to create an American Versailles," Oleg Cassini told her.

Jackie's push for glamour in the White House was not merely glamour for glamour's sake. It served the larger purpose of relaying to the world that the modern age was upon us in America. As Hamish Bowles, European editor at large of *Vogue* magazine, observes, "Cassini and Jackie Kennedy were very conscious that there was an image that needed to be presented. The clothes that they worked on together have a sort of clarity of line, a dignified restraint, but at the same time they are modern and forward looking.... With Mrs. Kennedy's visual self-presentation you certainly have the sense of a new era dawning, a new decade and all that it promised, from space travel to the twist."

Now that she had come into her own, Jackie was truly a style leader, representative of the best our country had to offer. As few other first ladies did, she realized and acted upon the notion that the White House was not just a home she shared with her family, but a symbol of our nation. She was proud to be an American, eager to show the world we were no longer Europe's stepchildren. The decor of the White House, the entertainment at state dinners, even the clothes she wore on presidential trips abroad furthered this aim. And when she stood beside her husband at a state dinner wearing a one-shouldered evening gown (a Cassini construct for which she had to secure her husband's permission), she was not merely a well-dressed woman but a forward-thinking representative of her country.

When Hugh Sidey and Jackie were writing an article for *Life* about her restoration work in the White House, he met with her. "I was upstairs in the yellow Oval Room... and all of a sudden she looked out over the Truman Balcony and said, 'You know, this is what it's all about.' And I said, 'What do you mean?' And she said, 'This is what it's all about — these men *battle* in politics. And here it is, the Washington Monument, the Jefferson Memorial, the White House, the meaning of that whole struggle.'

"Now, that," Sidey recalls almost forty years later, "takes a great mind. To sum it up like that, in an artist's way. Poets define our civilization and tell us what we are all about and where we are going, and that was one of those moments."

Jackie looked out over the Washington Mall. She had always dreamed of being a writer. But her art was bigger than the page. Her art was her life and those she inspired, and whether she acknowledged it or not, the example — of courage, beauty, individuality, and single-mindedness — she set for others.

the pillbox hat

> You're only as good as the
> people you dress.
>
> — HALSTON

The pillbox hat. Has there been another fashion accessory so memorable, so debated, so utterly associated with a public figure? Like the bishop's miter, Jackie took that silly pillbox and made it *hers*.

The most surprising thing about Jackie and hats is that she did not even like them — but in the 1950s, hats were part of the proper uniform for the wife of an up-and-coming politician.

Part of the problem was that Jackie had a large head and, in the late '50s and early '60s, preferred a bouffant hairdo. A hat, she felt, would be simply *de trop*. Halston, who designed hats at Bergdorf Goodman, devised an ingeniously simple, small chapeau that would mirror whatever outfit she was wearing. The pillbox hat was born.

Of course, like so many things in fashion, this particular style had been around — in Paris — for several years. The Hollywood costume designer Adrian first introduced the pillbox hat to the American public by placing one on Greta Garbo in the 1932 film *As You Desire Me*. Balenciaga, Dior, and Givenchy all showed pillbox-style hats in their collections in the mid-1950s. And Jackie, of course, knew exactly what was appearing on the Paris runways. Mini Rhea, Jackie's dressmaker when she lived at home

in Merrywood, recalls seeing Jackie wear a pillbox (then called a domed or soft hat) as early as 1954, when she accompanied her husband to the hospital for back surgery.

Although it is hard to imagine now, until the late 1960s hats were a very big deal in fashion, as essential to completing an outfit as shoes. In 1961, Halston and Ethel Frankau, the head of the custom salon at Bergdorf's, traveled to Paris and viewed seventeen complete couture collections plus five devoted solely to hats.

Bergdorf's had the largest millinery workroom in the United States. The designer Adolfo (who, like Halston, got his start designing hats for Bergdorf's) remembers 40 women sewing only hats. At its peak, Halston's custom millinery department employed 150 custom milliners, 12 salesladies, and 16 assistants.

Bergdorf's second floor was Halston's kingdom. He was the only person Greta Garbo would talk to. Barbara Hutton's chauffeur would carry the ailing heiress into the store and set her in a chair in front of Halston where she would spend hours. Even Andrew Goodman, president of the store, admitted that Bergdorf's customers adored him. "Mrs. Paley and the duchess of Windsor would have lunch at the Colony and then they'd spend the afternoon at Bergdorf's trying on hats," he said. "Halston would talk to them about fashion and they respected his taste. They listened to him." At the age of twenty-nine, he was the star of the millinery department.

In studying the sketches Halston produced before Jackie went to the White House, we see that in the late 1950s pillboxes were very much on his mind. His earliest sketches, preserved at the Fashion Institute of Technology, show pillbox designs in Fall 1959. By Fall 1960 (shown the spring before the election), he was King of the Pillbox, producing dozens of styles that were variations on the same theme — black pillbox with jet beads, fuchsia pillbox, apple green pillbox, straw pillbox, pale blue pillbox with double bow.

Oleg Cassini also claimed credit for designing Jackie's distinctive pillbox hat, saying it had evolved from inspirational conversations he'd had with Diana Vreeland about how best to dress Mrs. Kennedy.

Another early fan of Halston's was Jacqueline Kennedy, and Halston adored the wife of the future president of the United States. He recalled visiting her at her suite at the Carlyle and finding her listening to Frank Sinatra records on the stereo.

In addition to his talent, there was another attribute that made Halston vital to his fashionable, but busy, client — he and Jackie wore the same hat size, and he used to fit her hats on his head. "He was the only one who could do her hats because of her strange head size," recounts Tom Fallon, who was Halston's assistant from 1966 to 1968. "Before the hats were sent to her, Halston would put her hats on his head and look at them with two mirrors...turning his head at different angles to make sure they looked right. It was funny, this wonderful big palooka of a guy with these ladies' hats on."

"That's a pile of shit," says Leonard Hankin, Bergdorf's executive vice president, who was there. "Halston designed it." Andrew Goodman concurs. "I remember the day Halston brought the pillbox to Mrs. Kennedy at the Carlyle, 'You're so young to be so successful!' she said to him."

In 1991 author Steven Gaines was researching his biography of Halston. In an attempt to answer the question of who designed Jackie's pillbox hat once and for all, he went to the source and wrote a letter to Onassis at her office at Doubleday. "I know in the scheme of things, this is not a big deal," he said, "but it is a matter of some great importance to me and to people that are involved." He wondered if Jackie could set the record straight.

He came home one day to find a message on his answering machine. "Mr. Gaines, this is Mrs. Onassis..." That distinctive voice. There was a pause as if she were sharing a private joke with him, enjoying the buildup to the punch line.

Halston," she said with a smile and hung up.

In the acknowledgments, Gaines thanks Jacqueline Onassis for her one-word contribution to his book.

Style is what you are.
It's your essential self—
it's what makes you a Bouvier.

— JOHN VERNOU BOUVIER III

fortune's child

As the daughter of two strong-minded individuals, Jackie wanted what she wanted. She admitted she was a willful child. "I read a lot when I was little, much of which was too old for me," she confessed, sneaking out of bed during naptime to read Chekhov and Shaw, then carefully scrubbing the soles of her feet so she would not be found out. She was winsome, proper, strong-willed, a great mimic. With her dark coloring, high cheekbones, and wide-set eyes, she was a miniature version of the father she adored, John "Black Jack" Bouvier III.

Much like her future mother-in-law, Rose Kennedy, Jackie's mother, Janet Lee Bouvier, was a stickler for details: there was a right way and a wrong way to do everything. Later, there was the story, apocryphal perhaps, that Janet threatened a maid at Merrywood with a knife for not emptying the wastebaskets properly. She taught her daughters discipline, the importance of the thank-you note and of associating with the right people. But Jackie's father was her first style mentor in the more important art of life. He had an unerring eye for color and form, and he lectured his daughters, Jackie and Lee, four years younger, on everything from antiques to courtship to men, which was, after all, the raison d'être of the whole game. ("All men are rats," he warned them in an inadvertently comic bit of projection: "All men are rats, don't trust any of them!")

For Jackie and Lee, sex reared its head early. Because of their father's excessive and continued interest in other women and their parents' volatile relationship, they had ringside seats for the less savory aspects of the relationship

between men and women at a very young age. Beyond that, Black Jack was so invested in Jackie's beauty and her allure to the opposite sex that, by today's standards, it would probably be said that he crossed the boundaries of proper father-daughter relations.

But for some reason, no one in the Bouvier household seemed to find their relationship odd. In fact, Jackie's cousin John Davis, who explained Black Jack's behavior by his "Latin nature," found it touching. "It was a special love of a father for his daughter, the likes of which I have never seen witnessed in America before or since   To see Jack and Jacqueline strolling along Park Avenue arm and arm was to behold two lovers who delighted in each other's company. Only in southern France and Italy have I observed such closeness between father and daughter."

John Davis recalls a birthday luncheon at Lasata, their summer home in East Hampton, where Jack Bouvier sang his daughters' praises — "Jackie's got every boy at the Maidstone after her and the kid's not even ten. What are we going to do with her when she's twenty?" And gushing about Jackie's equestrian skills, he said, "The girl's taken all the prizes in her class so far this summer, the whole lot of them . . . and she's always the prettiest thing in the ring to boot." Jacqueline's adult relatives at the table were accustomed to Black Jack's grandiose fatherly tributes. To them, there was nothing excessive about his overlaudatory praise of his children. They had heard them so often, his comments barely merited a response.

At the head of the table, Grandfather Bouvier, the major, who happened to have his hearing aid on, gave a smile and a vague nod of his head as he worked through his first course of tomato stuffed with crabmeat. He and his wife and five children, their spouses (except for that tacky Janet Lee, whom Black Jack had fortunately gotten rid of), and their children were in his house, being served by his staff, and it was his money that subsidized their Park Avenue apartments, their country homes, their glamour, their dissoluteness, their artistically inflated opinion of themselves.

Black Jack then made the other cousins more envious by flattering his younger daughter, Lee. "Lee's going to be a real glamour girl someday — would you look at those eyes? And those sexy lips of hers?" Lee and Jackie thrived on the glowing praise of their father. In his eyes, they could do no wrong. It was no wonder they preferred his company to that of their hypercritical mother.

Black Jack treated Jackie more as if she were his number-one girlfriend than his daughter. A few years later, after her parents' divorce was final, whenever she visited New York he canceled all of his other social engagements to spend time exclusively with her. His interest in her was extreme. When Jackie was in her late teens, she got her hair cut in a "poodle cut," a short, feathered style popular at the time. She called him at the Yale Club to tell him about it.

He was beside himself with worry — what if the hairstyle made Jackie look silly and ruined her features? He need not have worried, but he did. "He was as obsessed with Jackie's poodle cut as he had ever been with the pursuit of women," noted a Bouvier in-law. A few hours later, they met up at his apartment at 125 East Seventy-fourth Street. Jackie looked fine.

Whatever the situation, Jackie's father taught Jackie invaluable lessons about style, lessons she would carry with her her whole life. As he told his daughter, "Style is not a function of how rich you are, or even who you are. Style is a habit of mind that puts quality before quantity, noble struggle before mere achievement, honor before opulence. It's what you are. It's your essential self — it's what makes you a Bouvier." Intriguingly, the subtext of Bouvier's definition of style — that it is not important how things actually are, but how they appear — is strikingly similar to that of Joseph P. Kennedy.

Jackie soon learned from her father — and later from her father-in-law — that style is not only how you choose to dress, it is also how you choose to view the world. At a very young age, Jackie possessed a formidable ability to allow only what she wanted into her life and to ignore what she did not want to see. In later years, as her fame grew to unimaginable proportions, she applied this talent to people, too. "She was the most emotionally self-sufficient person I have ever known," recalls her stepbrother, Jamie Auchincloss. Jackie herself admitted, "If something unpleasant happens to me, I block it out. I have this mechanism."

From early on, Jackie also had the ability to rework difficult or unpleasant events in her life into something more seemly, even noble. She cultivated a sense of optimism — through force of will or trick of imagination, she saw the world the way she wanted it to be. For Jackie, with her exceptionally domineering mother and self-absorbed (albeit dramatic) father, this was more a matter of survival than aesthetics.

Growing up in the Bouvier household, there were boxes within boxes, turbulent events that were overlooked or ignored. Jackie never discussed any of this with anyone, partially because of the reticence of her milieu. As C. Z. Guest admitted, "She was like me. We never discussed our personal feelings." To do so would be déclassé, almost impolite. But a greater part of Jackie's distaste for revealing things of a personal nature was that she, more than most little girls, had a good deal to hide.

In Jacqueline Bouvier's world, almost from the day she was born, things were *almost*, but not exactly, as they seemed. Her paternal grandfather, John Vernou Bouvier Jr., was referred to as "Major" after being commissioned at the age of fifty-two in the Judge Advocate Section of the Officers Reserve Corps in the U.S. Army and serving a five-month stint in 1918. A graduate of both Columbia and Columbia Law School, the major enjoyed a successful career as a lawyer before inheriting millions from his uncle, Michel Charles "M. C." Bouvier.

M. C. was a financial wizard who did business with the capitalist titans of his day — the Vanderbilts, Drexels, and Rockefellers — and was eventually named "dean of Wall Street," an honorific title given to the eldest member of the New York Stock Exchange. M. C. lived in true Gilded Age splendor with his three unmarried sisters in two adjoining New York City brownstones. A very religious man, he donated a magnificent altar in St. Patrick's Cathedral in honor of his parents, which can be seen there to this day.

M. C. died childless and left the bulk of his estate to the major, his nephew and the only male heir to his generation. In the best New World tradition, the major then honored M. C. by cobbling together a fictive genealogy called *Our Forebears* that bore the most threadbare resemblance to reality. In it, the Bouviers and Vernous are depicted as members of French aristocracy, even knighted by the Sun King himself, Louis XIV. None of it was true. In actuality, Michel Bouvier was a cabinetmaker who had immigrated to America after the Battle of Waterloo in 1815 and ended up in Philadelphia.

In terms of history, and style, the interesting thing is not that Major Bouvier wove an elite background for himself and his forebears (which practically every successful immigrant did). Or that the Bouviers were not in any way a first family of America. The key thing is that the Bouviers became American aristocracy by consciously deciding to *present* themselves as such. Yeats wrote that we eventually become the mask we choose to wear in the world; by the time Jackie was born, the Bouvier myth was accepted as fact. It was not until 1967, when John Davis critically researched the family history for his book *The Bouviers*, that Jackie's formative idea of herself was found to be largely mythical.

No matter. John Davis's discoveries did not change Jackie's perception of herself one bit. From her father and grandfather, Jackie believed she was special — whether she was in actuality is almost beside the point. She believed it, and it became true. Her father had taught her that lesson years ago.

Jacqueline Lee Bouvier was born into considerable comfort on July 28, 1929. Her father was a dashing stockbroker (if that is not too much of an oxymoron), who spent more time seducing women and tooling around in his black Mercury convertible than monitoring his investments on Wall Street. Her mother was a disciplined, emotionally volatile, socially ambitious woman who encouraged Jackie's love of horses. Janet Lee had Jackie on a horse at the age of one, schooling at age three, and jumping fences at age six.

From the start, the marriage was dicey. Bouvier was thirty-seven and a well-established roué when, to the surprise of many, he married Janet Norton Lee at St. Philomena's Church in East Hampton on July 7, 1928. Janet was twenty-one and a friend of his twin sisters, Maude and Michelle. Was it love?

Janet, like practically every other woman who ever crossed his path, was probably in thrall to the charming, inconsistent Bouvier.

For his part, Black Jack seems to have been attracted to Janet's money. The daughter of Margaret and James Lee, who had made a fortune in real estate and banking, Janet was educated at Miss Spence's in New York City, as well as Sweet Briar and Barnard Colleges. Although her parents were Catholic and the children of Irish immigrants who came to America from County Cork at the time of the potato famine, by the time she married Bouvier, Janet had somehow transmogrified into an Episcopalian descended from the "Lees of Virginia." It is almost touching how desperately she wanted to be part of society.

The Bouviers, who were listed in the first edition of the *Social Register* in 1887, never got along with the Lees. In spite of James T. Lee's considerable financial success, to the Bouviers they were just a bunch of micks. Black Jack's mother, Maude Sergeant Bouvier, practically wept at the thought of her beloved son marrying into that ridiculous family. The Lees' own marriage was in such disrepair that after Janet's birth, no one heard Old Man Lee speak to his wife, Margaret, again. Janet's grandmother, Mrs. Merritt, was right off the boat and spoke with a *brogue*, for God's sake! They kept her upstairs sewing and darning the family's linen. Once, before their marriage, Black Jack came to take Janet out. "Who is that woman?" he asked of the elderly woman peering down at him over the second-floor banister. "Oh, one of the maids," Janet answered, hurrying him out the door. In marrying Janet Lee, the Bouviers thought that Jack had definitely married down.

On the surface, though, the Bouviers led an enviable life. Jackie's sister, Caroline Lee, was born March 3, 1933, making their family complete. In the midst of the Depression, they divided their time between a rent-free duplex at 750 Park Avenue (courtesy of Janet's father) and Wildmoor, their summer home on Appaquogue Road in East Hampton (courtesy of Black Jack's father), with more than enough cars, horses, shopping, and socializing to fill their days, as well as a phalanx of servants to attend to their every whim.

But the place that captured the Bouvier imagination, then and now, was Lasata — Major Bouvier's fourteen-acre estate on Further Lane in East Hampton, New York. Lasata (from an Indian word meaning "Place of Peace") was a sprawling, artful seven-bedroom house with a huge living room and dining room and a glassed-in solarium where the Bouvier grandchildren played. For the Bouviers, Lasata was a magical, protected place. It reflected their image of themselves as part of an American elite.

Lasata's grounds were lovely. Tended to by two full-time gardeners and several assistants, they were spacious and, in the prevailing style of the time, highly manicured. As Jackie's cousin John Davis recalled, "The estate began not far from the Atlantic Ocean with a long weathered post and rail fence smothered with honeysuckle and swarming with bees whose humming could be heard from twenty-five feet away. The bluestone driveway led from Further Lane, curved through a vast green lawn under an arbor of young maples, passed by the main entrance of the house, skirted the four-car garage with the chauffeur's apartment above and the gardeners' shed, and eventually became a dusty dirt road running past a large cornfield to the stables and riding ring, where it finally ended in a back entrance on Middle Lane.

"Behind the house a brick terrace overlooked a delightful Italian garden, Lasata's chief glory and the winner of many horticultural prizes. Here a neat geometrical pattern of box hedges and brick walks guarded the flower beds — blazing yellow zinnias, blue hydrangeas, orange tiger lilies — and led to the carved stone sundial."

In the manner of the day, no estate was complete without a cutting garden with annuals, sunflowers, and roses; a vegetable garden with lima beans, lettuce, parsley, and tomatoes; and orchards of peach, pear, and plum trees. Behind the orchards stretched a long grape arbor, cornfields, and finally — for Jackie, the most vital part of her summer home — the riding ring and stables, where on most days Jackie and her mother could be found riding or grooming their horses.

Lasata was enchanting. Though the Bouviers' time there was brief, from 1935 until it was sold at the death of Major Bouvier in 1948, they saw it as nothing less than a physical manifestation of the fact that they were blessed with talent, social graces, beauty, charm, and (on the part of the major, anyway) business acumen. "We thought it would last forever," says John Davis.

But beneath Lasata's placid surface, things were not as they appeared. In spite of Jack and Janet Bouvier's glossy lives, they were fundamentally unsuited for each other. Black Jack was a self-indulgent ladies' man who had no interest in changing his ways. On their honeymoon, sailing to Europe on the *Aquitania*, he had engaged in a shipboard dalliance with tobacco heiress Doris Duke. During the summers, Jack worked at the family's brokerage firm in the city while Janet and the children stayed in East Hampton. After his day on Wall Street, he would head up to his favorite haunt, the Polo Bar at the Westbury Hotel on Madison Avenue. There, during cocktail hour, Black Jack had no difficulty persuading one of the young women to join him at his Park Avenue duplex for a private tête-à-tête. John Davis's father, who shared office space with Black Jack on Wall Street, and the same commuting schedule, used to tell young Davis about the gorgeous women he saw accompanying Uncle Jack to restaurants and cocktail lounges on summer evenings. "Your uncle has a veritable harem in New York," he confided to him.

Word of Bouvier's summer romances would, of course, make their way back to Further Lane, and Janet would fly into uncontrollable rages when he returned to East Hampton on Friday evening full of laughter and bonhomie. Knowing that Lee and Jackie preferred their father over their mother did not help matters. As the oldest, Jackie bore the brunt of her mother's roiling and, it seemed, continuous anger that would flare up like dark storm clouds no one could predict. In Janet's opinion, nothing Jackie did was right. In frustration, Janet hit her daughter and verbally abused her if she did not precisely follow her commands.

Jackie's mother's volatility was not helped by the fact that, in spite of considerable wealth on both sides of the family, Jack Bouvier personally was in a financially precarious situation. Trading his own accounts, he was more a gambler

than a broker on Wall Street—betting on stock tips and trading compulsively, in and out of the market, rather than following the more astute buy-and-hold method his father favored. Like Joseph P. Kennedy, John Bouvier Jr. emerged from the Depression with much of his considerable assets intact. After peaking at around $7.5 million in the 1920s, the major emerged from the crash with $3.8 million—$1.6 million in cash and the rest in very secure municipal, corporate, and U.S. Liberty bonds.

His son, on the other hand, with no discernible plan of action, tossed the dice every day on Wall Street. One month he might be worth $3 million on paper, the next, down to his last thousand dollars, or nothing. Regardless of the balance in his bank account, though, Black Jack kept up the front of a rich man with mistresses, fast cars, club memberships, and tailored clothes. After the Crash of '29, and through further bad investments, he was forced to go to his father and borrow twenty-five thousand dollars, a not inconsiderable amount of money for the time, but still barely enough to keep his family afloat.

Black Jack's rampant infidelity, the bitter parental fights in front of the children and servants, Janet's hair-thin temper and physical and emotional abuse of her children, particularly Jackie, might have caused Jackie's will to break. It did not. If anything, these childhood experiences served to toughen her and strengthen her inner resolve. At seven, as a student at the Chapin School in New York City, Jackie got very good grades (far better than either her husband or father at the same age) and was a champion rider. But Jackie was not a saint. At Chapin, she was quite the rebel. After racing through her schoolwork she would doodle and dream, often inciting her classmates to mayhem.

Janet Felton, a classmate who went on to work with Jackie after she became first lady, recalls, "She was naughty as everything, and she would disrupt whatever she could, but very talented. We would be taken on these ghastly bird walks in Central Park and we had to tiptoe, and of course Jackie would scream and yell.... I mean, she'd be sent to the headmistress every second week because she was so naughty!" Ethel Stringfellow, the headmistress, finally got Jackie to calm down and behave herself by comparing her to a thoroughbred. "I know you love horses," she said, "and you yourself are very much like a beautiful thoroughbred.... But if you're not properly broken in and trained, you'll be good for nothing." Years later, the beleaguered headmistress confided to Jackie's mother at one of their innumerable conferences about her behavior, "I mightn't have kept Jacqueline—except that she has the most inquiring mind we've had in this school in thirty-five years!" Whatever Miss Stringfellow told Jackie must have worked: Jackie would later call her "my first great moral influence."

At Chapin, Jackie made one of the most important friendships of her life, that of Nancy Tuckerman, whose mother was an acquaintance of Janet. They met in the fifth grade and later roomed together at Miss Porter's School in Farmington, Connecticut. Although they had no way of knowing it then, "Tuck" would remain Jackie's friend, guardian, and confidante her entire life. In time, she would almost become Jackie's alter ego; after Jackie's children, Nancy was one of her closest and most long-standing emotional connections. Her handwriting, voice, and even her outlook came to mirror Jackie's. In Jackie's world, where discretion is of the highest value, Nancy kept the secrets.

Jackie had tremendous control of her mind and did not let the tense situation at home upset her equilibrium. She refined this ability as she got older. Her sister, Lee, believes this talent — a coping mechanism, really — first came about in the aftermath of their parents unceasingly bitter divorce when Jackie was eleven years old. Lee feels that "Jackie was really fortunate to have or acquire the ability to tune out, which she always kept. It was like, for the years from ten to twenty, never hearing anything [from your parents] except how awful the other one was. I envied her so much being able to press the button and tune out."

Jackie responded to the upheaval in her family by disappearing into her room to read, spending hours on her horse, Danseuse, or going for long walks by herself on the grounds of Lasata or the beach. "Oh — to live by the sea is my only wish," she wrote in a poem at the time. To cope with her disruptive home life, Jackie turned inward. There was no one she could trust, no one she could confide in. And even if there were, would she have chosen to? "Her privacy and her shyness were very great," observes Jamie Auchincloss.

Janet obtained a Reno divorce from her husband in June 1940, leaving Jackie shell-shocked. A member of her East Hampton riding club remembers her that summer, "wandering around like a lost kitten, talking to the grooms and lavishing attention on the horses. You somehow sensed that she was a thousand miles away, existing in a world of manufactured dreams."

The pain of her parents' divorce stayed with Jackie a long time. When Jackie was in her sixties, her friend Peter Duchin, son of the bandleader Eddy Duchin, asked if she had any memory of his parents. She replied, "I'll never forget the night my mother and father both came into my bedroom all dressed up to go out. I can still smell the scent my mother wore and feel the softness of her fur coat as she leaned over to kiss me goodnight. In such an excited voice she said, 'Darling, your father and I are going dancing tonight at the Central Park Casino to hear Eddy Duchin.' I don't know why the moment has stayed with me all these years. Perhaps it was one of the few times I remember seeing my parents together. It was so romantic. So hopeful."

Two years after the breakup, Janet regained her social and financial standing by marrying the immensely rich Standard Oil heir Hugh D. Auchincloss Jr. (whom Jackie and Lee would come to call "Uncle Hughdie"). The girls went to live with them at Merrywood, an imposing brick Georgian home outside Washington, D.C., in what was then rural McLean, Virginia, and Hammersmith Farm in Newport, Rhode Island.

Like everyone who lived there, Jackie was captivated by Merrywood. Set on fifty acres high above the Potomac, the tall white pillars of the front portico reminded her of Tara in her favorite movie, *Gone With the Wind*. The estate, with its sun-dappled meadows, stables, riding paths, and dramatic views of the Potomac, gave her a feeling of peace and security after the tumult of the past few years. Author Gore Vidal, whose mother Nina Gore Vidal had been Auchincloss's second wife, described Merrywood as "peaceful...a bit Henry Jamesian,

a world of deliberate quietude removed from the twentieth-century tension. It was a life that gave total security, but not much preparation for the real world."

His son, Hugh D. "Yusha" Auchincloss III, recalls meeting Jackie before their parents got together. "I first met Jackie in December 1941, when she was twelve. She, her sister Lee, eight, and their mother Janet Bouvier came from New York to visit my father and me at our home, Merrywood, for a sight seeing tour of Washington ten days after Pearl Harbor.

"Janet B. and my father, both recently divorced, were friends and obviously attracted to each other, and I quickly gathered that each thought it would be nice if the girls could meet a shy, young teenager home for Christmas vacation from Groton school." During their first week together, Jackie and Yusha became fast friends. He wanted to give her a Christmas present but did not know what to buy her. Besides, he had already used up his quarter-a-week allowance. He romantically offered to share half of his polo pony, Chief, with her the next time she visited Washington.

"Which half would I be responsible for," Jackie immediately wanted to know. "Feeding or cleaning up?"

Even in their early negotiating, Yusha noticed, Jackie positioned herself to have the upper hand, and her questions and answers were to the point. A few years later, her quick thinking saved Yusha from a speeding ticket on the Merritt Parkway driving from Washington to Newport. When they were stopped by a young Connecticut state trooper, Jackie leaned over, looked seriously into his eyes, and in a quiet voice informed him, "Excuse me officer, but your fly is undone." Embarrassed, he thanked her and neglected to give Yusha a ticket.

On their last walk at Merrywood that Christmas vacation, Jackie and Yusha stood on a rock overlooking the cold rapids of the Potomac. Jackie thanked Yusha for accompanying her and invited him to visit her in New York over Easter vacation so she could show him the Empire State Building and the Statue of Liberty, and they could go ice skating at Rockefeller Center. Yusha readily accepted and, when he returned to school, wanted to send her a letter confirming everything. But his French was poor and he was not sure how to spell Bouvier. Fortunately, his teacher told him to look through a recent *National Geographic* article on unusual dogs and find a picture of a Bouvier Deflandre. Jackie had told him about her dog, Cappy, so at least he knew what they looked like. He was able to address the envelope correctly, and so their correspondence of more than half a century began.

Although he was only two years older than Jackie, Yusha noticed how enormously self-possessed she was even as a young girl. He recalls, "I never heard or read of her complaining about herself, never saw her cry — only occasionally weep for others. She often thanked and she often praised. Her physical courage showed whenever needed, but the courage of her convictions was always present. She was determined, self-disciplined, with a sense of clear purpose that she carried out with a desire for perfection. Her capacity for concentration, whether it be exhibited in amusing storytelling, both real and imaginative, her thoughtful writing, her whimsical drawing, was finely focused. Her sense of humor, often mischievous, was never cruel and often directed toward herself."

Although Janet was still high-strung, she and Hughdie settled comfortably into their vast country estates, with their children, horses, dogs, servants, bridge partners, and family retainers — a kind of WASP Brady Bunch. For Janet, it was Auchincloss's money that made the difference. Hughdie may have been dull, with none of Black Jack's inconstant spark, but he was safe and reliable.

Auchincloss had three children from his previous marriages to Maria Chaprovitsky (Yusha's mother) and Nina Gore Vidal (mother of Nina and Tommy), while Janet brought Jackie and Lee. Janet and Hughdie then had two children of their own, Janet Jennings and James Lee. Remarkably, everyone seemed to get along, and Jackie took a strong motherly interest in both Janet and Jamie.

After the self-involved drama of the Bouviers, this was the closest thing Jackie ever had to a normal family life. At Christmas, Lee and Jackie recruited the Auchincloss children to participate in the annual Christmas pageant they staged for their mother. Yusha played Joseph, Jackie was Mary, and Lee, the only one who could carry a tune, was an angel who sang all the carols. Jesus was played by one of Janet's dogs, usually a pug or a poodle wrapped in a satin-edged baby blanket; in later pageants Janet or Jamie would be given the role.

Jackie was a rambunctious, fun-loving adolescent with an irreverent view of the world. As the eldest girl in the blended Auchincloss coterie, she did not take any nonsense from anyone — least of all Yusha, even if he was two years older. In the first summer together at Hammersmith in 1943, with the war on, the children had chores — Yusha helped milk the Guernsey cows and Jackie collected eggs from the chickens. Once Yusha, a bit lazy and dreaming of a back scratch and a head rub, asked Jackie if she would mind waking him the next morning. Jackie thought his request presumptuous and entered his room the next day with a damp washcloth soaked in hydrogen peroxide and vigorously rubbed his head with it. In the shrieks that followed, Jackie explained that she got the idea from seeing Yusha's adorable baby picture when he had been a blond. She only wanted to help and thought it would be nice to bring his hair back to its original color. Really.

By the time Yusha finished milking the cows and riding his bicycle to Bailey's Beach, the sun had caused his hair to turn even blonder. He got lots of compliments and even forgave Jackie (sort of), but he hid the peroxide and from then on got himself out of bed.

In many ways, Jackie was a typical American girl. She loved movies: *The Wizard of Oz, Casablanca* (Humphrey Bogart and Ingrid Bergman were two of her favorite actors), and anything to do with a horse or a dog—*National Velvet* or *Lassie Come Home. Gone With the Wind* was a particular favorite; she had read the book three times by the age of nine. She confided to Yusha that Rhett Butler reminded her of her father, Scarlett O'Hara of her mother, and Ashley Wilkes was sort of Yusha and his father combined. She was not exactly flattered when Yusha said that he thought she was like Melanie— but felt better after he quickly explained that he meant their similar strong characters.

By the age of twelve or thirteen, the essential Jackie was in place. She was smart, an exceptional reader, and a cutup. She had befriended Nancy Tuckerman. While she had an up-and-down relationship with Lee and her mother, she consistently loved ballet, reading, horses, her father, and the sea. Yusha recalls that during their first sight-seeing week in Washington, "Jackie loved the Smithsonian. One of her special interests was the American Indian, although she was also fascinated by pirates. . . . She greatly loved her father and imagined him as a swashbuckling pirate." Even her husband John F. Kennedy, a man not generally given to introspection, noticed "she's got a father thing."

Early on, Jackie made the connection between money and security. Her mother taught her the importance of "marrying well," which, in her mind, meant rich. Having witnessed the hurtful, self-involved dramas of the Lees and the Bouviers, Jackie knew how precarious familial relations could be. Now that she divided her time between the Auchincloss worlds of Merrywood and Hammersmith, the influence of East Hampton and the Bouviers, and even her father, receded.

But again, like life at Lasata, things were not precisely as they appeared. No matter how glamorous and well situated the Bouvier girls' lives appeared in the bright, pretty rooms of Merrywood, as the stepdaughter of a very wealthy man Jackie knew she and Lee were dependent on his largesse. As the oldest male, Yusha would inherit the houses and the land; the remainder of the money would be divided between him and his Auchincloss siblings. Jackie knew she would have to make her own way in the world. She realized that her father—no matter how much she idolized him—could not, in the end, be relied upon.

Nothing in Jackie's young life was really secure. Her mother's love was entirely conditional—upon her grades at school, how she behaved, the ribbons she won at horse shows. Her father's, while unconditional, was powerless against the daunting Auchincloss establishment, while he himself was largely absent from her life now. Although it appeared she came from a stable WASP background, Jackie was like Cinderella, the stepdaughter. Outside of her belief in herself, nothing was certain.

Perhaps because she was the keeper of so many secrets and so many conflicting emotions, Jackie had the habit of being maddeningly elusive — even to those closest to her. In later years, her good friend Oleg Cassini observed, "Jackie was famous for her shifting moods. She was an original and difficult to decipher. She might be warm one day and freeze you out the next. . . . She seemed quite a challenge to me. You never really knew where you stood with Jackie."

She also had a very strong need to be by herself. "I think most fascinating people often are solitary so their batteries get recharged," says Jamie Auchincloss. Not surprisingly, Jackie's elusiveness drew other people to her. Although she was the life of the party and could, if she chose, charm the birds out of the trees, Jackie held herself separate, a little apart.

Given her background, and given the ethos she picked up from the Bouviers, Jackie invented herself. She took an unfortunate situation — her parents' divorce, her mother's abuse, her father's drinking and verbally incestuous manner — and neatly recast it by either putting it out of her mind, in her mother's case, or perceiving it as something more romantic (her father did not have a drinking problem, he was just extremely sociable). While her background was not exactly as it seemed, her *belief* in herself, from the love of her father and the mythical Bouvier past, was absolutely grounded.

In terms of fashion and style, growing up, Jackie was a tomboy who lived in her riding outfit of breeches and boots. As Jackie said in an essay she wrote in 1951, "I lived in New York City until I was thirteen and spent the summers in the country. I hated dolls, loved horses and dogs, and had skinned knees and braces on my teeth for what must have seemed an interminable length of time to my family."

Sylvia Whitehouse Blake, one of Jackie's closest Newport friends, noted that "Jackie didn't care a whit about fashion in those days. She and I ran around in shorts and sneakers all summer. The only time we dressed up was during Tennis Week, Newport's social highlight. But even then we weren't exactly your typical *Vogue* fashion plates."

Jamie Auchincloss thinks Jackie's mother influenced her sense of style. "Our mother was always very carefully and superbly dressed, and made sure that she didn't fall into the trap that women in the 1940s and 1950s did with wearing big hair or corsages or too much jewelry. I remember at my mother's funeral, there was a woman minister who barely knew her, and the main thing about this minister's eulogy was the hats that mummy wore and the fact that she was never seen without her perfect white kid gloves."

Jamie mentions an interesting subtext to their relationship—that his mother was always the center of attention until Jackie came along. "My mother had a lot of social charm, so I think Jackie got that from her," he says. He thinks, too, there may have been some competition involved between Janet and her daughter because "maybe one of the reasons that they were barely together was that they didn't want to share the spotlight."

At Jackie's coming out party at Newport's Clambake Club in August 1947, she wore a lovely white tulle gown with an off-the-shoulder neckline and bouffant skirt that she had picked up at a New York department store for fifty-nine dollars. Her mother, still recovering from the birth of Jamie in the spring, was unable to shop with Jackie for the dress. Instead, she told Jackie to buy "the most glamorous one possible." The simple gown Jackie wore was lovely, but Janet, who expected a more ravishing creation to reflect Jackie's position as her daughter, was disappointed by her choice.

Her sister, Lee, on the other hand, trying to look sophisticated at the age of fourteen, had no compunction about going for glamour. According to Sylvia Whitehouse Blake, "Lee was shorter than Jackie but more rounded, with a classically attractive heart-shaped face and tiny, delicate features. She never left the house unless dressed for Ascot."

Lee had been invited to attend the party after dinner and showed up in a racy dress of her own design that she had coaxed a local seamstress to make for her. Instead of the little girl dress she was expected to wear, Jackie recalled that Lee arrived in a "strapless pink satin [gown] sprinkled generously with rhinestones and sirenishly accessorized with elbow-length black satin mitts, fingerless, but tethered by a pointed strap over her middle finger." Janet, needless to say, was not pleased with the spectacle Lee was making of herself. After a moment, Jackie saw the humor of it—pink satin and rhinestones in boring old Newport! The stag line made a determined rush for the curvaceous, flirty Lee. That night, on her sister's evening, Lee got the lion's share of attention. It was the last time she, or anyone else, would outshine Jackie.

Although it may not have appeared this way, Jackie was an outsider, separated from others by her intelligence, her shyness, her family's secrets, and her exotic good looks. Among the Auchinclosses she was a glamorous interloper. As a bystander to her parents' turbulent marriage, she had a lot to hide. She was enormously proud of her Bouvier heritage and, after her marriage to John F. Kennedy, held herself apart from the Kennedys, refusing to take part in their incessant roughhousing and touch football games. Still later, she would be separated from others by tragedy, by what life had asked of her and how she responded. But in her early adolescence, she felt apart from others by her sensitivity, her intelligence, and her quest to survive.

Although they were educated at the "best" schools (Jackie at Chapin, Farmington, and Vassar; Lee at the Potomac School, Farmington, and Sarah Lawrence), members of all the "right" clubs, and even listed in the *Social Register*, Jackie and Lee were outside society in a way that is difficult to imagine today. In the 1920s, Irish Catholics were rare in WASP society, while Jews were unheard-of. One particularly onerous bit of society gossip about Janet Lee Auchincloss circulating at the time was that her original surname was not Lee, but Levi. It was not true, but Janet flew into a rage when her ten-year-old stepdaughter, Nina, repeating something she had overheard, said, "I wonder what will happen when Hughdie finds out that Janet's father was Mr. Levi."

Having grown up under this not-so-polite prejudice, Jackie never forgot what it was like to be discriminated against. Near the end of her life, Jackie had lunch with Peter Duchin, who had been raised in the shadow of great wealth by Averill and Marie Harriman after his parents' untimely death. Peter was just beginning the process of writing his memoirs. "You're about to embark on a very difficult journey," she confided in him. "I could never do a book like this. It would be too painful."

And then she made a fascinating observation about the world she had grown up in, a world she seemed very much a part of. "You know, Peter, we both live and do very well in this world of WASPs and old money and society. It's all supposed to be so safe and continuous. But you and I are not really of it. Maybe because I'm Catholic and because my parents were divorced when I was young — a terribly radical thing at the time — I've always always felt like an outsider in that world. Haven't you?"

"Yes and no," Duchin replied.

Jackie felt separated from others not only by her religion and her parents' divorce, but, more acutely, by her intelligence and her shyness. Although cloaked in a beguiling aura of femininity, she also had a fierce sense of discipline, focus, and intelligence. It wasn't until her junior year of college, when she studied at the Sorbonne in Paris, that she "learned not to be ashamed of a real hunger for knowledge, something I had always tried to hide."

Even as a young girl, Jackie knew that the socially cloistered worlds of East Hampton, Newport, Bailey's Beach, and all they represented were too small for her. As a teenager, Jackie predicted she might end up as "a circus queen... who married the young man on the flying trapeze."

She and Vivian Crespi dreamed of bigger things than Saturday night dances at the club. As Vivian recalls, "We wanted to move beyond what was expected of us. It's just that we grew up in a rather limited, shall we say, WASP world and both of us happily escaped it at an early age. She did say that to me in Greece. We were sitting there, saying how lucky we were to have gotten

away from the narrow little world we were brought up in. She kept moving forward — she had to."

By the time she left for college, Jackie had matured into a striking young
woman. As she described herself for *Vogue* magazine, "I am tall, 5'7", with
brown hair, a square face, and eyes so unfortunately far apart that it takes three
weeks to have a pair of glasses made with a bridge wide enough to fit over my
nose. I do not have a sensational figure but can look slim if I pick the right
clothes. I flatter myself on being able at times to walk out of the house looking
like a poor man's Paris copy, but often my mother will run up to inform me
that my left stocking seam is crooked or the right-hand top coat button is about
to fall off. This, I realize, is the Unforgivable Sin."

Jackie turned eighteen in July 1947. At the end of the summer, amidst
all the fun she was having in Newport, all the beaux, all the parties, all the
boys ("She had more men per square inch than any woman I've ever
known," recalls Letitia Baldrige), she had to pack up and head to Poughkeepsie, New York, where she would attend Vassar College. In the fall of her
freshman year, she was voted Deb of the Year by newspaper columnist
Cholly Knickerbocker (the pen name of Igor Cassini, Oleg's older brother).
He described her as "a regal brunette who has classic features and the dainti-
ness of Dresden porcelain. She has poise, she is soft-spoken and intelligent,
everything the leading debutante should be." Jackie was more embarrassed
than anything else by the honor. Her Vassar friends do not ever remember
her mentioning it — she was too self-possessed for that. She did, however, get
a giant kick out of the fact that she happened to be wearing the "siren suit"
Lee had worn to her coming out party when Knickerbocker decided Jackie
was going to be his Deb of the Year.

the whispering sisters

They were the original American geishas.

— TRUMAN CAPOTE

If anyone could give Jackie a run for her money in the style department, it was her younger sister. In fact, in terms of taste, originality of design, and beauty, by all accounts Lee surpassed Jackie.

Although the Bouvier girls squabbled as children, by the time they had married and were starting their own families (Lee married her first husband, Michael Canfield, said to be the illegitimate son of the duke of Windsor, in the spring of 1953), Lee and Jackie were as close as any two siblings. People who knew Jackie and Lee then were struck by their friendly intimacy. Once, in New York's Central Park, they were taken out in a rowboat by Michael Canfield. As he wielded the oars, the two sisters sat in front, whispering intently behind their hands. Later, Michael asked Lee what they had been discussing, imagining some grave family crisis.

"Gloves," she told him, in all seriousness. From then on, he dubbed them "the whispering sisters," which Jackie loved. After the Canfields moved to London where Michael represented Harper & Row Publishers, Lee and Jackie stayed in touch visiting back and forth across the Atlantic.

Lee married her second husband, Prince Stanislas "Stas" Radziwill, in March 1958. A Polish émigré who insisted on using his technically defunct royal title, as did Lee (much to the amusement of the British upper echelon they circulated in), Radziwill was a real estate developer in London. Nineteen years older than Lee, friends thought Stas (pronounced "Stash") bore a marked physical resemblance to Black Jack Bouvier, with his stocky physique, broad face, and thin mustache.

Jack Kennedy once said that "the White House is no place to make friends." And he was right. After her sister and brother-in-law moved to 1600 Pennsylvania Avenue, Princess Lee was a frequent guest, always staying in the Lincoln Bedroom, a place of honor.

During these hectic, public years, Jackie loved Lee because she did not have to *explain* everything to her. They had grown up in the same rooms, walked barelegged together at Lasata in July, known the same cast of characters that were the Bouviers. And besides Jackie, Lee was the only one who knew what it was like to have Janet Auchincloss for a mother.

When Jackie was living in the White House and her entire life was so publicly dissected she could not stand it, Lee was her confidante. When the whole world wanted a piece of her, Lee did not. She asked no favors.

On technical points, Lee was prettier than Jackie. Vincent Ropatte, who styled both women's hair at the Caruso Salon in the

1980s, said that Lee is actually more delicate than Jackie. "Lee is truly a raving beauty. There were times when I would see her in the morning when she didn't have any makeup on, and every feature was just *so!*"

In terms of fashion and style, Lee was the trailblazer, taking more risks than her conservatively dressed sister. As early as 1962, she was one of the first to discover Corrèges and Ungaro. With her sister in the White House and promising to wear only American designers, Lee smuggled Givenchy suits to her from Paris, thinking no one would be the wiser.

Jackie often turned to her for fashion advice. A friend who spent the weekend with the Radziwills at Turnville Grange, their country home outside London, remembers Jackie calling hourly from the White House about what to wear to this event and that event. "They were on the phone *constantly*," she recalls. "And this was when transatlantic calls were expensive."

In the White House, Jackie was careful to give her sister her due. She hosted a dinner dance in her honor on March 15, 1961. With guests ranging from LBJ to Prince Aga Khan, it was the highlight of the social calendar. When Lee accompanied Jackie to India, she was referred to as Princess Radziwill.

But despite Jackie's efforts, Lee was quickly, and some would say permanently, eclipsed by Jackie's celebrity. As Jamie Auchincloss observes, "Lee was *always* being called the kid sister of Jackie — you know, the Princess Margaret Syndrome." For a woman as talented and finely tuned as Lee,

this must have been excruciating. Still, she did the best she could. "If I wanted to compete with my sister," she once quipped, "I would have given up when I was twelve."

As an adult, Lee attempted to carve her own path, away from Jackie. She tried acting, decorating, and, most recently, has been a fashion ambassador for Giorgio Armani. Like many wellborn women, she made the mistake of befriending Truman Capote, not realizing his gossipy stories, once so entertaining, could easily be turned against her. After a bitter falling out, he took to referring to her as "La Princess Manqué" on national television.

These days, in the midst of a divorce from her third husband, director Herbert Ross, Lee divides her time between New York and Paris, with her niece Caroline including her in her family's activities. Fated to survive two of her husbands, her older sister, and, most tragically, her son Anthony, Lee is still fragile, beautiful, and largely misunderstood. "It is strange to speak with her now," says a friend. "She sounds just like her sister — it's like listening to a ghost." In publishing circles, it is known that she has been working on her autobiography these past few years. Will we ever see it?

In many ways, Lee Bouvier is still the gamine young woman whispering about gloves while the world wonders. Regardless of the vagaries of their relationship (Lee, more beautiful; Jackie, more famous), Lee has kept her sister's confidences, inconsequential as they might be. And in Jackie's world, this is the highest way of showing your regard for someone.

I hate this pink and gray college.

— EDNA ST. VINCENT MILLAY, '17

that damned vassar

When Jackie entered Vassar through Taylor Gate on Raymond Avenue in September 1947, she was an eighteen-year-old wearing what every other well-dressed young woman of her era and class wore: a neat traveling suit, white gloves, small purse, and an even smaller cloche hat perched upon her tidy coiffed head.

By the time Miss Bouvier arrived, Vassar had long figured prominently in the American imagination. According to Mary McCarthy, '33, it signified "a certain *je ne sais quoi*; a whiff of luxury and the ineffable, plain thinking and high living." In terms of luxury, the campus, designed by Frederick Law Olmsted, was almost cinematically picturesque, featuring two lakes, a golf course, an apple orchard, and a riding stable. The library looked like a cathedral, with a stained-glass window devoted to the Italian scholar Elena Lucrezia Cornaro Picopia, the first woman to receive a Ph.D., in the fifteenth century. There were also the social niceties everyone's parents expected, with tea served every afternoon in the Rose Parlor.

As one of three hundred freshmen, Jackie lived with her roommate, Edna Harrison, in an unadorned room on the third floor of Main Building. A dramatic brick structure, Main was modeled after the Tuileries and, at one time, housed the entire college, with the top floor devoted to the college's first Art Gallery. Dramatic inside, the halls of Main were ten feet wide to accommodate the hoop skirts of the Civil War era, with twelve-foot ceilings.

Considering the places Jackie would eventually live, Room 312, her one-room double, was exceedingly simple, just twenty-six by eleven feet, with

glazed oak molding its only decorative touch. There were two walk-in closets, one for each girl, with the bathroom down the hall. The lone window — did they flip a coin to see who would get the desk beneath it? — faced the quad in the direction of Strong House, another dorm, and Rockefeller Hall, where Jackie attended Shakespeare class.

The school was founded by Matthew Vassar, a brewer, as the first American institution devoted solely to the higher education of women. English has been the most popular major since the school's inception in 1861. Not surprising in a crowd of such literary strivers, mnemonics abounded. Like generations before her, Jackie learned "Dear Robert Louis Stevenson," the phrase used to remember Davison, Raymond, Lathrop, and Strong — the dorms on the quad.

Of course, Vassar had its own sartorial style, which could best be described (then as now) as bohemian prep. Once the parents departed, everyone dressed, well, pretty badly, unless you were going to the prom or New York City for the weekend. Much to the dismay of alums, students of Jackie's day favored jeans rolled to mid-calf, or gray flannel Bermuda shorts worn with white socks and beat-up sneakers, with a camel hair polo coat tossed over one's shoulder. No matter how badly you dressed, a single-strand pearl necklace (the requisite debutante present) was de rigueur. Except for the lab rats in the Sciences, everyone's hair shone. Blondes abounded.

Selwa "Lucky" Showker Roosevelt, who got her nickname because she was a talented card player at Vassar ("I took the name Lucky as a kind of talisman —

and it's worked!"), was a good friend of Jackie's. In later years, she went on to become a journalist and author, working as chief of protocol for the Reagan White House, but for now, she and Jackie were just two girls living on the same hall on the third floor of Main.

She remembers, "We wore skirts and bobby socks, baggy sweaters, and a string of pearls. Then we got very dressed up on weekends. I remember I had all these dresses. They were the first sophisticated clothes that I ever owned, and certainly inappropriate! They were very sexy, glamorous things that I bought in New York."

As for shopping, there was a surprisingly large selection in Arlington, the tiny town that catered to the college. Peck & Peck, the famous New York store, maintained an outpost on Raymond Avenue near the edge of campus, where students were allowed to open charge accounts sent to their parents. ("I have paid Peck & Peck & Peck & Peck," wrote F. Scott Fitzgerald, then a struggling screenwriter in Hollywood, to his daughter, Patricia "Scottie" Fitzgerald, '42, when she was an undergraduate.) Shops like Luckey Platt's, Edythe Harris Lucas ("College Sport and Dress Wear"), and Beatrice Kaye & Co. ("House of College Fashions") featured Braemar sweaters from Scotland and other collegiate favorites.

The finer New York department stores like Bergdorf's and Best & Co. came up from the city once a season and staged fashion shows at the tea shops that lined Collegeview Avenue to induce the young women to buy the latest fashions. "There was also a wonderful store called Alexander's in the city," Lucky rhapsodizes, "that used to have line-for-line wonderful copies of the French designers like Givenchy that we were absolute crazy for."

Lucky Roosevelt has fond memories of Jackie. "When I went to Vassar, I was very unsophisticated, and to me Jackie was just the most awesome person. First of all, her beauty was incredible. She didn't wear any makeup — she didn't have to! I mean, to me she was *breathtaking!* Incredible wide-set eyes, and this mouth which was very sensual. Yet, she also seemed unaware of her physical beauty."

The young Jackie's combination of modesty, humor, shyness, and beauty made her an extremely appealing friend. "Oh, always — she had such wit! Jackie was so funny! Every now and then she would say something and I wasn't sure if she wasn't being a little bit observant and cute, or whether she was just being funny.

"She had a very broad mind. And very modest. She never projected herself. She had that incredible beauty, but she never pushed herself to the forefront. I remember what I thought was so lovely about her was this enormous beautiful hair. It was so dark and alive. She drew beautifully, darling things. She had a great sense of humor. Even then, she had a star quality — you just knew something wonderful was going to happen to her!"

Lucky also recalls that Jackie effortlessly got good grades. "I remember when our first marks came and everybody was so nervous. I was so sure that I was going to fail out.... Jackie got her grades — everyone was talking about it and she didn't say anything. So one day we were walking across campus and I said, 'Jackie, is anything wrong?' I wanted to console her in case, you know, things hadn't gone so well.

"'I made Dean's List.'"

And Lucky had been worried about her! "Actually, I thought she looked rather embarrassed about it. She was never the sort to jump up and down, she was pretty self-contained."

Slight, gray-haired, pretty Helen Sandison, the Elizabethan specialist, taught Jackie's freshman Shakespeare class. An English professor from 1913 to 1950, she was legendary for having taught Edna St. Vincent Millay (who received the Pulitzer Prize for poetry in 1923), Mary McCarthy, and Eleanor Clark, as well as the scores of Roosevelts, Rockefellers, and Mellons who tripped through. Professor Sandison was renowned for her hatred of imprecision, foggy thinking, and bowdlerization of texts. She imbued Jackie with a love of Shakespeare that found its way into JFK's senate speeches and, later, the White House.

Carmine Calenti, a World War II veteran, was one of about thirteen men in the sophomore class attending Vassar at the time on the GI Bill. He sat next to Jackie in Sandison's class, on the second floor of Rockefeller Hall.

He remembers Jackie as reserved and shy, graciously making him, the only man in the room, feel more comfortable. She didn't contribute much to class, but neither did Calenti. "I was intimidated," he recalls. They both knew French, and Sandison chastised them for speaking it to one another.

Seated alphabetically beside Jackie next to the door, Calenti remembers that Jackie was "the first to leave and the last to enter." Like the rest of her class-mates, she "wore mostly baggy sweaters, wool Bermuda shorts, and knee socks — they all dressed that way. She was quite attractive. She didn't need any makeup."

At eighteen and nineteen, Jackie was a natural beauty. She wore little makeup because she felt (as she told *Vogue*) that "beauty care for a college girl should be confined to the minimum essentials. Any elaborate plan will be ignored in the frenzy of studying during the week and going away on weekends."

As a college student, Jackie believed that "the health and cleanliness of hair, skin, teeth, and nails are the basis of any beauty care. If these are attended to regularly and with a little discipline it should be possible to achieve what is more important than beauty...namely good grooming." Jackie felt you should take one night a week for the time-consuming jobs of sham-poos, manicures, hair removal, and so on. She believed that "you can never slip into too dismal an abyss of untidiness if once every seven days you will pull yourself up short and cope with ragged ends." Thursday night, in her opinion, was a good time to do this.

In later years, Jackie had famed hairstylists Alexandre and Kenneth to do the heavy lifting. As a college girl, she was strictly do-it-yourself. ("We didn't go to the hairdresser in those days," says Lucky Roosevelt "We were all just normal girls.")

Hair—should be brushed every night, fifty to one hundred strokes, depending on the oiliness of the scalp. Bend over while brushing and grab the scalp with the brush at every stroke. Jackie suggested an oil shampoo if your hair is dry and a vinegar rinse to cut hard water and leave a sheen. And steer clear from too many permanents.

Skin—"Soap and water and one good nourishing cream is all that a healthy young skin needs.... Wash your face at night with hot water and a rough wash cloth and really rub, with upward strokes on the cheeks and forehead.... Rinse with cold water: the shock will stimulate circulation and leave it tingling. With the same upward motions massage in a rich cream before retiring. Do this for about two minutes and wipe off what is left so that you won't find it on the pillow the next morning."

Makeup—Although she later favored Erno Laszlo, in college Jackie thought Dorothy Gray's Special Dry Skin Mixture was "excellent" for her. After applying a very small amount of this moisturizer, she patted on translucent powder with a cotton ball, using the other side of the cotton to remove the excess. She found this gave "an even surface that looks smoother and will last longer and clog up your skin less than any pancake concoctions.

"Grin, and on the part of your cheeks that are in relief, use a powder rouge if you need it. It should be the same tone as your lipstick and nail polish. If you can't maneuver a lipstick brush get one of the new long lipsticks, a not too greasy brand ... it should stay on through hours and corn on the cob."

Hands—Jackie advised keeping a bottle of hand lotion on your bureau and using it whenever you come into the room. "This is especially important after washing the hands and before going to bed."

Teeth—Floss and use ammoniated toothpaste. If you smoke (as Jackie did), brush with a peroxide rinse weekly—"Nothing will be counted against you faster than a dingy smile."

Hair Removal—*Don't* use a razor, advised Jackie. "It may be cheaper but will catch up with you in the end and leave you with a case of lifelong stubble." Instead, she recommended depilatory cream. "Smooth it on the legs, underarms, arms if you need to, and give yourself a manicure while waiting for it to work."

Finally, Jackie advised young women to "eat and sleep sensibly, remember that cleanliness and neatness are what you are working for." With a little extra time each week, Jackie believed, "you should never have to scream in anguish and take an hour to get ready when told that your best beau has arrived unexpectedly and is waiting downstairs."

When Jackie was at Vassar, *everybody* smoked. (They also knitted, played bridge, went sledding down Sunset Hill, and waited for some Yale guy to call, but that wasn't so medically treacherous.) In a way, cigarettes were perfect for college — they helped you stay thin, and they helped you concentrate, relax, and stay awake. In a class photo taken in 1947 during Freshman Serenade (a yearly event where the freshmen had to sing to the seniors) Jackie stands with her pals from Main North, half hidden in the second row, second from the left. Everyone, nicely dressed, seems caught in mid–cigarette break.

Cigarettes were such a part of their bright college years that on the last page of the Class of '51's yearbook there is a full-page ad for Camel ("So Mild — and they taste so Good!"), with a woman in an evening dress smiling and looking over her shoulder, as if she is off to New Haven for the weekend.

In Jackie's day, anyone who could leave on weekends did. With a father in the city, Yusha Auchincloss at Yale, Bouvier cousin John Davis at Princeton, and a scattering of friends on the North Shore of Long Island, Jackie was well set for weekend socializing. For her part, Jackie rode her horse, Danseuse, made Dean's List, and disappeared on weekends. "She wasn't much of a joiner," recalled a friend.

For beyond tea in the Rose Parlor, the library-as-cathedral, and the riding stables, Vassar resembled an extremely *luxe* prison, and this may have started to rankle Jackie. If the college was characterized by a great deal to do, there were also a myriad of rules telling you what you could *not* do. Jeans had to be changed for dinner; only skirts were permitted in the dining halls. You had to sign out for weekends and return from vacations on a designated day. If you were late, or there was some kind of an infraction, you got demerits.

"You needed to get permission for *everything*," recalls Lucky Roosevelt. There was even a warden (during Jackie's years, Mrs. Elizabeth Drouilhet) to make sure the rules were obeyed.

At Miss Porter's, where she boarded from tenth through twelfth grade, Jackie wrote that her ambition was not to be a housewife. One would have thought Vassar was perfect for her — as McCarthy characterized her, the Vassar girl has "a passion for public service coupled with a yearning for the limelight, a wish to play a part in the theatre of world events, to perform some splendid action that will cut one's name in history like a figure eight in ice."

By the end of her sophomore year, Jackie was tired of being, as she put it, "a schoolgirl among schoolgirls." She considered giving up school entirely and moving to the city and becoming a photographer's model. Her father, who

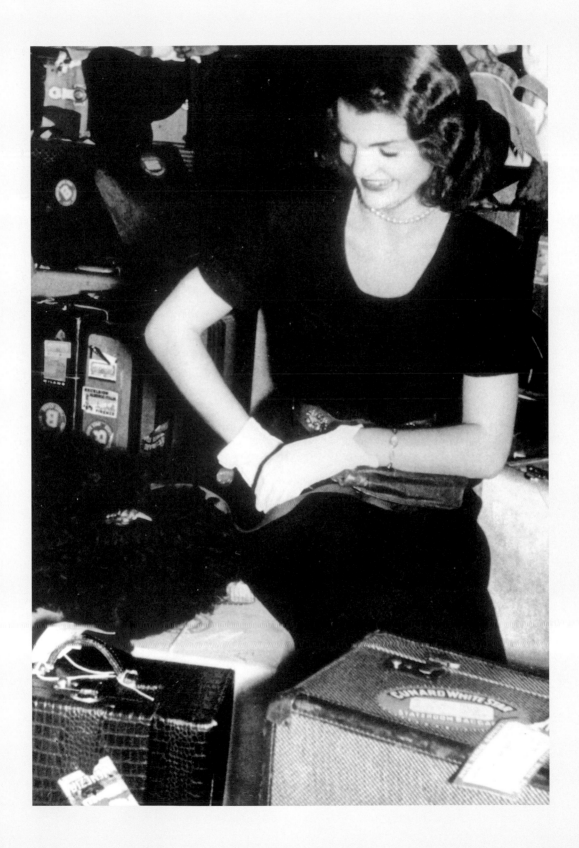

knew a good deal about the activities of young models in the city, quickly nipped that idea in the bud. Jackie came up with another plan and instead spent her junior year in France, studying at the Sorbonne.

Although the Kennedy mythmaking machine (and even her cousin John Davis) recounts the story of Jackie spotting a notice on a bulletin board advertising the Smith College Junior Year Abroad Program and deciding to study at the Sorbonne, the truth is that while she did study at the Sorbonne, Jackie never got permission to go abroad. According to Colton Johnson, Vassar's current dean of students, Jackie essentially went AWOL and never applied for or received permission from the college to study in France for the year.

When it came time for Jackie to return to Vassar, the story has always been that she decided not to: she was tired of Poughkeepsie and wanted to return home to Merrywood. In light of the fact that she took an extended road trip — abroad — without their permission, the college refused to allow her to graduate with her class.

A typical twenty-year-old, Jackie must have assumed she would somehow be able to talk her way back in — after all, she *did* make Dean's List.

Jackie's father, furious with her, drove up to Vassar to plead her case. It meant a great deal to him and the Bouvier pride that his daughter graduate from Vassar — she was an excellent student, he wanted to keep her close to him in New York City, and besides, what other school had as much prestige?

Fortunately for Jackie, unfortunately for him, Black Jack's vaunted charm did not hold much sway with Miss Marion Tate, the dean. Jackie had gone to study in Paris without obtaining the proper permission and was not allowed to return. And *that* was her final answer.

Lucky Roosevelt had never heard Jackie's true reason for not returning to college. Once she learned it, she said, "You know I never understood that.... I mean, here was this brilliant girl, she got wonderful marks, and then she went to Paris, which makes sense. Then she never comes back!"

So, much to her father's dismay, Jackie never graduated with her class. And although she kept in touch with her roommate and a small group of Vassar friends her entire life, she ignored later overtures from the college and never set foot on the campus again.

As an interesting side story, Colton Johnson also reveals that Jackie's college file "disappeared sometime during Kennedy's run for the presidency, although I don't see how the Irish Mafia could get past Vassar's president and the warden. At the time, the college was much more in loco parentis and the file contained biweekly letters to her father and personal things about how Jackie was doing. But that has been missing for forty years."

While it might seem important now, in the era she lived in, Jackie's leaving college was not that big a deal — most of her classmates did not graduate either. As Vivian Crespi recalls, "To attend college or have a career was rare; there just were not that many options for women — I was married at eighteen!" In those days, you could not attend Vassar and be married, and that caused a mass exodus after sophomore year. By the time Jackie left, the Class of '51's ranks were much depleted. By senior year, the yearbook noted that "Marriages and the lure of France had diminished our own number, and we hastened to write our missing friends of the changes that had taken place...." Jackie was not the only one to leave. Out of an original class of 397, 270 graduated and 127 (nearly one-third) did not.

After a certain point, though, Jackie must have decided to let bygones be bygones. "I spent two years at Vassar," she once recalled, "and still cannot quite decide whether I liked it or not. I wish I had worked harder and gone away less." It is telling that during the Kennedy administration, most of the women in the East Wing went to Vassar. When the guest list for the 1962 Nobel Prize dinner was drawn up, Sarah Blanding was the only women's college president in attendance, along with the heads of Harvard, Princeton, and Yale.

After studying at the Sorbonne, Jackie moved home to Merrywood and attended George Washington University in Washington, D.C., for her senior year. Switching her major to French literature, she studied journalism and creative writing as well. She had always loved to read and was thinking of becoming a writer. To her, journalism seemed a good way to get into it. Growing up in the house she did, she was also fascinated by people and their motives — why they behaved the way they did. Although she was shy, she also knew journalism would force her to get out and meet people.

Another milestone occurred, fashionwise, on November 3, 1951, when Jackie met who would be for her the precursor to Oleg Cassini and Hubert de Givenchy — Mini Rhea, a Georgetown dressmaker her mother frequented. Even as a young woman, Jackie was vitally interested in fashion. She pored over rare copies of French *Vogue* and studied what was happening in Paris. She would sketch out an idea she had for a dress and bring it to Mrs. Rhea's (and it was always Mrs. Rhea, until Jackie went to the White House) to be produced at her home at 1820 Thirty-fifth Street, NW. Even then, Jackie had an idea of what she wanted, and she depended on Mrs. Rhea to help execute it.

To assure a perfect fit, Mrs. Rhea took a muslin fitting of Jackie's figure, as they did in Paris. As Cassini would in years to come, she also cut out in muslin the pattern of each individual dress, so she knew exactly what she was doing when she cut into the good material. Mrs. Rhea pinned the muslin on Jackie so it formed a second skin, commenting that Jackie was lucky to have a figure "like a model right out of a Parisian salon of haute couture."

Jackie didn't think so. Like too many young women, she did not think she was perfect or ideal — even though Mrs. Rhea thought she was the most beautiful girl ever to walk through her door. As Mrs. Rhea remembers, "Jackie was quite critical of herself. She wished her feet were smaller, her waist slimmer, her bust larger, her legs straighter, and her face more oval. I felt like spanking her."

Jackie and Mrs. Rhea worked well together, falling into a familiar rhythm. As her dressmaker recalled, Jackie would dash in and show her a design.

"I have a terrific idea for a gown," she would say. "I think it should have this kind of a top," as she pulled out a mere suggestion of a sketch. "The skirt should be like this — you understand, don't you, Mrs. Rhea?"

She did.

As Mrs. Rhea noted, Jackie "wore a lot of black, in suits and daytime clothes, but not so much for evening. Pink — hot pink — was her favorite color, to match her lipstick."

Because she knew her own mind and what worked for her, Jackie was easy to work with. "She could look at something and make a quick decision: yes — no. A little higher — one inch more to the right."

And it is almost historic to note that one of the most influential looks of Camelot was invented in Mrs. Rhea's little shop. One afternoon Jackie had a muslin on and she and Mrs. Rhea were experimenting with different necklines and shoulder-lines.

Jackie, whose upper arms were toned from years of horseback riding, looked in the mirror and said, "I definitely look better with this sleeveless effect."

Mrs. Rhea agreed, although she continued, "It's a pity the style isn't that way for daytime."

Jackie went over and retrieved a magazine from her pile of things on the couch. It was the first time Mrs. Rhea had seen a French fashion magazine.

"Look here, Mrs. Rhea," she flipped a few pages. "You'll find almost any look you want — why *can't* you wear a sleeveless dress for daytime?"

While Mrs. Rhea leafed through the magazine, amazed at the variety of clothing styles the French were wearing and the extreme look of French dresses, Jackie fiddled with the muslin at her neck and shoulder, deciding which neckline looked good on her and how deep the armhole should be cut.

"I like the slim, sleeveless look. I think the shoulder should come about here." She pointed to the tip of her shoulder bone. "And I think it should barely cover here," as she ran her finger along the ridge of her collarbone.

Shortly thereafter, wanting to test her theory, she ordered a sheath for daytime and Mrs. Rhea suggested a little jacket to cover her arms. "That would be losing the whole point," Jackie said. "I think I'll just have the dress."

And so, a look was born.

Mrs. Rhea noticed that Jackie followed her own style, influenced by the more sophisticated French magazines and New York designers, rather than the prevailing Washington fashion. The general style for dresses at the time was a big skirt, becoming wider at the hem, falling to a few inches above the ankle; sweetheart or scalloped necklines; and big, loose cape sleeves. Puffy sleeves were also common, but sleeveless dresses were unheard-of. As Mrs. Rhea recalls, "There was a general Southern belle look about most dresses, particularly as they gathered into a tight waist.... This was certainly not the Jackie look. Jackie, even then, insisted on cleaner, neater, more compact lines and material with firmer body, so that the garments would hold their shape."

Jackie also started shortening her dresses before any of Mrs. Rhea's other clients. "An inch off can make all the difference," she said.

Mrs. Rhea eventually learned that although Jackie's ideas seemed a little strange when she first suggested them, she would inevitably hear more about them later from New York designers and smart specialty shops and, eventually, from the general public. Even in her early twenties, "Jackie was never intimidated into wearing what others were wearing. Some sixth sense told her where fashion's trend was leading."

In addition to being her dressmaker, Mrs. Rhea had a ringside seat during John F. Kennedy and Jackie's courtship. But it was Jackie's mother who in fact met Kennedy before Jackie did. She sat next to him at a dinner at the Edward Macauleys' on Twenty-third Street, in 1950, when Jackie was still in Paris.

Years later, the thing Mrs. Auchincloss remembered about that night was leaving the dinner party. She and Hugh were driving down the street "and I saw this tall, straight purposeful man striding down the street and I said to Hugh D., 'There's Jack Kennedy. Shall we see if we can give him a lift?' He didn't seem to have any car or any place to go and he was just walking on into the night. So we stopped the car and said, 'Can we take you anywhere?' And he said, 'Thank you very much. That would be nice,' and hopped into the car."

Something about the young man not bothering to ask anybody for a lift or calling a taxi struck Mrs. Auchincloss, even years later. "But just finding him marching on, blocks from the Macauleys' house — that was very endearing. I can't describe it to you, but he had a sort of Lindbergh quality to me at that point."

Kennedy had made a memorable first impression on Mrs. Auchincloss, but, as she recalled, "I certainly had no idea that I would ever see him again."

Jacqueline Bouvier and John F. Kennedy were first brought together at another dinner party in Georgetown hosted by mutual friends of theirs, Charles and Martha Bartlett. Actually, Bartlett had tried to introduce Jackie to Jack as early as 1948, at his brother's wedding on Long Island. He was escorting her through a great crowd to introduce her to Kennedy and about halfway across she got involved in a conversation with Gene Tunney. By the time she was done speaking with the heavyweight champion, Kennedy was nowhere to be found.

Still, Bartlett kept the two of them in the back of his mind. Although Jackie was much younger than Kennedy, "it was always in my mind and I think it was a very good concept." Charlie found Jackie enormously attractive and recalled that she "always had these sort of English beaux and I must say they were not up to her."

That first dinner went well, with everyone flirting and drinking and getting along. Jack was attracted to Jackie's beauty, of course, but he was intrigued

by her intelligence, too. "I asked her for a date over the asparagus," he would later recall. "There *was* no asparagus," she responded.

At the end of the evening Bartlett walked her out to her car, a second-hand black Mercury convertible, while Jack came sort of trailing after, muttering shyly, "Would you like to go someplace and have a drink?"

But while they were still inside having dinner, a young friend of Jackie's had walked by and noticed her car parked in front of the Bartletts'. He ducked in the backseat to wait, then stepped out of the car to greet her when she appeared with Kennedy and Bartlett. It was all a bit awkward, but funny, three men out on the sidewalk talking to Jackie. *What the hell kind of a guy sits in a backseat and waits for a girl?* Kennedy wondered. She and her friend got in the car and left. So, no drinks.

After that, Jack and Jackie liked each other; they just did not, like many modern couples, have time to see each other. Jack's Senate campaign was just getting off the ground, and Jackie left for Europe shortly thereafter. As Bartlett recalls, "He was really absent from Washington for most of the next year and she was absent for part of it, so there really wasn't much hope. The credit for the next phase really belongs to Martha, because Jackie was engaged to a fellow whom we didn't think too much of. He was a nice fellow, but he didn't seem to be worthy of her hand."

The Bartletts had another dinner party on May 8, 1952, and since her fiancé could not make it down from New York, they urged Jackie to invite Jack. She did. As Bartlett recounts it, "I think it was fortunate that Martha applied the pressure. This was the beginning of really the serious courtship which went on to the priest. [Jackie's] engagement was broken sometime during the winter. And by the spring we were happy to feel that this thing was pretty well moving along. And of course, they got married in September."

Just as Jackie had worked with dressmaker Mini Rhea in Georgetown, she — or rather her mother — employed another fashion secret for her wedding. Ann Lowe, an African American who had quietly sewed clothes for many prominent women in American society, created Jackie's wedding dress and outfitted her wedding party. Unfortunately, disaster struck when there was a flood in Lowe's Lexington Avenue workroom days before the wedding. As Lois K. Alexander, a friend of Lowe's recalls, "Ten of the fifteen gowns were completely ruined. The fifty yards of ivory silk chiffon from which the wedding dress was made, the bridesmaids' pink silk faille and red satin had to be replaced by the supplier. The bridal gown, which had taken more than two months to make, was completed in two days of cutting and three days of sewing. An estimated seven-hundred-dollar profit turned into a twenty-two-hundred-dollar loss because Ann refused to discuss the accident with the Auchinclosses."

The gown that Jackie wore for her wedding day was, to be kind, exceedingly busy. Even considering the fact that it was a 1950s society wedding, there was a *lot* going on. Made with fifty yards of ivory tissue silk taffeta, there were ruffles, tucks, stitching, giant circular pincushions cartwheeling around the skirt, flowers, a diamond brooch, pearl necklace, white gloves, and a veil. The costume—and this is a rare instance of the clothes wearing Jackie instead of the other way around—lacked her characteristic simplicity and straight lines. Even Mini Rhea did not think it looked like Jackie at all.

There may be a reason the dress did not look like Jackie. She preferred a simpler wedding gown of straight lines and elegant material, but her husband and mother wanted to see her in a traditional gown. Years later, she told her friend the designer Carolina Herrera that she did not like the dress she was married in, but had worn it to please her mother. While Jackie was a radiant bride, this was a rare fashion misstep for her. (However, she righted herself by the time she and Jack left for their honeymoon in Acapulco, saying good-bye to the guests in a gray Chanel traveling suit and diamond bracelet her new husband had given her the night before.)

Wartime photographer Toni Frissell, who took the picture that became Churchill's official portrait on Coronation Day, 1953, was given the assignment of shooting the Kennedy's wedding reception for *Harper's Bazaar*. It was not easy. Even the irascible Churchill was mild in comparison with the rambunctious Kennedys.

As Frissell recalled, "The Kennedy family was somewhat overwhelming. There are so many of them and they are so vital that they are bound to take over any place like a swarm of locusts. At a quarter to one, a big limousine drove into the portico. It was a radiant Jackie and her handsome newlywed husband. When she saw me with my camera she said, 'Toni is a good friend of mine. Let's give her a chance to get a good picture before the guests arrive.'"

Later, after taking group pictures of the thirty-plus members of the wedding party, Toni got the new Senator and Mrs. Kennedy by themselves. She persuaded them to walk out onto a stretch of lawn overlooking the water. Jack and Jackie *hated* posing for these corny shots. "I'm not exactly a flowers and candy guy," admitted Kennedy. But they knew they had to; everyone expected it.

According to Frissell, "They walked out and I suggested they face each other from a distance and hold hands looking into each other's eyes. A slight breeze came up and blew the veil behind her. How did I know I was photographing such people of destiny?"

As we can see from Jackie's honeymoon pictures, Audrey Hepburn was Jackie's first true style influence. Although her hair was short and full for her wedding, by the time she returned from her honeymoon, she had cropped it even further.

Then came the full skirts, little white blouses, and ballet flats. Jackie even had — shades of Sabrina at the Glen Cove train station — a black poodle named "Gaullie" for Charles de Gaulle, whom she would charm so thoroughly as first lady in less than a decade.

Jackie's style, still vaguely collegiate when Jackie was a young married woman living in Georgetown, can best be described as Hepburnesque — Audrey, not Katharine. *Roman Holiday* was released in August 1953, a month before her wedding to Kennedy. *Sabrina* appeared a year later. Like the rest of America, Jackie took note. (So did her husband; asked by *Time* magazine to name his favorite movie, he answered *Roman Holiday*, and named Audrey Hepburn as his favorite actress.) Yusha Auchincloss recalls that Jackie loved *Roman Holiday*, *Sabrina*, and *Funny Face*, and that Audrey Hepburn was her favorite actress.

In the early Georgetown years, Jackie, like thousands of other style-conscious young American women, wore the ballerina skirts of *Sabrina* and the leotards of *Funny Face*. Jackie could not have imagined that in less than ten years, these same women would be following *her* lead.

After graduation, Lucky Roosevelt married Theodore Roosevelt's grandson Archibald and settled in Washington, D.C. "Right after I got married, then she got married and we had lunch at the old Willard and she said, 'Oh, Lucky, isn't it wonderful to be married and to be in love!' She was so — I mean, she seemed to me to be just so happy, like she was on a cloud!"

Jackie's marriage to Jack changed him, in many ways for the better. For starters, the senator, who used to affect chinos, a seersucker blazer, and mismatched socks in the halls of Congress, now wore impeccably tailored suits. Jackie also made sure her husband ate properly — before they met, a hot dog or even a candy bar was lunch. Now, Jackie often prepared a lunch basket and had George, the longtime family butler, deliver it to Kennedy's office.

In matters of style and gracious living, Jackie helped her husband enormously. As their friend Lord Harlech recalled, the Kennedys "did not pursue excellence in style. Until he married Jackie he really had no idea about how you should decorate a room or what was the difference between a pretty house and an ugly house. And he certainly had no great feeling about good food or good wine."

Harlech also observed that unlike the rest of the in-laws (and the children, factotums, and hangers-on of Joseph P. Kennedy, for that matter), Jackie never followed the Kennedy line. She had her own standards about "the manners of the children, about having good food, about having beautiful furniture, the house well done up."

But first, Jackie needed a home to do up. In the early years of their marriage, Jack and Jackie did not even have a place of their own. Instead, they lived out of suitcases, shuttling between Merrywood and rented town houses in Georgetown. They lived for a short time at Hickory Hill in McLean, Virginia, which Jackie found too lonely and isolated, particularly after their first child, Arabella, was stillborn on August 23, 1956.

After selling Hickory Hill to his brother Bobby and his wife, Ethel, Jack bought a red-brick Federal town house at 3307 N Street in the heart of Georgetown, while Jackie was in New York Hospital having given birth to their daughter, Caroline, on November 27, 1957. He and Jackie had looked at "millions" of houses over the summer, Mrs. Auchincloss said, but Jackie could not make up her mind. Finally, with Jackie in New York, Jack picked the N Street house because, Mrs. Auchincloss recalled, he liked the door knocker.

Jackie returned and was thrilled, at last, to have her own home. She wanted everything to be perfect and embarked on a massive facelift for the house. For a time, it seemed everyone was assisting Jackie with her decorating project. She worked on it, her sister, Lee, worked on it. Everyone who passed by had an opinion.

Mrs. Auchincloss, for one, considered Jackie's entire N Street decorating scheme "an example of Jack's great patience with the foibles of women.

"I remember that when she got the N Street house, it was going to be just right. It was a house with a lot of feeling about it and a lot of charm, but she did that living room — the double living room downstairs — over at least three times within the first four months they were there. I remember you could go there one day and there would be two beautiful needlepoint rugs [and] the next week they would both be gone. They had been sent on trial. Not only that, but the curtains were apt to be red chintz one week and something else the next!"

One night when Mr. and Mrs. Auchincloss were there for dinner, Jack came home so late he had his meal off a tray. Jackie was trying yet another look for the living room. "At the moment the room was entirely beige," Mrs. Auchincloss recalled. "The walls had been repainted a week or so before.... Rugs, curtains, upholstery, everything, was suddenly turned different shades of beige.... I can remember Jack saying to me, 'Mrs. Auchincloss, do you think we're prisoners of beige?' "

Finally, help arrived in the form of decorator Keith Irvine, who had come to work for Sister Parish from John Fowler in London. He had been in the country only ten days when he traveled to Washington, D.C., with Mrs. Parish to do some work for Lorraine Cooper, the glamorous wife of Republican senator John Sherman Cooper of Kentucky, and a very good friend of Jackie's.

When lunchtime arrived, Mrs. Cooper asked Sister, "Will Mr. Irvine be joining us?" "Oh no, he can go out and get a hamburger somewhere." Mrs. Cooper stepped forward and said, "Mr. Irvine, you will lunch with us," and he found himself seated between Jackie and Madame Pandit, Nehru's sister. ("Your typical high-powered Georgetown lunch of the time," Irvine wryly notes.)

After lunch, Jackie wanted Sister to stop by the house on N Street, but Sister (as Keith tells it) "had sniffed a new client that she thought was going to spend more money, so she waltzed off to Virginia with her and said, 'Mr. Irvine can go with you!'

"So I got stuck going to N Street, and then I went over things with her. And I was so interested because she questioned everything and made little lists of 'wouldn't it be nice to have a lacquer table, and is it going to annoy people if the surface is uneven?' I mean, she went into everything in extraordinary detail." Keith and Jackie — of course, at that time, they referred to one another as Mr. Irvine and Mrs. Kennedy — got along very well, and then it was time for him to return to New York.

"I didn't really think about it, and then, typical of Mrs. Parish, she left me with no money and no airline ticket! So I had to borrow the money from

Jackie to get back to New York. In those days, the shuttle was fourteen dollars and I had to borrow it to get home!"

Irvine recalls Jackie's reaction, "She was amused! She knew I'd only been in America ten days, and hadn't gotten the money worked out yet."

A week later Jackie called Keith and said, "I'm going to be in New York, could you meet me at Schrafft's? I'd like to go over what I think we're going to do." So Irvine sat with her at the luncheonette with all those marvelous Irish waitresses (Schrafft's is where the Kennedys used to hire their maids) and together they went through her entire list.

Irvine feels that in those young days, "Jackie was uncertain about her knowledge, the background of some things, but she was always very assured. The first couple of times I met her she was always so assured—she knew what she was aiming for. She just saw it!" Jackie wanted her rooms to look like a painting, a watercolor. To help Jackie achieve the look she wanted, Irvine unearthed some French fabrics from Suzanne Fontagne in Paris that were very fresh, beautiful, high-quality white cottons with florals dashed on them. Jackie was very taken with them. Didi and Leslie Tillett also made a lot of special printed fabrics, from canvas to silk, very young and new at the time, that Jackie loved.

Irvine found Jackie an enjoyable client, and later friend, because she challenged him. Whenever he suggested something, she always wanted to know why. Was there a better way to do it? She wanted to learn from him. She begged him to tell stories about his days with John Fowler, who was responsible for the great rooms of England, and about his other clients and *their* style.

After they had worked out the entire scheme, Jackie dashed off to Europe. The day before she returned, Irvine arrived in Georgetown to put the rooms together. "In those days things were done fast. You could do some-thing—the curtains or what have you—in a couple of weeks. Now it's *years!* Anyway, I was installing these three rooms and she was going to come back the next day. So I arrived, and none of the trucks had arrived. I was waiting in the living room, and someone had gotten me some coffee when suddenly Senator Kennedy ran down the stairs in the hallway, just past the living room. He stopped and came back—'Who the hell are you?' I said who I was and he looked very bemused, and he said, 'Oh, it looks marvelous!' And it was a mess, nothing had been done! I said it would all be done by tonight and he said, 'Oh Jackie will be very pleased.'"

As Lord Harlech noted, before Jackie arrived, Jack had pretty simple taste. He *still* had simple taste—he could have Boston clam chowder any time of the day or night, and at the end of the day enjoyed a Heineken. But Jackie elevated the whole operation. Suddenly there were decorators running around and the overall *motif* of the living room became of vital importance. As curious

as he was about most things, in their early years together Kennedy really did not see the point of decorating. To him, a chair was just a chair.

As Harlech recalls, "He was very happy just to have a steak and some ice cream. Certainly he had no worry about furniture. I remember him saying when Jackie had gone off and bought some French eighteenth-century chairs or something, 'I don't know why. What's the point of spending all this money — I mean a chair is a chair and it's perfectly good, the chair I'm sitting in — what's the point of all this fancy stuff?'"

With Jackie in the picture, he was about to find out. Richard Nelson, who was Sister Parish's assistant, recalls the time they got a table from Paul Jones, who was the first to do beautiful glass and steel tables in New York. "We sent a table down and I remember that Senator Kennedy was distressed at the cost, he thought it was too expensive. He had an insurance person look at it and they said it's only worth this much. And Mrs. Parish just said, 'Okay, we'll let them have it for that amount and we'll pay the difference, because we want the table there!'" Nelson laughs. "It was in the living room. It was a pretty table and it was the first of its time."

In 1958, Kennedy handily won reelection to the Senate and was moving forward in his quest for the White House. Although she had been raised in a die-hard Republican family, Jackie switched her party affiliation and campaigned extensively with her husband. She traveled throughout Ohio, spoke French at a Cajun rice festival in Louisiana, and attended local Democratic dinners in Nebraska and Iowa. In Wisconsin, she "borrowed" the public address system in a supermarket and told the ladies to keep shopping while she told them why they should vote for her husband.

Perhaps without her intending it, people noticed Jackie wherever she went. Joseph Cerrell, director of the California Democratic Party, says, "I remember Mrs. Kennedy causing a great stir there because it was one of the few times I think Californians had seen somebody with a hemline above the knee. Her glamour and her unconventional beauty attracted attention and enticed the news media."

Her sister-in-law Joan Kennedy says Jackie was a lifesaver when it came to politicking. In the spring of 1960, when Jackie had to curtail some of her activity because she was pregnant, there were no family members to accompany JFK to West Virginia, a crucial primary. As Joan recalls, laughing, "Jackie was pregnant, Ethel was pregnant, Eunice was pregnant, everybody was pregnant!"

It was decided that Joan would go. It was her first campaign appearance and she was nervous about what was expected of her. To make things worse, she had just given birth to her daughter, Kara, in February of 1960 and had nothing to wear. Jackie stepped in. As Joan remembers, "She said, 'Look, I'm

not going to need these clothes, so they're all yours.' And fortunately, we were the same size. So I wore all of her clothes — all of her Givenchys, and all of her fabulous Parisian clothes." Jackie even advised Joan what shoes to wear: "Don't wear high heels, even though you look great in them — it's a long day."

After delivering the clothes Jackie had another idea, "Maybe you should take all my clothes and shorten them a bit. You have great legs!"

As the presidential campaign against Richard Nixon became more heated, the media's interest in All Things Kennedy was growing. Jack Kennedy, but more particularly his father, understood the power of images. Having worked in Hollywood, Joseph Kennedy Sr. understood that images could be used to sell his son to the American people "like a box of soap flakes." Jackie, and now Caroline, were important assets to the senator, giving him the aura of a dynamic family man.

Knowing that pictures of her family would have to be taken for the national newsweeklies like *Life* and *Time*, Jackie used her photojournalism skills, artistic eye, and attention to detail to help her husband. When *Life* wanted to shoot the Kennedys, like any good editor Jackie insisted on reviewing the photographers' books to decide whom to work with. She chose Mark Shaw, a highly decorated air force pilot in World War II who was now a leading photographer, appearing in *Harper's Bazaar, Mademoiselle,* and a host of other fashion magazines. Shaw began contributing to *Life* in 1952, and in sixteen years shot twenty-seven covers and over a hundred stories.

Jackie already knew Shaw's work shooting the Paris fashion shows for *Life* magazine in the 1950s and 1960s (he was the first to shoot the couture shows in color), so his wife, Pat Suzuki, thinks this may have given him an edge.

The black-and-white photographs Shaw shot of the Kennedys at home in Georgetown are classic. Suzuki agrees. "They're very articulate. I think they were the most beautiful pictures of all because after you have so much experience of being photographed a certain thing comes in, you know how to set your face a certain way. It's a defense." In the last weeks before the 1960 election, when these pictures were taken, Jackie had not yet learned to be wary of the press and photographers. Shaw's photos may be the closest we can ever come to knowing what it might have been like to hang out with Jackie when she relaxed in her own home – lounging in the living room late at night with a drink and a cigarette, Frank Sinatra on the stereo after a long day.

Jacques Lowe was another photographer who worked closely with Jackie prior to the election and later, in the White House, becoming the Kennedys personal photographer. In fact, he took the senator's favorite picture of Jackie in Hyannisport in the summer of 1960, when she approached the camera fresh-faced and confident (wearing her favorite pink lipstick) in a yellow and white gingham sundress.

While Kennedy appreciated the fact that Lowe was keeping a record of the Kennedys for historical purposes, Lowe felt that Jackie considered photography as art rather than mere documentation. "She looked at a photograph and saw composition and the qualities of light and shadow. She was the more creative of the two and appreciated my work for its artistic value."

With Lowe, or any of the White House photographers she worked with later, Jackie thought like a magazine editor. Studying proofs of their 1960 Christmas card, taken in Hyannisport the summer before, Jackie wrote a detailed note to Lowe, wondering if it would be possible to replace Caroline's head with one from another frame that she preferred. To let him know what she wanted, she marked the image with XXXX's and gave him the exact page and exposure numbers. Unfortunately, it was technically impossible to do that at the time, and Jackie went ahead with the original.

By December 1960, Jack had won the election and was busy planning his cabinet. Their son John Jr. was born on November 25, 1960, and Jackie was in Palm Beach trying to rest and, more important, attending to the serious matter of what she was going to wear to the inauguration balls.

She had one of two choices, and that was her problem.

With a great deal of input from Jackie, Emeric Partos, the fur designer for Bergdorf Goodman, had produced one gown. The dress, though it appeared simple, was composed of several parts. There was a silk crepe floor-length white gown on which the bodice had been painstakingly embroidered with silver thread. Then, over the sleeveless bodice, came the white sheer chiffon overblouse, also sleeveless. Over this came a white floor-length cape of the same crepe material as the dress, which stood high at the neck with a little mandarin collar.

When the fitters from Bergdorf's, Miss Frankau and her assistant, arrived, Mary Gallagher noticed that Jackie seemed subdued. In spite of all the trouble Bergdorf Goodman had gone through in bringing her idea to reality, executing it beautifully and bringing it down to Palm Beach to be fitted, Jackie quietly let it be known that at that point she was more interested in Oleg Cassini.

The gown Cassini designed for Jackie to wear to the inaugural balls was a showstopper. If anyone had any doubts about Oleg Cassini's ability to fulfill the role of first couturier, he silenced them with this extraordinary gown. A full-length evening gown of graphic simplicity, it was made out of sumptuous Swiss double satin, unadorned except for a simple rosette treatment at the waist. As Cassini recalls his inspiration, "The most emphatic thing about it was the fabric. The lines were unusually modest — there was a cleanliness to it —

but the quantity of the fabric and the luxury of the satin made it regal and altogether memorable." Cassini must have been checking in with Mini Rhea, or reading Jackie's mind. *This* was what she wanted. Their perceptions of fashion were perfectly in sync.

The gown Cassini presented was less ethereal than the Bergdorf creation, more substantial, and in character with the powerful woman Jackie was on the verge of becoming.

Of course, there was one minor problem, which was that Jackie had already promised she would wear the Bergdorf dress to the inaugural balls. Now she wanted to wear Cassini's. "Now I know how poor Jack feels when he has told 3 people they can be Secy. of State," she wrote Cassini. Jackie compromised by wearing Cassini's gown to the inaugural gala and the Bergdorf gown the following night to the inaugural balls.

In spite of Partos's work, Cassini's creation remained Jackie's favorite. She liked it so much she kept a framed photograph of herself leaving the Georgetown house in the snow, the night of the gala, in her White House dressing room. Years later, she tried to buck tradition and have the Smithsonian feature the gala gown rather than the inaugural one in its First Ladies exhibit, but the museum could not be persuaded, in spite of her and Mary Gallagher's best efforts.

In later years, there was so much interest in Jackie's inaugural gown, even if it wasn't her favorite, that the Smithsonian had to install heavy-duty carpet in front of her mannequin to cope with the crowds.

The night before the inauguration, Washington was like a fairyland, all white and snowing. The mood was magical; there was a sense of a new beginning. Leaving 3307 N Street, the little house she loved so much, to go to the inaugural gala, Jackie delicately lifted the hem of her gown and ducked her head, smiling shyly as a chauffeur held an umbrella over her.

En route to the Armory, Kennedy asked the driver to put the lights on so the people could see Jackie. He even made her sit forward in her seat so they could see her dress.

Living with her husband in London, Lucky Roosevelt saw a photograph of Jackie walking out her front door into the snow, and recalled meeting her at eighteen. "I think she was just fated to be always a star. There are very few people that I feel that way about. You can say, 'Oh well, you just have hindsight,' but I thought it at the time. She was the most glamorous person I had ever met, and yet the nicest."

prix de paris

I'm counting on her for the copy room team!!!

—CAROL PHILLIPS, VOGUE EDITOR

In 1951, Jackie beat out more than twelve hundred of the ablest college women in America to take first place in *Vogue*'s Prix de Paris competition, a contest to help college students make the transition from the groves of academe to the real world by offering them jobs in the Condé Nast magazine empire. But *Vogue*'s most famous winner almost didn't get her application in at all.

It was her mother's idea, and Jackie began her application with an apology for being late, and a plea for an extension. On October 10, 1950, she wrote *Vogue* with a classic The Dog Ate My Homework explanation. "Dear Sir," she began, "I do hope you will consider my entry.... I returned from Europe only a week ago and then it took several days to get hold of an August issue of *Vogue* as there were none left on the news stands."

She said she had completed three years at Vassar but would be living at home this winter and finishing at George Washington University. Like the talented head girl who is forgiven everything, Jackie optimistically closed her handwritten note, "I will go ahead and do the first quiz in case I don't hear from you before November 1st, and I do hope you will let me compete as a

career on a magazine is what I have always had in mind and this seems the perfect way to start training for it."

Soon after this note was written, Jackie spoke with Mary E. Campbell, the Prix de Paris director. On October 31, another handwritten plea arrived from Merrywood.

"Dear Miss Campbell," she began, "I am ashamed to be asking you for an extension of my Prix Papers this early in the contest.... I cannot type myself. I am taking a Secretarial Course this year but as yet it still takes me ten minutes to peck my way through a sentence." Jackie was sorry she was late, but she had a really good excuse—she had taken her articles to be typed by a GW student who *promised* she would do the typing on Monday and have them back to Jackie the next morning. But it was Homecoming Week and last night the typist had to go to a rally, and then there was a cornerstone-laying ceremony, but she promised she would have them to Jackie by Thursday at the latest. "I do hope you will accept them," Jackie concluded. "Very Sincerely, Jacqueline Bouvier."

Talent is its own excuse, and Jackie's essays—twenty neatly typed pages of foolscap held together with a paperclip—covering topics from fashion nostalgia to the three men she would most liked to have known (Baudelaire, Oscar Wilde, and Serge Diaghilev), wowed them at *Vogue*.

After reviewing the applicants, *Vogue* staffers weighed in with their opinions. Managing editor Carol Phillips was an early

This is IT — for my vote. A most impressive set of papers. Each paper is excellent — There is no exception. She is a writer; she definitely has the editorial point of view. My only worry is that she might marry some day — and go off on one of those horses she speaks about. But I'm counting on her for the copy room team —!!! Incidentally, I showed these papers to Margaret Collette + Kate Rand and they were absolutely wowed.

supporter, giving her a grade of AAAAAA. "This is IT for my vote. A most impressive set of papers. Each paper is excellent — there is no exception. She *is* a writer…my only worry is that she might *marry* some day — and go off on one of those horses she speaks about." Miss Talmey gave Jackie's papers a B+: "would definitely consider this girl — has range; easy writing; bright mind." Miss Daves thought Jackie showed *"Wonderful possibility. We must consider her seriously."* Miss Heal awarded Jackie's efforts an A and found her "intelligent, good background, fashion flair."

Carol Phillips felt most strongly about Jackie's future as a *Vogue* editor and pushed for her acceptance. She showed Jackie's papers to Margaret Collette and Kate Rand and they were "absolutely wowed." But, this being the publishing business — and *Vogue* magazine — there were a few dis-

senters. Miss Weston gave Jackie a flat B⁻. She noted grudgingly that her work was "uneven — but some of it isn't bad." And Mrs. Gleaves *really* wanted to nip Jackie's writing career in the bud. She found her style "flat footed. Biography uninviting. Other papers are sensible and thorough." *Ouch!*

Carol Phillips's assessment must have won the day, because on April 25, 1951, Mary E. Campbell wrote Miss Bouvier to let her know, "you are among the top finalists.... I think you have done a swell job and deserve a lot of credit for the hard and painstaking work you have done." Campbell then invited Jackie to New York City on May 10 to meet Edna Woolman Chase, editor in chief of *Vogue*, at a dinner hosted at the Cosmopolitan Club (casual), as well as lunch with previous Prix de Paris winners now working at other Condé Nast publications.

THE CONDÉ NAST PUBLICATIONS INC.

Office Memorandum

TO   Mrs. Gleaves   FROM   Mary E. Campbell

COPY TO   DATE   March 9, 1951

Name: Bouvier, Jacqueline   (George Washington U.)

Grade:

Remarks:

Flat footed. Biography uninviting. Other papers are sensible and thorough. No flair.

Unfortunately, Jackie was not able to make it to New York on the tenth because she had finals. But Campbell encouraged Jackie to come meet with the *Vogue* editors since "we all feel that you had one of the most interesting papers submitted." She wondered if it would be possible for Jackie to arrange to fly up to New York any time within the next two weeks so they could have lunch or dinner together—or just a brief meeting, if that's all she had time for.

Clearly, *Vogue* was interested in her. Jackie sent a telegram saying she could fly up to New York on Thursday, May 3, if that was convenient for them. It was. Communicating back and forth by Western Union, they made plans to meet at *Vogue*'s offices at 420 Lexington Avenue around noon.

After a quick tour of the offices, Jackie was taken to lunch by Mary Campbell, Carol Phillips, and Miss Heal at Schrafft's in the Chrysler Building, the "in" place for young career women at the time. Carol Phillips, who championed Jackie's efforts and went on to become founder of Clinique, remembers Jackie as a "sweet, darling

girl with not a great deal of confidence."

Over a lunch of sandwiches and tea, they talked about poems they had written and new books they had read. Growing up in Tucson, Miss Heal confided that she had always wanted to work for Condé Nast. Sensing their excitement, and seeing how much they loved their work, Jackie realized "what an exciting thing it must be to have something important to do with putting out a magazine." Jackie was also unsure of where to live after college, but was considering Washington, D.C.

"Go to Washington," Phillips advised her, "that's where all the boys are."

When she got back to Merrywood, Jackie wrote a long letter to Campbell, thanking her for taking the time to meet with her and apologizing for giving what she thought was not a very good impression during lunch. "After I left you I had the feeling that my chances of winning the Prix had been much better at the beginning of our meeting than they were towards the end of lunch." Campbell had asked Jackie what she wanted to do with her life, and did she have any questions they might answer? A standard conversation with a twenty-one-year-old job applicant, but because of nerves and shyness Jackie gave Campbell no answer and did not ask any follow-up questions. Now she regretted it and was afraid she had spoiled her chances for the prize.

"I don't want you to think I am blasé and apathetic—or that I don't appreciate what an unbelievable opportunity it would be to win the Prix," Jackie confided. "I have always known that I wanted to 'do something' with my life but I could never visualize just how to go about it. I had vague little dreams of locking myself up somewhere and turning out children's books and *New Yorker* short stories. . . .

"In the four days since I've been home," she said, "I have been thinking very hard about 'my career' and it has changed from vague ideas of puttering around, to something very definite. . . . In ten years, or twenty if it takes that long, I would like to be a top editor at Condé Nast—and for two reasons. I think when you have several bents, none of them pronounced enough to make you a great novelist or painter, and you love keeping up with new ideas, a magazine is the ideal place to work."

Jackie concluded her handwritten note by saying she would love to get her foot in the door and that if she didn't win the prize, she hoped they might remember her next year.

She need not have worried. *Vogue* remembered her that year. On May 15, 1951, a telegram arrived at Merrywood, telling her she had won first prize in the Prix de Paris. "Congratulations," cabled Edna Woolman Chase, the editor in chief. "Award is year's job with Vogue . . . we welcome you to our staff." A week and a half later, on May 21, Jackie was back at 420 Lexington filling out her employment application and having her portrait taken. On her Condé Nast employment application, she declared she was not a Communist, had never been affiliated with an organization that advocated the overthrow

of the U.S. government, owned a car but not a house, and had no business experience. Jackie could type but not take shorthand; the last book she read was *From Here to Eternity*; and she did not like science or math.

Six days later, her mother, who started the whole thing, pulled in the reins. After Jackie won, Mrs. Auchincloss decided she did *not* want her going to Paris for six months, since she had been away from home so much in the past year. "She feels terrifically strongly about keeping me 'in the home,'" Jackie explained to Mary Campbell.

Jackie still desperately wanted that *Vogue* job. "I would rather work at what interests me than have a home base," she told her. "I will stay home next fall—and learn to type, I guess—and then in January . . . I can move to New York." She would just have to gamble that there would be an opening then. "Yes," Campbell scribbled in the margin of her letter.

So that was that. Jackie's dream of becoming the next Diana Vreeland had ended. But *Vogue* kept an eye on her activities. Mary Campbell, ever the good sport, sent Jackie a copy of the studio portrait taken of her when she was in New York in May. In January 1952, Campbell wrote her a short note, congratulating her on her engagement to John Husted.

Jackie's *Vogue* file ends quietly with a brief two-paragraph newspaper clipping pasted on Condé Nast office memorandum paper: "Bouvier Kennedy Wedding September 12." Well, at least everyone in the copy room knew what she was up to after the *Vogue* thing did not work out.

She was the most difficult
first lady I've ever worked with—
but also the most talented.

— HUGH SIDEY

"goodnight mrs. kennedy— wherever you are"

T HE KENNEDYS WERE THE FIRST JET-SETTERS in the White House. They were also the first presidential couple of the Jet Age, making extensive use of the presidential airplane. In addition to Paris, Vienna, and London, the first couple traveled to Mexico, Puerto Rico, Venezuela, and Colombia. The first lady traveled with her sister to Pakistan, India, Greece, and Italy, causing one broadcaster to close the national evening news with, "Goodnight Mrs. Kennedy — wherever you are."

Nothing was more emblematic of the Kennedys' style than Air Force One. Working with Jackie, American industrial designer Raymond Loewy designed both the exterior paint treatment and the interior decoration of the plane. The style Jackie implemented for Air Force One was so comfortable, so quietly luxurious, that Kennedy forbade photographers to take pictures on board, for fear it would alienate average American voters.

But Jackie's talent was not limited to interior decorating. John F. Kennedy did not realize what a political asset his wife was until their trip to Canada in late May 1961. It was their first official foreign trip and Jackie was not sure how she would be received. Fortunately, she had Cassini in her corner. Because of his work as a studio costume designer, he was able to visualize Jackie's movements as if she were on a stage set, a tableau.

This is intriguing, since so much of Jackie's style was transmitted to the American public, and the world, through still photographs. In these photos, Jackie is often the one bright spot in a sea of gray suits. In being so acutely conscious of the "third eye" of the photographer, Jackie and Cassini came up with

public costumes that successfully transmitted her style (and, vicariously, the style of a new America) to the world.

In an inspired moment, Cassini came up with a regal red suit that mirrored the uniforms of the Royal Canadian Mounted Police. It was a hit. In one stroke, Jackie used clothing to broadcast her own sense of style and score a diplomatic coup.

Cassini says, "The idea was that I envisioned Canada with red coats, so it had to be red. At that moment, President Kennedy realized the weapon he had in his hands. That was the trip when she took another dimension in his eyes. She was Ambassador Numero Uno!"

Tish Baldrige recalls that the State Department repeatedly warned them not to expect a boisterous welcome from our northern neighbors, who were subdued even when Queen Elizabeth visited. Tish says, "When the day of the visit arrived, and as the motorcade bearing the Kennedys started through the crowded streets, the noise of shouting, clapping, screaming, joyous people almost deafened us. One strong chant came through above the others: 'Jac-kie, Jac-kie.'

"The Canadian welcome was a total upset — the Ottawans acted like Italians at a soccer game, and the Kennedy charm was proved once again to be totally, immeasurably effective."

Before she went to Canada, Jackie was uncertain about her ability to carry out her duties as first lady. After receiving the adulation of the crowds, she gained enormous confidence in her public persona. She would need it, because a few weeks after Canada she and her husband traveled on one of their most important state visits: to France.

Jackie was not the only person anxious for her trip to France to go well. Cassini was feeling the pressure, too. With the first lady's celebrated preference for Givenchy and all things French, Cassini was under the gun to show that he could come up with a wardrobe suitable for the woman he considered "the queen of America." And he outdid himself. Using the most luxurious materials and classic designs, he designed a look that was the equivalent of any French couture. The pink straw evening dress with matching wrap he created for her to wear at the state dinner at the Elysée Palace is one glorious example of his creativity.

Just as she did in the White House, Jackie augmented her Cassini collection with a few select pieces from Givenchy and Chez Ninon. For her visit to Malmaison, she wore a favorite Chez Ninon blue-gray suit with fringe detailing at the neck. But it was Givenchy's luxurious white evening dress and coat of silk-embroidered zibeline with a floral embroidered bodice that she wore for the dinner at the Hall of Mirrors that was most extraordinary. Interestingly, the sweep and dramatic nature of the silhouette was reminiscent of the gown Jackie wore for the inaugural gala. The double-breasted lightweight pink wool coat and sleeveless navy blue silk dress he created for her to wear to Notre Dame was another French classic.

Givenchy recalls that the day after the famous gala at Versailles, Jackie was so grateful she sent him a letter "in which she shared General de Gaulle's reaction on seeing her: 'Madame, you are truly lovely, you resemble a Watteau.' This, from a man who was not frivolous or a society-goer, was for me the most marvelous compliment."

While the president and first lady's official trip to France was initially seen as a fashion show for Jackie (Tish Baldrige recalls that it was quickly dubbed "the Jackie French Trip"), there were bigger stakes at hand. And Jackie knew it.

At the time of his election, Kennedy was not well known in Europe. As an isolationist or, worse, an appeaser during World War II, his father, Joseph P. Kennedy, had not helped to further our European alliances. In the eyes of world leaders like de Gaulle and, more important, Khrushchev, whom the Kennedys would be meeting in Vienna after France, JFK was a lightweight with a rich father and a good haircut who had ambled into the White House. This European trip was meant to prove them wrong.

France was a perfect stage on which to present President and Mrs. Kennedy to the world. From the first, the French were gaga over Jackie and seemed particularly caught up in the Kennedy mystique. In a French newsreel made shortly after the election, Hyannisport, where the Kennedy family maintained their summer home, was referred to as "le Saint Tropez d'Amerique." Much was made of Jacqueline's French heritage, as well as her fondness for French couture, culture, and even interior decorating. But what really won them over was her ability to speak their language.

A few weeks before their trip to Paris, Jackie gave an interview, in French, to a French television station. Seated at a small table under the trees on the White House lawn, while kitchen staff carrying trays of champagne glasses scurry in the background (it seems they are preparing for a state dinner), Jackie turns on the charm full blast. The interviewer is slim and suave, a continental on the Cassini model. He hangs on Jackie's every word, transfixed.

Jackie is wearing a favorite cream dress with a fringe-edged self-tie — the same one she wore for the first official campaign photo Mark Shaw took of her in Georgetown, as well as on the cover of the issue of *Life* in which she discusses the White House restoration. Her voice is low and modulated. She is assured as she speaks in simple, impeccable French, adroitly mixing in French-accented English when she cannot think of the correct word. (She charmingly describes "Voici le diplomatic reception room" and "un petit peu de punch.") For once, her voice is not breathy and fearful.

On a political level, Jackie's proficiency in French was invaluable during their trip abroad. At one point she sent de Gaulle's translator away and sat between the prime minister and the American president, translating their conversation.

The Kennedys' trip to France was Jackie's fashion apogee. Although she rued the fact that journalists seemed to regard her merely as a fashion plate, there was no denying the seismic effect she had on the French people. More than two million spectators lined the streets to watch the Kennedys' motorcade, and every scrap of information about their trip was detailed in the French newspapers and magazines.

Jackie had long had a schoolgirl crush on Charles de Gaulle, even naming the black Standard poodle she had when she was first married "Gaullie" after the great man. So it was fitting that she especially charmed the self-centered general and World War II leader ("There are moments in history," he famously quipped, "and I am one of them."). Socialites tittered that he was so taken with the Cassini pink evening gown Jackie wore at the Elysée Palace that he even put his glasses on to survey her visage. At one point, she told him, "My grandparents were French," to which he replied, "Madame, so were mine."

Manolo Blahnik was a young schoolboy when he first became aware of Mrs. Kennedy during her trip to Paris. "I was in Geneva in school, so I remember very, very well, and I remember the *style* — oh!" he trills. "I remember, it was in the Pathé News, before the movie — they don't have that anymore," he laughs. "So I remember in black and white in the beginning, and then in color. Yes, I was in my teens. The idea of seeing this — these were just images that I could never ever shake from my mind. Isn't it funny? I have the pictures somewhere, black and white, like sepia now."

Blahnik followed the first lady's travels with the resoluteness of a Beatles fan. "Do you remember the visit to Paris? I was absolutely totally *possessed* by this image, and I followed her all the time. All the time! I looked for magazines that she was in, I bought them all!" He laughs at the memory.

In twenty-five years, Jackie would be wearing Manolo's shoes. For now, he was an anonymous schoolboy cutting her picture out of *Paris Match*.

Jackie's trip to Paris was such a resounding success that she accompanied her husband (or he accompanied her) on a goodwill tour of Bogotá, Colombia, on December 17, 1961. Again, her wardrobe got as much attention as the political nature of the visit when her decision to wear someone other than Cassini made the AP wire. "President's Wife Gives Boost to Young Designer" read the newspaper headline. "Mrs. Jacqueline Kennedy gave a big boost to a young California designer by wearing one of his dresses at Colombian ceremonies. Her costume was made by Gustave Tassell. It was a pale yellow-green wool coat dress, double-breasted with an empire line and a bow in front. This is the first time Mrs. Kennedy has announced the name of any American designer for her clothes other than Oleg Cassini. A few of the clothes she wears come from a New York specialty shop, Chez Ninon, but no other names have been released as sources of Mrs. Kennedy's wardrobe."

The article concluded, "With the Tassell coat, she wore a large-brimmed hat, upturned and off the face in front, of a shade that almost matched the dress but seemed closer to yellow."

Almost forty years later, Gustave recalls in unerring detail how the first lady came to wear his clothes. He was brought to Jackie's attention by

Diana Vreeland, then fashion editor of *Harper's Bazaar*. Tassell had a show-room in New York on East Fifty-fourth Street and he had a vendeuse who helped him with the collection. One Friday, he took the day off to have lunch with an old friend. He called the office to see if there were any messages. There was one in particular: "Mrs. Vreeland called and would like to speak with you."

Mrs. Vreeland? That was like being discovered in Schwab's drugstore in Hollywood in the 1940s. Gus called her right away.

Gus was based in Los Angeles, and the first thing Vreeland wanted to know was, "When are you leaving New York?" Monday.

"Oh, Mr. Tassell," she implored him over the telephone with the lan-guid drama only she could muster. "Can you *pleeeease* send some clothes, I've been *tellllling* Jack-leen about your clothes, and they'd be *aaaaaaaaabsolutely* perfect for her!" Vreeland sounded as if she was about to throw herself on top of a funeral pyre if he did not send Mrs. Kennedy something to wear.

"Yes," he said, "of course we will." Arrangements were made for Pamela Turnure to come view the collection. She saw Tassell's work, knew Jackie would like it very much, and wondered, "Can you send the clothes to Washington?"

In those days, Gus produced a small collection for his society clientele such as Babe Paley, Nan Kempner, and Chessy Raynor. He packed up his samples and made arrangements to have them sent to the White House. "The funniest thing," he recalls, "is that the shipping service came to pick up the wardrobe boxes, saw the label, and said, 'Mr. Tassell, is there a store in Wash-ington called the White House?'" Gus laughed, "There is now."

He sent the clothes to 1600 Pennsylvania Avenue and they were eventu-ally sent back. Nothing was really said; they were just sent back, although Gus thinks Mrs. Kennedy may have kept a few pieces. About three weeks later, he got a phone call from Pierre Salinger at 6:00 A.M.

"Mr. Tassell, I have to tell you something," said the press secretary he watched on the evening news most nights. "Mrs. Kennedy wore one of your costumes to South America and would like to give you credit. And I would really appreciate it if you could possibly refer everyone to me, because you are going to be besieged by calls and I think it would be a more sensible approach for me to handle it." Tassell agreed.

Salinger was not kidding. As soon as Jackie announced she had worn Gus Tassell, his phone rang off the hook. "My God—it was madness!" he recalls. "They wouldn't leave me alone—they wanted to know *everything* about Mrs. Kennedy and I said, absolutely not! It was even at the point where I was going to be on the cover of *Time* because I was the second designer she mentioned, and then Kennedy's father had a stroke, so they threw it out."

For weeks, Tassell's little design studio was in a state of siege from aggressive journalists around the world. He never dreamed the attention would be this intrusive; it reached a point where he could barely get any work done. "My secretary would answer the calls. The reporters even tried to contact my accountant, to go through the books to see what she had bought. I gave them nothing, because that is the way I assume Mrs. Kennedy wanted it. We told them to call the White House — we never gave out any information concerning Mrs. Kennedy."

Tassell's discretion served him well. After Bogotá, Pamela Turnure attended his collections every season, and he sent many outfits for Mrs. Kennedy to wear. He even got involved in her India trip after Lee Radziwill visited his collection at the Gotham Hotel, where many California designers showed in New York City.

"I've got a crush on Jackie Kennedy."

As Gus recalls, "Lee Radziwill came up and wanted to see the clothes, possibly for India. We showed her clothes, Joe Eula was there.... She looked at things, she took numbers, and then she left." Unfortunately, the respected and powerful fashion journalist Eugenia Sheppard was in the lobby. She happened to see Radziwill pass by and put two and two together.

Minutes after Lee left, Eugenia called Tassell, whose work she knew well, from a house phone in the lobby. "Gustave, how are you?" she began. He said, "Fine." She said, "I just saw Lee Radziwill coming down the elevator—was she to see you?" Gus thought he should keep everything related to the White House quiet, so he said no. This infuriated Sheppard—"You're lying to me!" "I am not!" "You're *lying*—" and she hung up.

Sheppard was the most influential fashion journalist in America. She could have done a great deal to help his career. Instead, she did not speak to Tassell for many years, until he returned to New York a decade later to take over Norman Norell's line. Then she supported his work once more. But what could Gus do? He knew that if he were foolish enough to speak to the press—and he was not—he would never work with Mrs. Kennedy again. It was an honor to have the first lady wear his designs. He respected her too much to betray her confidence.

It undoubtedly did not help matters with Sheppard when Mrs. Kennedy was spotted wearing several Gustave Tassells in India, among them a pink brocade dress she wore when she and Lee rode a camel together.

Tassell's experience is interesting, because it shows how Jackie wore the designers she wanted to, yet protected her privacy in terms of what she was wearing, how much she bought, and what she paid for it. Although she and Tassell never met during the White House years, she certainly knew who he was and appreciated his work. As he recalls, "After the president passed away, I wrote her a sympathy note, and she wrote me back a personal note. So she did recognize who I was."

Mrs. Kennedy was about to make even more international fashion news. In planning her 1962 trip to India, she wanted color. As Cassini recalls, "For the trip to India we both felt that the visual impact of color was important. She and I discussed the colors of Mogul miniatures—marvelous pinks, apricot, green, and, importantly, white. These colors would make an impact, and they were in keeping with the climate and the wonderful vivid beauty of the country."

Manolo Blahnik was completely enraptured by Jackie's ensembles. Almost forty years later, Cassini's work still holds his attention. "I remember she went to India—the idea of wearing a hat, coat, gloves, and then this kind of Indian Nehru jacket, long, like a little coat, and a dress at the same time! It was, to me, beyond a fairy tale! Beyond! I mean that was, to me, the essence of chic and modernity."

By the time Jackie went to India, the press was clued in on her style too. Not only did they struggle to describe it, some of them began to emulate it. By the end of her trip, even the "traditionally dowdy female press corps" (*Life*'s description) were sprucing themselves up. In addition to their portable type-writers, two lady reporters now carried hatboxes containing wigs, while three took notes wearing little white gloves.

Everything Jackie did in India was news. When she slipped off her shoes and put on violet velvet slippers to visit the memorial to Mahatma Gandhi, *Chicago Daily News* correspondent Keyes Beech was quick to peek inside the shoes, triumphantly cabling home: "I can state with absolute authority that she wears 10A and not 10AA." The newsmen (and -women) became so clothes con-scious they even asked the U.S. ambassador to India, John Kenneth Galbraith, who had designed *his* suit.

The seventy-odd reporters and cameramen, who were kept away from Mrs. Kennedy and rarely had dealings with her, were reduced to commenting on what she wore during her two-week trip. One scribe recalls counting twenty-two different outfits by the end of her stay in Lahore. Unlike at the White House, where she often wore a favorite outfit repeatedly, only two of her outfits were worn a second time, and greeted with the enthusiasm of a rare-bird sighting. On one record day in New Delhi, reporters with too much time on their hands noted that Mrs. Kennedy changed costumes five times, but this was partly because she slipped off to ride a horse on the palace grounds.

Even though the trip was not supposed to be a fashion show, the whole thing was just so exotic, so *picturesque* — what with Lee and Jackie on the ele-phant, Jackie frightened by the snake in Nehru's garden, Jackie greeting chil-dren in a hospital ward with the traditional Indian greeting *namaste*, Jackie awarding the cup to the handsome winners at a polo match — how could it not be? It also put three designers on the map in India — Oleg Cassini, Chez Ninon ("What color is that?" wondered one male reporter), and Gustave Tas-sell. While Cassini, as ever, held the slight edge, Anne Chamberlain of *Life* recalled that "a reliable source also assured us that at least two dresses were by Joan Morse of New York." On a side trip to a textile showroom in Banaras, Jackie also wore a sleeveless pink unbelted and high-waisted sheath by New York designer Donald Brooks.

In addition to Cassini's perfect suits and Halston's hats, Jackie unveiled another upper-class secret to middle America: Schlumberger. Like Gustave Tassell and, later, Manolo Blahnik, Jean Schlumberger ("Johnny" or "Schlum," as he was dubbed) was a Vreeland discovery. A master craftsman, Schlum-

berger created the most renowned and beautiful jewelry in the world, worn by his friends Countess Bismarck, Gloria Guinness, Babe Paley, Bunny Mellon, and the duchess of Windsor.

Diana Vreeland met Johnny in Paris before the war, when he was making buttons for Schiaparelli. She even remembered his first creation made of precious material. It was a gold fish cigarette lighter, destined to become a classic, and an essential accessory for elegant women in New York and Paris.

After serving in the French army, Schlumberger made his way to New York City with the help of Countess Bismarck and opened a small shop at 21 East Sixty-third Street. Vreeland called Schlumberger a realist because he depicted nature as he saw it. He used natural motifs, rendering flowers, seashells, monkeys, and even palm trees in precious jewels. Schlumberger's clientele grew to include the most fashionable women in the world. In 1956, his burgeoning success caught the eye of Walter Hoving, the new chairman of Tiffany's, who set Schlumberger up in his own salon on the mezzanine level of Tiffany's (where Audrey Hepburn tried on jewelry between takes shooting *Breakfast at Tiffany's*).

Bunny Mellon, a great patron not only of Givenchy but of Schlumberger, introduced Jackie to his glittering artistry. Jackie responded to his work immediately. Although she rarely sponsored any society events, she opened a loan exhibition of Schlumberger's work at the Wildenstein Gallery on East Sixty-fourth Street in early November 1961, just after her husband was elected president. The opening benefited the Newport Preservation Society, and her mother and stepfather, Mr. and Mrs. Hugh D. Auchincloss, were on the committee, so that may have helped. (The press, who thought they knew Mrs. Kennedy's taste, assumed she would be going to the opening of the National Horse Show at Madison Square Garden, so she threw them off by showing up at the gallery.)

With pieces loaned by Bunny Mellon, Babe Paley, Diana Vreeland, Marietta Tree, Mrs. Whitney, and even photographer Richard Avedon's wife, Jackie must have seen one or two things she liked and perhaps dropped a few hints. Later that week, Kennedy ran into Harry Platt, president of Tiffany's, at a party in New York. "I'd like to come by tomorrow and pick up something for Jackie for Christmas — is that okay?" he wondered. Certainly it was. Without any fanfare, Kennedy ducked into Tiffany's on Fifty-seventh Street the next morning and picked out a Schlumberger piece called the "two fruit clip," a cluster of two strawberries made of rubies with stems and leaves of diamonds. The tiny diamonds were set in platinum, while the rubies were set in yellow 18-karat gold. He gave it to her for their first Christmas in the White House. Jackie often wore the "berry brooch," as she called it, and kept it in its original blue leather box the rest of her life.

Schlumberger's gold and enamel bracelets became something of a society bibelot. Marie Harriman, beloved second wife of Averill, who raised the orphaned Peter Duchin, had one in red. D. D. Ryan owned the first one Schlum produced in white, made especially for her. By the mid-1960s, Jackie was photographed wearing hers so often that the press dubbed them "Jackie bracelets." (Kenneth Jay Lane made a fortune knocking off Schlumberger in costume jewelry.) In time, Jackie came to own the sapphire and emerald "sixteen stone" ring, his enameled bracelets in several colors, and a pair of white enamel and gold "banana" earrings, her favorites.

Jackie recalled Schlumberger as "a gentle and sensitive man, a brilliant designer, and a loyal friend." Although she never wore much jewelry, Schlumberger was perfect for her: exquisite, costly, not widely owned (or known), and — like a Givenchy dress — with great lineage.

In addition to her penchant for travel and notable taste in fashion, Jackie was renowned for the hospitality she showed guests in the White House. With the Kennedys in residence, entertaining went into high gear — everyone wanted the honor of being received by this particular president and first lady. In less than three years, Jack and Jackie played host to seventy-four foreign leaders and hosted no fewer than sixty-six state dinners and receptions. Pat Suzuki, who attended several gatherings with her husband, Mark Shaw, recalls attending an early party in honor of artists, soon after the Kennedys moved in.

"I remember it was the first artists' party—not the Nobel Dinner, just pals. There wasn't a formal receiving line or anything when you walked in downstairs. The dressing room was crammed with these ladies who could barely put on their lipstick—'Oh, this is so exciting!' And they'd gone to everything in the world! Jackie had planned wonderful things like the Marine Band playing jazz stuff in the lobby, and they had all these guys wearing white gloves to dance with—it was really a giggle!"

Pat says that the fun began after the party had ended and some friends were invited up to the Yellow Oval Room on the second floor in the Family Quarters. Like any good hostess, Jackie liked to dish about the party. "She kicked off her shoes after everybody left and talked about, 'I thought it went off pretty well,' and stuff like that."

On their way to the White House, the Shaws saw something funny at the airport they could not resist buying—ceramic plates with Jack and Jackie's faces painted on them. They were *terrible*, but they were funny, too. They had the cashier wrap them carefully in tissue paper, not telling her where they were headed. Upstairs, after the party, Mark handed the package to Jackie, "Look at this Jackie, you've really made it!" Jackie opened the gift and almost shrieked she was so horrified. She held up the plate to her husband, as the whole room erupted. "Throw it away! Throw it away!" She was laughing, as she pushed the plates back at Mark, "Get them out of here!"

Hours later, on their way out of the White House, Pat gave the plates to the coat check girl on the ground floor. She thought they were beautiful.

The Social Office, headed by Tish Baldrige, oversaw every breakfast, luncheon, tea, press reception, state dinner, private birthday party, and social event. The organization needed to pull it all off to the exacting standards of both the president and Mrs. Kennedy (but mostly Mrs.). And all of this work was done before computers, Palm Pilots, cell phones, answering machines, Microsoft Outlook, self-correcting typewriters, or even Xerox machines.

Every move in the East Wing of the White House was plotted on yellow legal pads and handwritten memos in blue and red pencil. The RSVPs to state dinners (or any social event) were carefully checked off by Tish Baldrige and Sandy Fox of the White House Social Office with either a blue "A" ("accept") or a red "R" ("reject") next to each invited guest's name in perfect Palmer script, as well as an occasional underlined <u>to remind</u> notation.

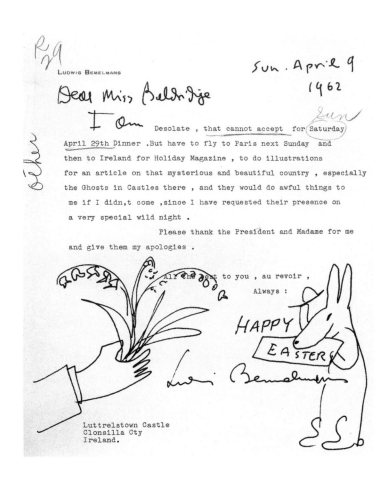

LUDWIG BEMELMANS

Sun. April 9
1962

Dear Miss Baldrige

I am Desolate, that cannot accept for Saturday
April 29th Dinner .But have to fly to Paris next Sunday and
then to Ireland for Holiday Magazine , to do illustrations
for an article on that mysterious and beautiful country , especially
the Ghosts in Castles there , and they would do awful things to
me if I didn,t come ,since I have requested their presence on
a very special wild night .

    Please thank the President and Madame for me
and give them my apologies .

        All the best to you , au revoir ,
        Always :

HAPPY
EASTER

Luttrelstown Castle
Clonsilla Cty
Ireland.

There was much repetition of work, page after page of carefully typed (and, one imagines, retyped) lists. Before the computer, mistakes were more difficult to correct. But today, it is immensely helpful for historians to have these records.

The rule of etiquette when invited to a White House state dinner is that, barring absence from the country or dire illness, you must attend. This being the Kennedy White House, the rare letters of regret were as illustrious as the people who accepted. The famously reclusive Mr. and Mrs. J. D. Salinger of Windsor, Vermont, sent their regrets. No surprise there. Ludwig Bemelmans ("Bems"), the illustrator and creator of *Madeline* (he wrote the first lines of his famous children's story at Pete's Tavern in Gramercy Park and worked off his 1946–47 stay at the Carlyle Hotel by drawing the murals in the bar) was a friend of Jackie's. She dreamed of writing a children's book about the White House that he could illustrate. Although she had little free time, he gave her a blank notebook with a charmingly illustrated cover to inspire her. Bems was on the guest list for the Nobel Dinner but could not make it because he would be in Ireland. His RSVP is as winsome as any of his books.

. . .

While the Kennedys became known for the elegance and style of their public entertaining at the White House, equally fascinating are the private luncheons, dinners, and birthday parties they hosted for their friends. Since it was difficult for Jack to get out, Jackie liked to invite amusing people to the White House to take his mind off his responsibilities.

At one o'clock on Thursday afternoon, September 21, 1961, the president and Mrs. Kennedy hosted a small, off-the-record luncheon for Mr. and Mrs. Otto Preminger and the cast of *Advise and Consent*, who were filming in Washington, D.C. Of the twenty-two guests invited, the only person who could not make it was the president's sister, Pat Lawford, who was in California, but her husband, actor Peter Lawford, was there.

It was a fun group. In addition to the president and first lady and the Otto Premingers, there were Mrs. and Mrs. Walter Pidgeon and Mr. and Mrs. Howard Lee. In the Small World Department, Mrs. Howard Lee, better known as actress Gene Tierney, was once married to Oleg Cassini and a former flame of JFK's.

In this sophisticated crowd, the rest of the luncheon guest list was filled out by married men and married women, *sans* their spouses. Jackie must have had a great time figuring out the seating arrangement. For the most part, the men were Hollywood actors — Frank Sinatra, Henry Fonda, Charles Laughton, Peter Lawford. With the exception of Ethel Kennedy, all the women lived in Georgetown — Mrs. Stephen E. Smith, Mrs. Mary Pinchot Meyer, Mrs. Husted Chavchavadze, Mrs. R. Sargent Shriver Jr.

The luncheon menu was a salmon mousse and tomato and cucumber garniture to start, followed by noisette d'agneau, potatoes soufflé, and green beans, three kinds of wine, and Piper Heidseck '53 with dessert. It was the kind of entertaining Jackie enjoyed — a lovely meal, accomplished Hollywood types, and no press to badger you.

It was also the kind of luncheon impossible to imagine the Trumans or the Eisenhowers hosting.

May 29, 1963, the president's forty-sixth birthday, was a day of celebration at the White House, and Jackie's touches were everywhere in the planning. There was going to be a staff party and another, more intimate dinner on the presidential yacht, the *Sequoia*, that night.

In the Kennedy tradition, JFK's birthday was characterized by a lot of laughs. One of the presents he got from his staff was a JFK doll. Sitting in a rocking chair and wearing a suit, the president unwrapped the box holding the JFK doll wearing a suit, sitting in a rocking chair. Holding it, he looked quizzically at Jackie, seated to his left. She laughed uproariously. Jackie gave him a basket of perfectly clipped sod from the White House lawn — one of their ongoing concerns was how lousy the lawn looked, compared to what they were used to at the other Kennedy homes. Jackie was always threatening to send a few gardeners up from Palm Beach to straighten things out.

Over tea sandwiches, champagne, and little cookies, JFK opened the rest of his presents from his staff, which included a toy airplane, a tiny toy space-ship ("recover your own space capsule"), a miniature pair of boxing gloves, which he promptly handed off to Pierre Salinger, as well as a cartoon of Kennedy with a bandaged finger standing behind a podium addressing the press corps, "First a word of thanks to the White House Correspondents for the new bread slicer." Kennedy was also given a large brass plaque that looked as if it had been stolen from a railroad waiting room: "Complaints Ignored." He thought that was hilarious.

The last event of the day was the president's birthday party on the *Sequoia*. There were a little over a dozen guests, the president's closest friends: his brother Bobby and sister-in-law Ethel, Ben and Tony Bradlee, Bill Walton, David and Hjordis Niven, the Shrivers, the Charles Bartletts.

Bare-armed in light-colored shifts, with tanned legs, good jewelry, and impeccable hair, the women were like brightly colored birds next to the somber-suited men. The vivacious Ethel, pregnant with her eighth child, Christopher, wore a loose dress with a strawberry print, an oversized bow at each shoulder, and bright pink shoes with pointy heels to match. Over coffee and cake in the long dining room, decorated with red-white-and-blue bunting, everyone was laughing as the president made a toast.

Jackie, looking impossibly young and happy, with David Niven on her right, had changed from the navy skirt, low shoes, and white top she had on during the day into a Cassini confection, a scallop-edged knee-length white evening skirt and an ice blue top with matching cummerbund. Tony Bradlee had on a beautiful brocade shift with a long matching jacket and Indian gold hoop earrings of delicate filigree.

The president and the men wore dark suits with occasional sartorial touches highlighting the fact they were on a boat. Charlie Bartlett and the waiters sported black tie. RFK, in a light blue sport jacket, smoked a cigar as he listened to the president. Bill Walton, the artist, wore a suit, tie, and pocket square with blue boating sneakers. Ben Bradlee, the most casually dressed, came in a turtleneck with a blue blazer, his hair slicked back, a cool look at the time.

The Secret Service guys, above deck, smoked cigarettes as Cecil Stoughton took their picture for the heck of it. They, too, are in dark suits, white shirts, and thin ties. Very Ian Fleming. You can tell they loved the president and thought they had the coolest job in the world.

And that was the thing about the White House: everyone there — from the gardeners to René Verdon, the chef, to the chief of staff — loved Kennedy. One Secret Service man, a young guy, recalled a time the previous winter when he was on duty outside the Oval Office. It was a freezing, bitter night. He was on duty, guarding the president, when JFK came to the French doors, opened them, and walked out saying, "I don't want you out here in this terrible cold. Come in here and get warm." The Secret Service guard told the president that his post was outside and he could not leave it. Kennedy returned to his desk and signed some more papers. About ten minutes later the president reappeared carrying a fleece-lined coat. "I want you to put this on, you're not warm enough, I can tell." To appease the president the guard put the coat on.

A little while later, the president came back with a cup of hot chocolate for the young man. Coatless, he came through the French doors, sat down on the icy steps, and the two men drank hot chocolate together.

Kennedy loved being president. His friend Charles Bartlett said that he used to worry a bit about what he would do afterward. He thought he might like to be ambassador to Italy if a friendly regime came up. He thought that would be a good place because Jackie would like it. One rainy Sunday at Camp David Jackie brought the subject up. "What are you going to do, Jack? I don't want to be the wife of a headmaster of a girl's school."

"Well now, let's not worry, Jackie," he said, humoring her. "Something will turn up."

Bartlett recalls, "I think he loved the presidency. He loved it so much. And he never made any bones about how much he loved the comforts of it. He loved the whole thing. He loved the people that were around him." One time, he joked that after he left, he was going to use his presidential allowance to bring the celebrated White House operators with him. They could find anyone in the world; they even tracked down publicity-phobic Charles Lindbergh and his wife to invite them to dinner.

"Of course," he said, "then nobody will want to talk to me, but at least I'll have them." Kennedy and Bartlett laughed at the thought of no one taking his calls.

That night, the *Sequoia* sailed down the Potomac and back to the dock five times as the president postponed his return to the White House. For the Kennedys, it had been a very good day.

On his last presidential trip abroad, Kennedy visited Ireland, the land of his ancestors, for a sentimental journey. There had been rumblings that this trip did not make any sense with a reelection year coming up. The current wisdom was that he should concentrate on political trips — out West, Texas, for example — that could help him in a tight race. "How many votes are we going to get in Ireland?" some wondered.

Kennedy did not care. There was something in him that wanted to return home. He went. For a few days in late June 1963, Ireland came to a standstill when President Kennedy, a few of his sisters, and as many White House friends and staff of Irish descent that he could muster landed on the island.

Dave Powers recalls their return to the Kennedy homestead in New Ross, County Wexford. "We went into this little room, with a fireplace, to see Mrs. Ryan. I was carrying the gifts Jack was giving them. He didn't realize he had that many cousins — there were more than we had presents for. Cousin Jimmy hands him a shot of Irish whiskey — it looked to me like a glass. He slipped it over to me and said to get rid of that — which meant to drink it. I downed it and — oh my God! In the helicopter he said, 'Imagine drinking so early in the morning.'. . . There was nothing like the days in Ireland."

Kennedy and his cousins had tea from a silver pot and cold boiled salmon. Mary Kennedy Ryan said, "The sisters were lovely, too. Not a bit of false pride in them for all their money. They sprang up and down to help with the serving." When it was time to leave, the last thing Kennedy said to his cousin was, "Cousin Mary, the next time I come I'll bring Jackie and the children."

A good family friend, Dorothy Tubridy, had encouraged Kennedy to visit Ireland. As he was leaving she asked, "Are you glad you came?" He said, "These were the three happiest days I've ever spent in my life." Mrs. Tubridy thought "he was really very happy — a little sad leaving, or lonely, I thought. I think he was very taken by the simple people about him who greeted him everywhere."

At a dinner the night before he left, his dinner partner recited a poem for him, "On the River Shannon," by Gerald Griffin. He was so entranced by it, he found a piece of paper, asked for a pen, and wrote it down:

'Tis it is the Shannon's brightly glancing stream,
Brightly gleaming, silent in the morning beam,
Oh, the sight entrancing,
Thus returns from travels long,
Years of exile, years of pain,
To see old Shannon's face again,
O'er the waters dancing.

Flying from Limerick to London the next day, Kennedy wanted to say a few words to express what these days had meant to him. Unselfconsciously, he stood in front of the crowd that had come to see him off, and recited the poem about the River Shannon from memory. "This is not the land of my birth," he said, "but it is the land for which I hold the greatest affection, and I certainly will come back in the springtime." The crowd erupted. A little shy now, he ducked his head, patted his hair, smiled more broadly, and lifted his hand to wave.

In August, the Kennedys endured a tragedy when their second son, Patrick, was born prematurely and lived only two days. The death of this baby, almost more than any other event in their lives together, almost broke their spirit. They got such joy from their two children: Caroline, at five, was a chatterbox, a natural leader, while John Jr. was developing his own personality. He was a real boy, always playing with guns and terrorizing the puppies. He loved watching the soldiers march around on the White House lawn. He was obsessed with flying, with planes and helicopters. "La-pa-ca" was one of his first words, "la-pa-ca": helicopter.

Unlike most two-year-olds, though, he got to ride in the real thing. Whenever the presidential helicopter landed on the South Lawn and his father had to go somewhere, John would throw himself on the ground, howling — he wanted to go with him. A compromise was worked out. John Jr. would fly with his father, sitting in his lap, to Andrews Air Force Base, where his father got on Air Force One to continue his trip. John then flew back to the White House in the helicopter. His father promised to buy him his own plane when he grew up that he could fly himself.

On August 7, 1963, Jackie had been relaxing on the Cape when she went into premature labor and was rushed to Otis Air Force Base Hospital, where their son Patrick was born by emergency cesarean section at 1:00 in the afternoon. A four-pound, ten-ounce preemie, the baby was having trouble breathing, suffering from a lung ailment known as hyaline membrane disease. Mrs. Kennedy and the baby were then rushed to the Children's Hospital in Boston, where the doctors did all they could to save Patrick. Mrs. Auchincloss was with

Kennedy at the hospital when he told her, "Nothing must happen to Patrick, because I just can't bear to think of the effect it might have on Jackie."

For Jack and Jackie, two enormously private people who were reticent about showing emotion to outsiders ("They both so rarely show any emotion, except by laughter," said Ben Bradlee. "They are the most remote and independent people we know"), their shared grief brought them closer than they had ever been.

The Kennedys' marriage had always been subject to a good deal of speculation, but Yusha Auchincloss, who knew them well, says, "The feelings shared by both probably began as mutual intellectual respect mixed with physical attraction, soon to be stimulated by private passion, matured through family devotion and concern, and by the time of the tragedy was reaching a combination of complete caring, mutual understanding, and strong binding love — shared in private, slightly showed in public, but obviously recognized by those fortunate few who were drawn to each through friendship and family ties."

A month later, on September 10, 1963, they had their tenth wedding anniversary at Hammersmith Farm in Newport. Mrs. Auchincloss, too, noticed a change in their relationship.

> I felt they were closer. I can't think of two people who had packed more into ten years of marriage than they had. And I felt that with all their strains and stresses, which any sensitive people have in marriage, had eased to a point where they were terribly close to each other. I can't think of any other married couple I've ever known that had a greater understanding of each other.... He appreciated her gifts and she worshipped him and appreciated his humor and kindness, and they really had fun together.

Knowing that the next election would be a tough one, Jackie wanted to travel with her husband when he went out on the campaign trail. Several aides spoke of the necessity of shoring up support in Texas, Lyndon Johnson's state.

They would travel to San Antonio, Houston, and from there, Dallas. Kennedy agreed. Sitting in on one of the planning meetings, Jackie wanted to go, too — when was the date? Plucking the little sterling silver pen from the side of her red leather Hermès date book, she scrawled "Dallas" across November 21, 22, and 23, 1963.

Shortly before the Kennedys went to Dallas, Susan Mary Alsop and her husband, Joseph, Georgetown friends, dined alone with them at the White House. Mrs. Alsop recalled that the president wasn't happy about taking Jackie to Dallas, because he thought she wasn't feeling strong enough — it was only a few months since she had lost the baby. But she was determined to go. She didn't enjoy political trips, but felt she had to do it for Jack. She put the best face on it by saying things like, "I love the idea of going to Dallas," and "It will be such fun, won't it?"

As Alsop recalls, "The president told her, 'You must show them the pretty pink Schiaparelli suit you're going to wear. You look ravishing in it.'" Fashion autodidact that he was, Kennedy was beginning to take pride in how well his wife dressed. He bitched about the bills, as any husband would. But he was proud of Jackie. Cassini's sartorial influence must have rubbed off; he was even beginning to imagine himself well-versed in French couture. When Prince Rainier and Princess Grace of Monaco came to lunch at the White House, JFK suddenly turned to her and said, "Is that a Givenchy you're wearing?" Grace Kelly was shocked. It was.

Jackie's suit was actually a very good Chez Ninon copy of a pink bouclé Chanel with navy blue collar, and one of Jackie's favorites. She had worn it in London when she visited her sister, to meetings about the reconstruction of Lafayette Square, and when the maharaja and maharani of Jaipur visited the White House.

"Oh, Jack, it's nothing much," she said. But she brought the suit down to show the Alsops anyway.

Susan Mary recalls, "We spent most of the night talking about the new house they were going to build in the Virginia hunt country — they were so excited about the house and showed us the architectural drawings. I made the president laugh when I told him, 'Oh, come on, it isn't nearly big enough for you!' It was a lovely evening — a cozy dinner in the residence. We said goodnight and wished them well in Dallas."

Riding in a motorcade in Dallas, with his wife beside him in the backseat of an open convertible, President John F. Kennedy, forty-six, was fatally shot by Lee Harvey Oswald on the morning of November 22, 1963. Two bullets pierced his brain and neck, killing him instantly. Rushed to Parkland Hospital, he was officially pronounced dead at 1.00 P.M.

On the flight back to Washington, Jackie sat beside her husband's coffin in the rear bedroom of Air Force One, with his best friends Dave Powers, Kenny O'Donnell, and Larry O'Brien. Her stockings and the front of her pink suit were stained with blood and brains. The most fastidious of women, she had refused when Mary Gallagher, or anyone else, suggested she change. "No," she insisted. "Let them see what they have done." She held a glass of whiskey someone had given her — funny, she had never tasted it before, but it did not seem to affect her now.

As the world beneath them was in chaos learning of the president's assassination, they drank whiskey and spoke of the past. Listening to Kenny's stories, Jackie was visualizing how she wanted the funeral to be. Lincoln. Her first thought was Lincoln, because he had been assassinated, too. And she remembered how much Jack said he had loved his trip to Ireland, and how impressed he had been with the Irish military cadets at a wreath-laying ceremony. They must be there, as well as his Irish cousins. Only nine days ago, they had enjoyed a performance of the Black Watch pipers on the White House lawn. They would be part of the ceremony, too.

All the world leaders must be invited, and they would walk from the White House to St. Matthew's Cathedral for Jack's funeral service.

Back at the White House, as an early winter dusk fell, helicopters ferried cabinet members and other dignitaries to Andrews Air Force Base to meet the presidential party. Nancy Tuckerman was with family members and a few close friends in the Yellow Oval Room, along with Caroline and John. John ran to the window and watched the helicopters landing and taking off, landing and taking off. He was so happy he took Maud Shaw's hand and pulled her over. He thought his father was coming home.

After landing at Andrews, Jackie accompanied JFK's body to Bethesda Hospital for the autopsy. Pamela Turnure recalls, "Jackie was thinking about the funeral, she said, 'I am going to walk behind the casket.' Whatever procession there was, the one thing she wanted to do was to walk behind it. Considering the emotional state she was in, she was thinking of all sorts of details and other people.... Her sense of history came through on this occasion, and she knew it had to be the most fitting possible funeral."

When Bobby asked what should be done with Jack's body after it was brought to the White House, all Jackie could say was, "It's in the guidebook"—the guidebook she had produced to show the history of the White House. In it was an illustration of Lincoln's body lying in state on a catafalque: that is what she wanted. With a phone call, the Library of Congress was opened in the middle of the night so William Walton could get the books he needed to research Lincoln's funeral.

Larry Arata, the White House upholsterer who worked with Mrs. Kennedy on her restoration projects, returned to the White House that night to help with whatever needed to be done. Following tradition, Jackie wanted the public rooms draped in mourning, but with very humble material. "Like Lincoln's," he recalled. Fortunately, Arata had recently ordered a hundred yards of simple black cambric, used to finish the bottom of an upholstered piece. He and his wife worked until 4:30 in the morning draping the windows, mantels, chandeliers, and catafalque in the East Room.

Jackie decided there would be a lying-in-state in the East Room on Saturday, transfer to the Capitol's rotunda on Sunday, and the funeral mass and

burial on Monday. The most pressing question, now, was where would Jack be buried? The family and the Irish Mafia were pushing for the family plot in Brookline, where baby Patrick was buried. "We're all going to be buried around Daddy in Boston," Eunice pronounced. Robert McNamara argued for the National Cemetery at Arlington.

The next day, in the pouring rain, Jackie was driven to Arlington. The view was magnificent. It was peaceful here, quiet. Already, an idea was forming in her head. There could be a broad green vista and the headstone grave marker, a gray New England stone, would be low, set into the ground so you would not see it until you came upon it. She had the idea of an eternal flame, like the Arc de Triomphe at Paris. She decided: Arlington.

For four days in November, Jackie's public dignity held the country together as Americans mourned the death of their young president. Pamela Turnure's overriding memory was how involved Mrs. Kennedy was in every detail. "Nobody wanted to go near her. They felt the one thing she must want is to be left alone.... Yet when the time came to make some important decision that only she could make, she was always available. I can always remember feeling that I talked to her more in those three days than I probably talked to her in the last three years."

Jackie decided on the mass cards. She wanted an excerpt from the Inaugural Address, then a little prayer and a picture of her husband. She chose the picture and wrote out the lines from the Inaugural Address, as well as the prayer, "Dear God, please take care of your servant, John Fitzgerald Kennedy." Picking up a memo pad headed "The White House" she wrote it all out with an illustration of where she wanted everything to go.

Jackie wanted the Kennedy coat of arms on the sympathy cards, but no one could find an illustration of it. She remembered that she had given Jack a signet ring for his birthday, so she went and got it to show what she wanted, and that was sent to the printers, too.

There were so many details, but the most important thing on her mind was Caroline and John. Although they had both been told that their father had died and was in heaven, she wanted their lives kept as normal as possible for the next few days. She asked Maud Shaw to have them wear their matching light blue English coats for the funeral. She would not think of having them wear black.

She told Pierre Salinger, "I have only one thing to do now — I have to take care of these kids. I have to make sure they grow up well." She confided to journalist Teddy White, "I want John to grow up to be a good boy. He loves planes, you know. Maybe he'll be an astronaut when he grows up, or maybe he'll be plain John F. Kennedy fixing somebody else's plane on the ground."

The morning of the funeral dawned bright and clear. Prior to the funeral service at St. Matthew's, Mrs. Kennedy arranged for all the help who had any contact with the president to meet in the private dining room, then go out to the North Portico and pay their last respects to him.

The coffin was loaded onto a caisson and the sorrowful procession made its way out of the White House grounds and down Connecticut Avenue to St. Matthew's. Leading the group of mourners, Jackie walked between her brothers-in-law, Bobby and Ted, followed by the leaders of the world—General de Gaulle, Emperor Haile Selassie of Ethiopia, Prince Philip of the United Kingdom, President Lyndon Johnson, as well as Joseph Karitas, the White House painter who did all of Mrs. Kennedy's painting projects, and the workmen who had worked with her.

Also in the column was a magnificent, skittish black gelding, bearing the sheathed sword and reversed boots of the dead commander in chief. Jackie did not know it then, but the horse's name was Black Jack.

John F. Kennedy was buried on Monday, November 24, 1963. His son John turned three years old that day. Overcome with emotion, Cardinal Cushing of Boston, who had married Jack and Jackie a little more than ten years earlier, added his own blessing to the end of the traditional Latin service, "May the angels, dear Jack, lead you to Paradise."

At the graveside at Arlington, Jackie lit the eternal flame. She passed the talon to Bobby, who touched the flame, too. Wreathed in black, Jackie was presented with the folded American flag that had draped her husband's coffin; her eyes bore the grief of centuries. She held it carefully in her gloved hands. It was over.

> Her life hinged on
> disappointments but she
> always sort of bounced back.
>
> — KEITH IRVINE

1040

IT WAS A PERFECT JULY DAY and Jackie and the children were out at Hyannisport, the first summer after Jack's death, staying at the little cottage they shared at the Kennedy Compound. She was dressed as she never would have allowed herself to as first lady. No more perfect Cassini suits, matching hats, and little white gloves for her. That part of her life was over. She wore loose wrinkled trousers and a yellow t-shirt untucked. She was barefoot with the wind blowing her hair. She owed the American people nothing. From now on, her devotion was to her children and her husband's memory.

Instead of the crisp, optimistic outlines of the New Frontier suits she once favored, her silhouette seemed blurry, indistinct. She wore white but revealed nothing. It was a bright sunny day; green sea grass waved against the cloudless sky. "Kennedy weather" they called it when Jack campaigned — *I should have known it was asking too much to dream that I might have grown old with him and seen our children grow up together.*

The day she left the White House and was driven over to the Harrimans' on N Street, she wore a black suit with tasseled buttons Oleg had made for her years ago. Caroline pulled her from the car to the house in her new blue coat, as if on another adventure. She owned so little black. As first lady, she favored bright pastel colors — yellow, pink, apricot — to draw every eye to her. Such faith they had then. Now, she just wanted to disappear. "When this is over I'm going to crawl into the deepest retirement," she said.

Days after Jackie left the White House and moved to Georgetown, Lyndon Johnson called her to offer her the ambassadorship to Mexico. She

politely turned him down. It was just too hard; she was fighting to keep her life together.

"They asked me to every state dinner automatically," Jackie recalled. "Then Mrs. Johnson kept the [White House] restoration committee going and I'd always be asked to that, but I explained to her in writing and on the telephone that it was really difficult for me and I didn't really ever want to go back. I think she understood, but out of courtesy they kept sending the invitations."

To return to the White House was unthinkable. The thought of crossing over the portal and seeing all her old friends was beyond her. As she confessed, "It was just too painful...I just couldn't go back to that place. Even driving around Washington I'd try to drive a way where I wouldn't see the White House."

In Hyannisport, looking out at the water she was able to think more clearly. Staying in Washington had been a mistake; she knew that now. She could not leave her front door and go for a walk without being accosted. Every day, hundreds of shivering people stood in the snow on N Street until 9:00 or 10:00 at night, filling both sidewalks and spilling onto the narrow street as far as the eye could see. They climbed trees and gazed through binoculars for a better view. Others set up picnic tables or brought boxes and ladders to stand on. Desperate for any mawkish souvenir, they snapped the ends off the shrubs; someone even pried off the house number next to the front door. After Dallas, Jackie had not counted on becoming a national institution; naively, she thought she would be allowed to disappear, quietly and sorrowfully, back into her private life.

"I'm a freak now," she told Robert McNamara, who came to visit. "I'll always be a freak. I can't take it anymore. They're like locusts, they're everywhere...I can't even change my clothes in private because they can look into my bedroom window." All those strangers watching her, waiting for her to stumble. It was Jackie's worst nightmare.

In Georgetown, she was surrounded by ghosts. The crooked brick sidewalks held too many memories. She thought she would go mad. There were times, in those first sorrowful months, when she half expected Jack to walk in the door with his breezy enthusiasm, as if he had just gone around the corner for a newspaper.

In the year after she left the White House, Jackie could no longer bear to see the friends they had shared. She let them go: Cassini, who had been so good to her, the Bartletts, Ben and Tony Bradlee ("The three of us had very little in common without the essential fourth," wrote Bradlee). It was all too painful. She was surrounded by ashes. She had to take care of herself and her children now.

No one knew what she was going through. "Can anyone understand how it is to have lived in the White House and then, suddenly, to be living alone as the president's widow? There's something so final about it. And the children. The world is pouring out terrible adoration at the feet of my children and I fear for them, for this awful exposure. How can I bring them up normally?"

She was isolated from everyone; her life was engulfed in shadows. No one understood. Not her mother, not even Lee, who had been such a help. Bobby was the only one she could trust. Trying to be helpful, even the Bradlees said the wrong thing. After spending the weekend in Middleburg

with them just four weeks after Dallas, she wrote them a hurt and anguished letter:

> Dear Tony and Ben,
> Something that you said in the country stunned me so — that you hoped I would marry again.
>   You were close to us so many times. There is one thing that you must know. I consider that my life is over and I will spend the rest of my life waiting for it really to be over.

Washington was the president's town. She should have realized that — walking along the beach clarified her thoughts and gave her courage. It was time to move on. With Lee's encouragement, having stayed less than a year on N Street, Jackie decided to move not to Boston, where the Kennedys expected her, but to her father's city, New York. When she and Nancy Tuckerman quietly looked at apartments, Jackie played a game with the ever-present, prying public by having Nancy act as the prospective buyer while she played the role of the children's nanny. It worked.

In September 1964, Jackie moved to a large, comfortable apartment at 1040 Fifth Avenue, a prewar cooperative building facing Central Park on the Upper East Side of Manhattan. After the *Day of the Locust* atmosphere of Georgetown, it was a wise move. Carnegie Hill was renowned for being one of the more peaceful sections of New York City. According to Pat Suzuki, "That was an area people didn't really go to. It was more residential — there were a few bookstores — it was a lot quieter then. They didn't have those Ann Taylor stores, and they wouldn't dare approach her."

Purchased for $200,000, Jackie's new home had fourteen rooms, including five bedrooms, a kitchen she barely set foot in, an impressive living room that overlooked Central Park (Arthur Schlesinger says it was like going into an English drawing room), fenced terraces facing Fifth Avenue where she planted crab apple trees in large wooden planters, and several fireplaces. She and her intimates referred to her New York base as "1040." It was the place she would live the longest.

Of course, being Jackie, her life had its amusing moments. Nancy recalls, "The day Jackie moved into the apartment, we spent the day unpacking, emptying cartons, putting books in bookcases. Around 8:00 in the evening, the doorbell rang and Jackie, in her blue jeans and looking quite disheveled, opened the door. There stood two distinguished-looking couples in full evening attire. When they recognized Jackie they were taken aback. They said they were expected for dinner at Mrs. Whitehouse's. It turned out that the elevator man, unnerved by the mere thought of Jackie's presence in the building, was unable to associate the name Whitehouse with anyone or anything but her."

Jackie's first concern was her children. The day she left the White House she asked J. B. West, "My children, they're good children, aren't they Mr. West?" It was a question, not a declaration.

"They certainly are," he said.

"They're not spoiled?"

"No, indeed."

They had lost their father at a young age, but thanks to Jackie, John and Caroline's lives were full of love. She had a map of the world in the dining room. When the children were little, she would sit with them while they had their dinner and tell them about the places their father had traveled when he was president. After school they played in Central Park. In the fall there were tennis lessons with Mr. Fenton, and in the winter, sledding on the hill behind the Metropolitan Museum. At about 4:00, they would come home hungry for a snack or tea. When it was cold, Caroline and John loved hot chocolate with marshmallows and whipped cream on top. That and cinnamon toast or chocolate chip cookies would keep them until dinner. John's favorite meal was sloppy joes. When Marta Sgubin, the children's French governess, first started cooking, she did not even know how to make it—she sautéed chopped meat and onions, then poured Ragú sauce all over it. John loved it and eventually Marta became a great cook.

Jackie was strict with her children. They knew she loved them, but they knew she kept an eye on things, too. John and Caroline were brought up far more conscientiously than some of their Kennedy cousins; they did not have the tiresome sense of entitlement some of them possessed. Jackie reminded Caroline and John that they were Bouviers, too, and raised them formally, the way European children were, to stand when an adult entered the room, shake hands when introduced to someone, ask permission before leaving the table.

Acting as both mother and father, Jackie was no pushover. When Caroline and John were growing up, she said she didn't want them to "just be two kids living on Fifth Avenue and going to nice schools. There's so much else in the world, outside this sanctuary we live in." But she knew how to have fun with them, too. They were her entire world. And with her inventive take on things, she was almost a child herself.

And what was life like at 1040? As one might imagine, with someone so hunted when she walked down the sidewalk, Jackie's home was her respite, a place to relax with those she loved and to do exactly as she pleased. As John Loring says, "Her apartment was for her enjoyment. Her favorite room was the library—

she loved books. Her favorite thing was to lie on the couch, reading and smoking."

Although she was loyal to her friends and confidantes, Jackie was fairly promiscuous when it came to working with interior decorators. As Mark Hampton diplomatically put it, "Jackie's apartment was a history of American decorating." The stars of interior design — Sister Parish, Albert Hadley, Billy Baldwin, Keith Irvine, Mark Hampton, Harrison Coultra, and Vincent Fourcade, as well as up-and-comers like Richard Keith Langham, all plumped Jackie's pillows over the years.

Right after Jackie moved into 1040, there was a bit of a disagreement with Sister Parish, who had done such lovely work for her in the White House.

Although it has been close to forty years since he helped Jackie with her New York apartment, Albert Hadley, Sister Parish's partner in the firm, recalls the experience exactly. "Whenever you went to 1040, the Secret Service men would let you in, but it was all very friendly. They were not intimidating or stuffy about it," says Hadley. "I remember the first time we went to that great room and the furniture had arrived. The fireplace was at the end of the room, and there was a sofa at right angles and some chairs, and behind the table was the *bureau plat*, and on it was the president's folio and there were two photographs, and there was also this marvelous straw basket that was filled with sweet peas, and it was just so beautiful! So simple. It is that mixing, bringing the sense of the country to Fifth Avenue. It wasn't a grand room, the way some of these places can be — it was comfortable. It was a beautiful room, with long windows looking right out over the park."

Sister and Albert were helping Jackie with the big drawing room. It had been pulled together at that point, and they'd gotten the directive to help with the curtains. They had come up with a sort of lettuce green unlined taffeta idea, and hung a big piece of it on the window so Jackie could see it. Then, Mr. and Mrs. Parish and Albert went on vacation to Ireland. They left the fabric hanging on the window for a week or so. By the time they came back, the fabric had been ruined by the dog — and somebody else was doing the work.

Hadley thinks, "Jackie couldn't wait and was sort of miffed that Mrs. Parish had left. In addition, there was the story that Sis had corrected Caroline for putting her feet up on the sofa. . . . I don't know how true it was, but she may have. So that was the end of it and we didn't do any more work for her at all."

Jackie may have had a few decorators jumping through hoops (and who wouldn't, given the chance to work with the most famous woman in the world?), but once the place was put together, that was it. A friend who knew both women observed, "Jackie's taste wasn't chic. Lee's taste was chic — and always changing." Much like her own style, once she found it, Jackie did not radically change the look of a room.

Keith Irvine, who had worked with Jackie on her first Georgetown home, had also done the Harrimans', where she had stayed after leaving the White House. After moving to 1040, Jackie called Irvine with an idea. "I've asked Marie Harriman, 'Can we copy your bedroom,' and she said, 'yes.'" And that's how Jackie's bedroom turned out, with a Scalamandré glazed cotton called "Tuileries" that the English decorator John Fowler had first used for Marie Harriman and Bunny Mellon. "And interestingly," says Irvine, "that bedroom was done three times before she died, all in the same thing — with the same fabric and everything. And that always impresses me because it shows a great deal of confidence. You've made the decision and it's part of your life. And I'm always knocked out when clients want to do that."

"Jackie was great fun to work with," Irvine says, "because if you had an idea, she always argued the point, 'Well, why would you do that?' Like, if you're making a valance or something, she wanted to know the thinking behind it. She never accepted anything on face value. The wheels were always turning, and she was fascinated by anything that had a historical reference."

In designing a room, Mark Hampton recalled that Jackie's "favorite colors were a sour yellow-green that she called citron and a pretty, faded red, slightly raspberry in cast. There were also some blues and crusty white paneling, probably original to the apartment. It was very French American in feeling — exactly what she was. It had the appearance of not being completely decorated. There was something very loose, very Holly Golightly about her style. Jackie had a sense of humor and was always making fun of things that were pretentious. There was a cerebral quality to the apartment, too — piles of books lining the edges of the room."

Albert Hadley remembers Jackie's "very feminine taste." In the apartment, the big sofas were covered in soft colors and very pretty floral chintzes. "She arranged flowers in baskets, and that was the beginning of that whole craze of flowers in baskets. She did that in the White House in those great rooms. Wonderful, wonderful simple flowers in baskets placed on those remarkable tables. She had a great sense of coziness about things."

Once Jackie got 1040 together, it suited her relaxed lifestyle perfectly. As a friend describes it, "I was expecting Versailles, but instead I saw an apartment that was simple, restrained, perfect — grand and humble at the same time. She had a great love for French furniture, but her taste was so quiet that, unless you had some knowledge, you would never notice how fine the pieces were. There were a lot of French and Italian old master drawings and watercolors, mostly of animals. It felt like a family apartment — cozy, warm, friendly. . . . She loved that place and wanted it kept as she had always known it."

Even though Jackie had a great talent for bringing her aesthetic vision to life, she did not win all of her decorating battles. When Caroline was a few years older, her mother wanted to decorate her bedroom with delicate French antiques. Caroline had a few style opinions of her own and wanted modern furniture. Keith Irvine's daughters ultimately ended up with the FFF (fine French furniture) originally meant for Caroline.

Immediately after leaving the White House, after seeing that her children were settled and well cared for, Jackie's first priority was her husband's legacy. To that end, she was deeply involved in the creation of the John F. Kennedy Library. Though a presidential library is traditionally a museum and

archive administered by the National Archives, the planning, fund-raising, building plan, and decision about where it would be located rested on Jackie's shoulders.

In preparation, Jackie flew around the country looking at various museums and cultural centers, meeting with architects and studying blueprints and scale models. After meeting with an advisory panel of internationally recognized architects to discuss the type of museum that would best capture Kennedy's spirit, Jackie visited with individual architects who presented their ideas to her. One of the architects, I. M. Pei, was an unknown talent at the time. As he recalls, "The day Mrs. Kennedy came to my office, I told her: I have no big concert halls to show you, no Lincoln Centers. My work is unglamorous — slum-clearance projects.... She didn't say much, but she kept asking 'Why? Why? Why?' about what I'd done."

After reviewing the top architects from around the country, Jackie had to make a decision. "I thought I. M.'s temperament was right. He was like a wonderful hunting dog when you slip the leash. I don't care that he hasn't done much. I just knew he was the one. I marshaled all these rational reasons to pick I. M., but it was really an emotional decision. He was so full of promise, like Jack; they were born in the same year. I decided it would be fun to take a great leap with him." Jackie spoke: I. M. Pei was the one.

While the architect and site were being discussed, Jackie planned a traveling exhibit of the library that went to twenty-five cities in the United States, to show people what would be in the library. As Nancy Tuckerman recalled, it was "a miniature Kennedy Library, an exhibit of things which some day will be in the Library — objects which were in the president's office: photographs, important papers such as the Test Ban Treaty, letters which he wrote his father during the Second World War."

Jackie not only decided which items to include in the exhibit, she was also involved in the actual layout and the catalog that accompanied it. In addition, she was actively involved in fund-raising for the library and wrote a personal thank-you note to anyone who donated more than a thousand dollars.

After she left Washington, Jackie relied on a few close female friends for moral support. Keith Irvine recalls that she was particularly close to Bunny Mellon, who had introduced her to Givenchy, Schlumberger, serious gardening (which would come in handy remaking Skorpios — Onassis had so many snapdragons planted, she thought the place looked like a Burpee's catalog — and planning her home on Martha's Vineyard), and even the Tuileries fabric that draped her bedroom. "Bunny Mellon became sort of a style mentor. I saw a lot of her influence. It was a competitive thing because Bunny not only had the same interests and flair, but she had all the money, whereas Jackie didn't. I think that's maybe what pushed her over the edge to marry Ari Onassis — to keep up with Bunny." Irvine recalls, "The two women wrote each other copious notes that were illustrated with absolutely charming watercolors. I thought that it was sort of like an early-nineteenth-century ladies' occupation — it's not E-mail!"

Jackie also remained close to Joan Kennedy. When they were together on the Cape, these two stylish women never spoke about clothes or fashion. As Joan says, "Actually, we talked about how we were *artistes*." She laughs at the recollection. "She used to say the rest of our in-laws just ran around and played touch football! They were really into sports — but they thought that we were sort of... weird, or different. The word was *different*, because we liked to be alone sometimes. They didn't—they liked to be surrounded by each other at all times. The more the merrier!

"After I married Ted, the first thing Jackie advised me was, 'Don't play touch football—whatever you do!' She had hurt her ankle. She said, 'Just don't even play!' When they were playing touch football down at the big house on the lawn, I would go up to my house, which was only ten minutes' walk, on Squaw Island, and play my piano and read. And the others would say, "*Read?!?*" And then she would go to her house and paint, to get a break from everyone. So we would giggle about that. . . . The things we liked to do are a little different than what everyone else liked to do. The Kennedys are very entertaining, but also a bit exhausting."

As two of the few people who understood what life was like inside the Kennedy maelstrom, Joan and Jackie remained friendly. "We talked about things [the Kennedys] would never talk about—they were so action oriented. We talked about more philosophical and artistic things. We always laughed about how we were different — not that *we* thought we were different, *they* thought we were different." She gives a light musical laugh. "*We* thought we were normal!"

Actually, Jackie did give Joan one style tip. They used to go waterskiing together. With the Secret Service agent driving the boat, Joan would read Jackie's signals—go faster, go past the wake. Jackie was in incredible shape; she would stay on the skis a good hour, then Joan would go out while Jackie rested on the boat, and then Jackie would go out again. After that, they would get dropped off about a mile past the breakwater and swim back to shore. Jackie was an excellent swimmer. She always used flippers when she swam — "If you wear flippers," she advised Joan, "it's a great way to trim your thighs."

Solange Herter, who had been Jackie's friend since she'd spent her junior year at the Sorbonne and remained close to her for the rest of her life, recalls that the first year she was in mourning Jackie took little interest in her appearance. "She was really in her shell then and Bobby made her give dinner parties. And she wore the same old yellow dress—it was practically unraveling—for every single dinner party she gave at 1040 Fifth Avenue. I don't think she cared much about herself in those days, like wearing a pretty dress or a new one." But little by little, with time, Jackie came back into the world and rekindled some of her old interests.

Now that she did not have the American public looking over her shoulder commenting on whose labels she wore, Jackie bid good-bye to Cassini and returned to her old haunt, Bergdorf Goodman. Rose Citron, her fitter at Bergdorf's (she worked there for more than thirty years until her retirement in 1999), says, "Mrs. Kennedy loved Givenchy—*everything* was Givenchy. When she came in, there were Givenchys lined up in the hallway!" She confided, too, that when Jackie was in the White House, she wore Givenchy, and logistically got around the "buy America" restriction by having everything shipped to her from Bergdorf's. In the mid-1960s, Jackie also wore a lot of Madame Grès; her salon was on the second floor, in the corner overlooking the Pulitzer Fountain. But after Dallas, there were no more Chanel-style suits.

Miss Citron has fond memories of her former client. "Mrs. Kennedy was a very nice woman. She used to come in after lunch, sometimes with Caroline. She was very low-key, unlike some of my clients, and knew what worked for her and what she wanted." One afternoon when Jackie came in, Rose asked if she was hungry; she said yes, and sitting on little gold chairs in the spacious fitting room they split a tuna fish sandwich.

Just as Jackie had lifted the curtain on the secrets of upper-class life in our country during her White House years, she now was beginning — just beginning — to loosen the strictures a bit, and relax them for us, too. In the 1950s, when Audrey, Grace, and Jackie came of age, style was linked to class in a way we cannot imagine today. The way you dressed reflected your school, your family, where you grew up, how you voted, even how much money you earned. To dress as if you were poor made no sense — what was the point of that? People dressed with formality. Men donned hats to go to the office. Women wore pearls while washing the dishes. But Jackie, by dressing so simply, helped break down the class barriers that set people apart — millions of women copied her style, feeling that if she could dress that way, so could they.

By the time she visited her sister in London in May 1965, hemlines were creeping up and coats, while still tailored, were not as stiff as before. In fashion, a change was in the air. As early as April 1963, designer Arnold Scaasi commented to WWD that "clothes have gotten boring because women have been afraid to go away from the trend. A dozen years ago, there were at least 25 fashion leaders, each with her own look, each with her own following among other women, and with her influence on designers. Today, there is only one leader — Jacqueline Kennedy — who looks marvelous, but it is only one look."

It was time, insisted Scaasi, for fashion to break out of its conformity, if only because "you can't sell a woman a dress for $800 that looks like the dress she bought two years ago.... The American woman is ready for a change," he announced. "She is well educated about fashion. She must simply develop some self-assurance."

There was one fashion trend Jackie was already on the front line of — women wearing trousers in lieu of a dress. Although she did not yet wear them in public, Jackie had begun wearing pantsuits a few years earlier in the White House, which was a very radical look at the time. Albert Hadley recalls meeting her there. "The elevator door opened and I heard this voice across the

hall — she looked so chic and trim! I remember she was wearing a pantsuit. It was dark, either black or navy blue, which was a little bit far out at that point." In Manhattan in the mid-1960s, fashionable ladies like Babe Paley, Nan Kempner, and Happy Rockefeller were turned away from better restaurants for wearing pantsuits by Courrèges or Yves Saint Laurent.

In 1964, around the time she moved to New York, Jackie also discovered an Italian designer, Valentino Garavani, from Voghera, a small town in northern Italy. After a five-year apprenticeship with Jean Dessès and a two-year stint at Guy Laroche in Paris, Valentino struck out on his own with his father's backing in 1960. Business was slow, but a few months later, that changed when twenty-eight-year-old Valentino met the twenty-two-year-old architecture student Giancarlo Giametti while on vacation in Capri. With the potent combination of Valentino's considerable talent and Giametti's equally considerable attention to the bottom line, things took off. Ultimately, Valentino went on to dress Audrey Hepburn, Catherine Deneuve, Nancy Reagan, and Princess Caroline of Monaco.

Valentino's passions were absolute: he loved flowers, pasta, and creating beautiful clothes for women. Valentino and Jackie shared the same elegant outlook on clothing. "The excessive must rest a moment," said Valentino, a sentiment Jackie clearly agreed with. "The importance of fashion," he once said, "is to make one dream a little, to soften one's imperfections." Jackie could not have said it better herself.

Valentino was just two years younger than Jackie when they met. As he recalls, "Jackie discovered my clothing in 1964, the year after the president died. Gloria Schiff told me that she had a friend who would like to meet me, could I bring some dresses to her house? Her friend was Jackie Kennedy. I took a vendeuse and some fitters to 1040 Fifth Avenue, and she chose six outfits in black and white because she was still in mourning for the president.

"We worked a lot together," continues Valentino "When I was in New York we would choose the outfits for the season. We discussed together what kinds of things she had to do, for example, when she went on that big trip with her brother-in-law Bobby Kennedy to Cambodia in November 1967. I did the entire wardrobe for that trip. She had been invited by the president and I knew from her what dinners and programs she had to participate in. We chose things together."

In the last week of September 1965, Jackie threw her own coming out party, a kind of thank-you to all the friends who had helped her through the past few turbulent years. Unlike the hastily chosen fifty-nine-dollar off-the-rack dress she wore to her first debutante party, this time Jackie put a bit more effort into her outfit. She wore white — a sleeveless ermine jacket over a glistening crepe sheath — almost as if to proclaim that she was back, that her life was resuming. "There'll never be another Jack," she confided to her friend Joan Braden — there would be escorts, companions, and even another husband, but there would never be another Jack.

Officially, it was posted as a small black-tie dinner party for twenty-seven guests in honor of John Kenneth Galbraith. After attending an art exhibit at Manhattan's Asia House (to which Jackie and Galbraith had each lent some of their North Indian paintings), Jackie and her group of friends headed off to Sign of the Dove, the secluded restaurant in a town house in the Turtle Bay section of Manhattan. Jackie had taken over the restaurant and turned it into a discothèque decorated with framed life-sized photographs of Galbraith (who is 6'7" tall). One wag immediately dubbed the gathering "Galbraith à go-go."

When Jackie's group joined up with the rest of her guests, the party really took off. The dancing started off sedately to Cole Porter, but then Jackie requested "the fastest music you've got" from the DJ. She shed her sleeveless jacket to reveal her glistening white crepe sheath, and did the frug and the watusi with dance instructor Killer Joe Piro, who had taught her the twist when she was in the White House. "All my nieces and nephews do these dances so well," she told him. "I'd like to do them well too."

It was a long way from waltzing with Yusha at Hammersmith as a teenager. Outside the restaurant, midnight strollers stopped and peered in the windows until Secret Service men lined up in a barricade to keep celebrity watchers away. Jackie's party was a blowout — by 1:45 A.M. there was a buffet of

smoked salmon, foie gras, French pastries, goulash, and spaghetti, then everyone went back to drinking and dancing. Jackie ducked out at 2:45 A.M., and the
crowd cheered as she walked to her waiting limousine. Everyone else stayed
until 3:30 A.M.

Jackie was back. She had put away her widow's weeds and was rejoining
the world. As John Galbraith, the raison d'être of the party, recalled, "Jackie
went to enormous efforts. It was an evening of pure fun. Time had passed, and
this was her expression of enjoying herself again."

Although few people were aware of it, Jackie and Aristotle Onassis had been
friends since she was in the White House. After baby Patrick had died, and
with her husband's support, she and Lee had gone for a cruise on Ari's yacht,
the *Christina*. At Jackie's directive, Ari was invited to the president's funeral. In
the years she lived in New York, Jackie and Ari stayed in touch. Over the winter of 1968, their relationship turned serious.

On March 16, 1968, Robert F. Kennedy announced that he would run
for the presidency of the United States. A few days later, perhaps being indis-
crete, Ari made an observation about Jackie at a party at the George V Hotel in

Paris. Jackie, he said, is "a totally misunderstood woman. Perhaps she even misunderstands herself. She's been held up as a model of propriety, constancy, and so many of those boring American virtues. She's now utterly devoid of intrigue. She needs a small scandal to bring her alive. A peccadillo, an indiscretion. Something should happen to her to win our fresh passion. The world loves to pity fallen grandeur."

Ari was a brilliant student of human nature and not a particular fan of Robert Kennedy. He knew his comments would find their way to Bobby. "That ought to set the cat among the pigeons at Hickory Hill," he chortled.

It did. Bobby called Jackie and wondered what Ari's curious comments were all about. Jackie admitted that they had discussed marriage, but nothing had been decided. Bobby blew up. He wanted the best for Jackie, but he did not want anything standing in his way of the White House. "For God's sake, Jackie — this could cost me five states!" he fumed.

If Bobby Kennedy did not support Jackie's relationship with Onassis, the possibility of the Greek winning over his possible mother-in-law, Janet Auchincloss, was even more distant. In 1963, she was staying at Claridge's Hotel in London and was informed that Lee was upstairs in Onassis's suite. If she thought Lee's racy pink dress at Jackie's coming out party was inappropriate, she really did not like the idea of Lee and Ari — too many antics like this could get them all kicked out of the *Social Register*. Janet stormed upstairs, walked into Onassis's suite with all the maternal outrage she could muster (which was considerable), and found Ari sitting at his desk, clad in his bathrobe.

"Where is my daughter?" she demanded, as if Ari had kidnapped her and stashed her in the armoire.

"And who exactly is your daughter, Madame?"

"Princess Radziwill!"

"In that case," Onassis said coolly, "you just missed her."

"Mummy stormed out," says Jamie Auchincloss. "She made up her mind then and there that he was a cretin. I think he may have reminded her a bit too much of Black Jack."

To placate Bobby and the rest of the Kennedys, Jackie agreed not to make any decision about Onassis until after the November election.

In America, violence was in the air. On April 2, 1968, at a New York dinner party, Jackie took Arthur Schlesinger aside and told him of her fears for Bobby. "Do you know what I think will happen to Bobby? The same thing that happened to Jack.... There's so much hatred in this country, and more people hate Bobby than hated Jack. I've told Bobby this but he isn't fatalistic like me." Two days later, as Bobby campaigned in Indiana, Martin Luther King was shot and killed in Memphis.

Jackie flew to Atlanta for the funeral and spent time alone with Coretta Scott King. "She came to my house," recalled Mrs. King. "She came to my bedroom . . . and I thanked her for coming and also for what her family and her husband had meant to us . . . I told her that I felt very close to her family for this reason."

Something terrible was going on in America and Jackie felt the darkness. After the Reverend Dr. King's funeral, Jackie told Bobby's press secretary, Frank Mankiewicz, "The church is at its best only at the time of death. The rest of the time it's often rather silly little men running around in their black suits. But the Catholic Church understands death . . . as a matter of fact, if it weren't for the children, we'd welcome it."

At 12:15 A.M. on June 5, as he walked through the kitchen of the Ambassador Hotel in Los Angeles, having just won the California Democratic primary, Robert F. Kennedy was shot and killed by a lone gunman. After Jack's assassination, Jackie's worst fear was coming true. With Bobby's death, her ties to the Kennedys and to America were cut.

Shortly after her husband was assassinated, Jackie had gone to stay with close friends Minnie and James Fosburgh in Katonah, outside New York City. Kitty Carlisle Hart, the ebullient actress, was also a houseguest that weekend. She had recently lost her husband, the director and playwright Moss Hart, and the two women spent hours together talking. Hoping to lighten the mood, Mrs. Hart asked Jackie, "What would you be if you could be anything at all?"

"A bird," she replied quickly, for then she could fly away and escape her destiny. With Onassis's money and promise of protection, now she could.

Events moved quickly. There was nothing holding her back now. On October 17, Nancy Tuckerman made an official announcement to the press. "Mrs. Hugh D. Auchincloss has asked me to tell you that her daughter, Mrs. John F. Kennedy, is planning to marry Aristotle Onassis sometime next week. No place or date has been set for the moment." The deaths of Martin Luther King and Robert F. Kennedy affected Jackie profoundly. "I don't want my children to live here anymore. If they're killing Kennedys, my kids are number-one targets. . . . I want to get out of this country."

She left.

jackie's closet

There is a realm of good things that don't go out of style.

— MARK HAMPTON

Jackie loved clothes. It may have been genetic. Her mother loved clothes, her sister loved clothes, even her father, "Black Jack" Bouvier, loved clothes. To get a sense of what Jackie was up against in her family, stylewise, her father quit his job on the New York Stock Exchange in 1953 and spent the summer at the Maidstone Club in East Hampton so he would have a proper tan for his daughter's wedding to John Kennedy in September.

But really, since when is it a crime to like clothes? Although the press had a field day with Consumer Jackie, the people who actually knew her say the shopping sprees were largely overrated.

Keith Irvine, who was in the rare position to actually *see* her closets, from her first home in Georgetown through 1040 Fifth Avenue, thinks the whole Jackie-as-Shopper myth is largely that, a myth. He says, "She got an awful lot of dresses, but I think they went back. I don't think she held on to too many, because those closets were never too full. Obviously, designers and shopkeepers were willing to give her everything she ever looked at just for the publicity of her being seen wearing it."

He observes that the "newspapers get a hold of things and try to make a story, and then after a while it becomes a reality that never goes away and then that becomes the truth."

That said, if you're not dating a Greek shipping magnate, here's how to get Jackie's look for yourself.

Sleeveless A-line dresses for spring and summer Irish linen or raw silk is best in light colors — white, pink, taupe. The American public was shocked when Palm Beach photographers caught JBK going into church barelegged, which caused JFK (and his mother) to hit the roof, but times have changed and *Vogue* editors now go stockingless in February. We won't tell Rose if you don't.

Lots of Valentino Hey, working girl! Sure, you're just starting out in publishing, but that's no excuse to walk around like a *schlub*. Jackie favored Mr. V's trousers and silk shirts and, boy, did she look fabulous. Whether you're at the top of the food chain or still battling your way out of the slush pile, you'd be wise to follow her lead.

A good French suit Falling to the middle of your knee with three-quarter sleeves on the jacket, this wildly nostalgic silhouette is what you remember your mother wearing your entire childhood. Chanel, Givenchy, Cassini, it doesn't matter — it's a classic. If you buy a modern version, make sure it's the best material you can afford.

Riding clothes Like C. Z. Guest and Lee Radziwill, Jackie got her hacking jackets from Huntsman on Saville Row. If you are going to ride, looking good is as important as watching your lead and keeping your heels down. And wake up the crew at the stables — people who knew Jackie say her horses were as well turned out as their owner.

White jeans Now is not the time to slack up on the yoga — and go easy on the carbs! In her New York years, Jackie favored belt-less white jeans and a black turtleneck, *never* tucked in, but pulled down over the hips. Always. Do you know anyone else who looked as good in this outfit?

Dark sunglasses This, you know. Once she was no longer a political wife, Mrs. Kennedy practically didn't take the dark glasses off for the next thirty years. She admitted that she loved wearing sunglasses because she could surreptitiously watch people (who were generally watching her). A publishing friend visited her at Double-day, opened her desk drawer, and saw a dozen pairs, ready for action. Truth or Urban Legend? He swears the former.

Hermès scarf Practice putting it on at home so you look like you know what you are doing. Former first lady trivia: Waiting in line on the Upper East Side to vote one rainy day, she covered up with a black Hermès "Horoscope" design.

House charge at Van Cleef & Arpels, Harry Winston, or David Webb After she became Mrs. Onassis, Jackie picked up some *serious* jewelry to offset those t-shirts she favored. Van Cleef was the sentimental favorite, since her engagement and wedding ring from JFK came from there. But Ari was no slouch when it came to giving her some major trinkets in the late 1960s. Who can forget the 40.42-carat honker from Harry Winston that put Ari firmly in Richard and Liz terri-tory? Jackie was such a New Yorker, she wore it to dinner at La Côte Basque one night, earning the enmity of wives, mis-tresses, and girlfriends everywhere.

Something Schlumberger Another very good reason to be kind to your batty aunt who drives you up the wall with her "Truman, DV, and me at the Colony" sto-ries. Enamel and gold jewelry with impecca-ble lineage — favored by Bunny Mellon, Marie Harriman, and D. D. Ryan. Although she never wore them all at once, Jackie owned several bracelets, the "sixteen stones" ring, and white banana earrings. Kenneth Jay Lane does knockoffs, but buy the origi-nal when your ship comes in . . . you're worth it. Johnny's stuff is still available at Tiff's and occasionally, rarely, at auction.

Three-strand pearl necklace from Kenneth Jay Lane You're twelve points down in the polls and you've got to get through eight states in two days? Don't let the demands of campaigning get to you. Slip on this first ladies' favorite from Jackie through Barbara, Nancy, and Hillary. In case mere sentimentality is not reason enough to own this, JKO's KJL faux pearl necklace went for $211,500 at the Sotheby's auction.

Vogal riding boots JBK loped around Vassar (and the halls of the White House) in jodhpurs and paddock boots for that recherché "I'd rather be anywhere but here" look.

Jack Rogers sandals With their distinctive lanyard edging and pink and green color scheme, nothing says "I summer in Southampton" like a pair of Jackie Rogers. Jackie — our Jackie — favored these distinctive sandals that took her from Piping Rock to Skorpios in style. Best of all, they're still around and made in the U.S.A. — get the original in several colors.

Hélène Arpels Hélène's been your friend forever. She let you and Lee try on her Givenchys when you could barely get into them, and she knew Ari ages before you did. Hightail it over to her shop on Park Avenue and pick up a few pairs of shoes. (N.B. Princess Diana favored the loafers.)

Manolo Blahniks Of *course* JKO wore MB's — are you surprised? Watch out for sharp-eyed *Women's Wear Daily* reporters just waiting to leak your shoe size to the entire world.

Keds sneakers For evading the Ron Galellas in your life and, after the court order, bicycling peacefully around the Vineyard.

T. Anthony luggage Moving between Fifth Avenue, Skorpios, Paris, and Peapack, New Jersey, you've got to find somewhere to *put* all your necessities, right? While we're not saying Jackie packed herself, you might (lots of tissue paper is the trick), so save the Louis Vuitton for Diana Vreeland and Joan Rivers, and opt for T. Anthony instead.

> What does she do with
> all those clothes? All I ever see
> her wearing is blue jeans.
>
> — ARISTOTLE ONASSIS

the most famous
woman in the world

JACKIE SEEMS TO HAVE spent the Onassis years behind a pair of sunglasses, hiding in plain sight. And who was the man she married? Like Joseph P. Kennedy, but far less provincial and infinitely more successful, Aristotle Onassis was his own creation. He was born on January 20, 1900, in Turkey, where his father was a prosperous merchant and prominent member of the Greek community that outnumbered the Turks in the port of Smyrna. Ari's mother died when he was eight, and ten years later he barely escaped a brutal massacre of non-Turkish citizens by the Turkish army in 1922. After an unhappy spell in Athens, Onassis immigrated to Argentina, where he made a fortune importing tobacco, and then to New York, where he built his multimillion-dollar shipping fleet.

Largely self-educated, "Tellis" (as Jackie called him) was well read in classical Greek history and spoke six languages: Greek, Turkish, English, Spanish, French, and Italian. A night person and an insomniac, he was a hypnotic raconteur and fascinated guests at dinner parties with his recollections of Winston Churchill. Friends, particularly women, considered him a perfect listener.

Unlike the beautiful women he squired, Onassis was no clotheshorse; he did not need to be. His baggy suits ("Made in London while he is in New York," sniped a critic) were always worn with a blue shirt and blue tie. On the yacht, he generally went shirtless and paid strict attention to his waistline. Ari was a shrewd operator whose enigmatic, almost Oriental facade hid a volcanic rage and a long memory for a grudge. Unencumbered by the world, he did as

he pleased, and this must have attracted Jackie greatly. He was generous, superstitious, and charming. He took from the world what he wanted. He spent five months of the year on a 325-foot yacht, the *Christina*, named for a daughter he rarely saw. With a battered briefcase, a red leather appointment book, and an encyclopedic memory for deals, he traveled the world, a latter-day Odysseus.

On October 20, 1968, less than five months after Robert Kennedy was killed, Jackie married Onassis in a small ceremony in the chapel on his Greek island, Skorpios, with her children, sister, and mother in attendance. Onassis was sixty-eight, she was thirty-nine.

Although Jackie truly loved Onassis and thought she was doing the right thing at the time, the marriage caused her reputation to suffer a rare setback from which it took her years to recover. "She went through two terrible times," says Letitia Baldrige. "Once by the tragedy [of the assassination], once by the criticism following the Onassis marriage. She didn't understand why the American public descended upon her."

Descend they did. Most Americans, and indeed the world, took her marriage to Aristotle Onassis as a personal affront. JACKIE, HOW COULD YOU? headlined Stockholm's *Expressen*. GOODBYE CAMELOT, HELLO SKORPIOS! trumpeted *Life* magazine. JACKIE WEDS BLANK CHECK! headlined one tabloid. The marriage even merited a rare joke from Mao Tse-tung: "If Mr. Khrushchev had died, I doubt if Mr. Onassis would have married Mrs. Khrushchev."

Warranted or not, Onassis was viewed as a foreigner and a pirate in contrast to the graceful all-American John F. Kennedy. "She's gone from Prince Charming to Caliban," said a former Kennedy aide. "He's not a man of the salon," one detractor said. "He's a man of the pier." Among Jackie's few defenders was Elizabeth Taylor. "I find Ari charming, kind, and considerate," she said. "I think that Jackie made an excellent choice."

To the rest of the world, the Onassis-Kennedy union was not seen as a love match, but a business deal Jackie had brokered for her own ease and luxury. Many were disturbed, or said they were, that she was marrying out of her church and culture. A certain lingering American Puritanism inspired her critics to condemn the frivolous, slightly louche jet-set world she seemed to be entering. "She feels she has not been very well treated by America," a Kennedy-ite said at the time with understatement.

"She married him for the island," says Peter Duchin bluntly. Well, yes, there was the island, but also Onassis's two hundred personal employees and servants, as well as his yacht and fleet of aircraft: two amphibians, a helicopter, and the entire Olympic airways system.

Lee, who had enjoyed a dalliance with Onassis in the early 1960s, noted the prejudiced, xenophobic response to her sister's marriage and set it right.

"Americans can't understand a man like Onassis," she said at the time of the outcry. "If my sister's new husband had been blond, young, rich, and Anglo-Saxon, most Americans would have been much happier.... He's an outstanding man. Not only as a financier, but as a person.... My sister needs a man who can protect her from the curiosity of the world."

From their mother, Jackie and Lee had learned to associate money with protection, with love. "She loves Onassis," Lee said, with a telling coda: "Onassis is rich enough to offer her a good life and powerful enough to protect her privacy." Her friend Peter Beard agreed, referring to this as her "privacy marriage." After the hell of Jack and Bobby's deaths, this was all Jackie wanted.

While the rest of the world was aghast at her decision, her old friends at *Vogue* thought the idea of Jackie O. was *fabulous*. In the December 1968 issue of *Vogue* the editors weighed in with their opinion: "The announcement of her marriage to Mr. Onassis, an international figure of power—granitic, laughing, adamant—came as a fist blow to her public all over the world who have been supremely happy on the lovely myths they have devised for themselves. The actual woman is far better—delectable, determined, emotional, strongly beautiful, questing. She can again be herself, eager to exult, prepared for exaltation, living in her natural element of vital excitement."

One senses the manicured hand of Diana Vreeland, then editor of *Vogue*, behind the pronouncement (*granitic?*). She always had a thing for vitality. Her sophisticated response to Jackie's union ran along the lines of the old society adage that the first marriage is for love, the second for money, and the third for companionship.

No longer respectfully referred to as "Mrs. Kennedy," the former first lady was now called Jackie O. For his part in the drama and his ability to foot the bills, Ari was referred to as "Daddy O."—as in Warbucks.

Much to Jackie's annoyance, *Women's Wear Daily* tracked her with the persistence of Woodward and Bernstein—after all, WWD had originally stirred up the Cassini-Givenchy feud and broken the news that Lee was smuggling Givenchy clothing to Jackie when she was in the White House. Once, asked if she read *WWD*, Jackie replied, "I try not to." Three months before her marriage to Ari she ordered a wardrobe from Valentino. *Women's Wear* called the designer shortly thereafter and asked, "What are you making for the wedding?" Valentino told them she had not ordered a wedding dress, but *WWD* had followed her one day and watched her buy a beige lace and chiffon hat by Adolfo. From this, they deduced that she would be wearing the beige and chiffon dress from his Spring collection. They were right. After Jackie's wedding, thirty-six brides requested the same youthful-looking lace dress and Valentino ended up selling one hundred fifty that year.

If Valentino wasn't talking, *WWD* could have picked up a tip from one of her decorators about what Jackie had in mind. As Keith Irvine recalls, "When it happened, the Onassis thing was interesting because Jackie was just about to redo a whole lot of things at 1040 because it had been quite a few years, and we went through all these things and got estimates, and again it was too expensive."

Jackie was always trying to get a bargain, but all the Kennedys were like that. "She would wear away at you like a water tap," says Keith Irvine. "And then when she realized you weren't going to move, she just went ahead and did it." Once the estimate for the work arrived, Nancy would call up and say, "Keith, Mrs. Kennedy said you were going to give her a special price," and he would say, "Well, no, I didn't say that." After a bit of silence, Nancy would call out and say, "Mrs. Kennedy says go ahead." Once the work was done and Irvine knew Jackie was pleased with it, he would send a bill. Nancy would then call and say, "Oh, but you said you were going to give her a special price." And on it would go.

Keith knew nothing about Onassis, but he knew something was up when suddenly Nancy called him and said, "Go ahead with everything!" after they had been arguing about the cost of his work for three months. Had Jackie won the lottery? Well, sort of. Keith recalls, "I got the paper, and there she was on

Skorpios! And I said to Nancy, well, what do we do? And she said, 'Just send the bills to Olympus.'" Irvine laughs. "And that's how I found out about the famous marriage!"

In the beginning, Ari and Jackie had fun together, as both tried to lead their version of a normal married life. With her usual intellectual enthusiasm, Jackie learned Greek and insisted Caroline and John learn it too. She polished up on Greek history and archaeology. Twenty years later, she ran into Robert Pounder, classics professor at Vassar, at a party at the Schlesingers in New York City, and he was "amazed by how much she knew about the history of the archaeological excavations I had worked on. We discussed the excavations at Samothrace; she had all the landscape and excavations from memory. My theory is that when she married Onassis she did a lot of homework because she didn't want to seem like the dumb American who didn't know anything about her new country. She was very, very well informed and very funny."

Jackie even studied a cookbook, *Those Entertaining People* by Florence Prichard, very 1950s with lots of rich sauces. It was all marked up in the back with notes to herself and sample menus Ari might like. Marta Sgubin, who had begun work as the children's nanny but was now doing the cooking at 1040, did her bit by baking a chocolate cake for Ari when he was with them in New York.

Marta did not really know how to bake yet, so she used a Duncan Hines mix. A few minutes after it was served, Charlie, the butler, came into the kitchen. "Mr. Onassis would like to see you," he said. "It's about the cake."

She went into the dining room with some slight trepidation, but Onassis was beaming. "This is the most wonderful cake I ever ate! How did you do it? I want you to give me the recipe for my chef."

From then on, Marta kept General Mills in business shipping boxes of Duncan Hines chocolate cake mix to Onassis's homes in France, Greece, and aboard the *Christina*. Clement, the chef, was very upset — no self-respecting man of the kitchen adds water, Crisco oil, and three large eggs to a mix, stirs it, and calls it baking. "This is the first time in my life I had to cook with powder!" he raged. "I can't cook with powder!"

Onassis told him to get over it, he liked the cake.

From then on, Duncan Hines chocolate cake was served at every meal to the richest man in the world.

After her marriage to Onassis, Jackie the Shopper went into high gear. Hélène Arpels recalls Ari and Jackie stopping by her exclusive boutique, a jewel box of a shop on Madison behind the Pierre Hotel decorated like an intimate pied-à-terre, where everything from the clothes to the shoes and handbags was designed by Hélène. They were on a shoe shopping expedition. Jackie wanted low shoes, while Onassis liked high heels. "Hélène, please, give her very high heels," he begged. "Give her very high heels, I think they're very sexy!"

Jackie preferred shoes with low heels so she would not tower over her husband and was very conservative when it came to color. At size 10½, she liked black, blue, or brown shoes. They chose six — high for Ari and low for Jackie.

In the beginning, Ari encouraged her to buy and do and get whatever she wanted — after all, he was the richest man in the world. The Kennedys and Onassis viewed money differently. JFK was somewhat penurious and had little concept of the joy of money (except insofar as he never gave it a moment's thought). Friends knew that the Kennedys spent money on political campaigns and that was it. As a businessman, Ari saw Jackie as a symbol of his success and showered her with jewelry, including a crass (or wonderful, depending on your taste) 40.42-carat diamond ring from Harry Winston, so large that Jackie could not bend her finger when she wore it.

Working with both Billy Baldwin and Keith Irvine, as well as Bunny Mellon's decorator, Paul Leonard, Jackie decorated the Pink House on Skorpios. "Once she married Onassis it was very different," Keith Irvine says, "because Billy Baldwin and I were called every morning and told, 'find this, find that, find that, tell Nancy about it — if it's all right, it's got to be on the Olympic flight tonight!' and they'd just bump the passengers and clear the seats out. At that point in time, I was a thrift shop! I was in direct competition with Billy Baldwin — she was asking me to find the same things she was asking him to find, and whoever came up with the cheapest one fastest, she bought!"

While Ari and Jackie were reveling in newlywed self-indulgence, America was exploding. Diana Vreeland showed the first bare-breasted model in *Vogue*. (Of the outcry that ensued she said, "My God, you'd think people's lives would be so full they wouldn't even notice.") The exceedingly ordered world of Jackie's mother, Janet Auchincloss, and Bailey's Beach were in disarray. For the moment, the black and orange *Social Register* was most useful as a doorstop. Fashionable women of a certain social strata no longer changed several times a day, with separate outfits for at-home, lunch, cocktails, and dinner. The safe little suits, gloves, and hats — like those Jackie and her classmates had worn to a tea with the president of Vassar in 1947 — were gone.

In 1968, Harvard merged with Radcliffe. In 1969, Yale went coed. That same year, after flirting with the possibility of selling their thousand-acre land-marked campus to IBM and moving to a patch of land next to the Yale Divinity School (thereby guaranteeing the wrath of her formidable alumnae forever), Vassar admitted men. Clearly, something was up.

The late 1960s were the beginning of mixing high and low, in society and in fashion. In society, artists hung out with debutantes while Lee Radziwill trailed Mick Jagger and the Rolling Stones on tour. In 1967, Truman Capote hosted his Black and White Ball in honor of Kay Graham at the Plaza Hotel. Described as "just a nice party for friends," the guest list of four hundred included a Kansas City detective he had met while researching *In Cold Blood*, half a dozen presidential advisers, some performers, some artists, several heiresses, and a sprinkling of royalty, with the elfin Capote overseeing all of it in a thirty-nine-cent mask from F.A.O. Schwarz. It was a remarkable evening.

This breaking down of class barriers was reflected in fashion, too. Walking around New York City, Jackie wore black turtlenecks from Jax (a shop Audrey Hepburn also favored) and white jeans, with an exquisite Schlumberger bracelet.

Sensing that a fashion era was over, Jackie wrapped her white gloves in tissue paper and put them away, too. It was as if she woke up one day and realized that the whole ladylike look, which had dominated America in various incarnations from the 1900s through 1969, was finished. Eleanor Lambert says, "Jackie's taste was very unaffected, very distilled, and she had a sense of when to let go of a look. For many, many years she wore little white gloves, but she knew the moment when they looked passé, and she never wore them again. She did wear jeans, but never at the wrong moment."

In the late 1960s and early 1970s, Jackie's style was slavishly imitated, just as it had been in the White House. Less than a decade after the era of proper French suits, white calfskin gloves, and pillbox hats, Jackie's style morphed into what could be described as High Kenneth (after her favorite hairdresser), a sort of Fifth Avenue chic that was as at home in Beverly Hills as Greenwich, Capri, or Mayfair. Jackie was on top of every fashion trend, not just white jeans. She followed designers' work like a market editor. She favored white at night, wore sleek bell-bottom pantsuits with "YSL" stitched on the outside pocket, suede go-go boots (with matching pocketbooks), modified miniskirts, Roger Vivier "Pilgrim" shoes that Vreeland favored, and — remember the maxi coat?

Valentino describes Jackie's style at this time as "the quintessence of American beauty — a mix of naturalness and sophistication, an outdoorsy kind of beauty." On Skorpios and on the *Christina*, Jackie wore "tight white blue jeans and a t-shirt, black sunglasses and her hair pulled back in a chignon. She often went barefoot, carrying her sandals in her hand in order to outrun the paparazzi. Her style was her own, based always on the same elements. She had a magical, simple way of updating her clothes according to where she stood at a particular moment in her life."

During the Ari years, Jackie no longer had the flawless, safe, accessorized look of the White House. She was more confident of her own taste, no longer depending on Cassini or Givenchy or her sister to guide her. She was sybaritic, looser, no longer held back by what her husband or the American people expected of her. In short, she looked rich. She could do what she wanted, and did. If she saw a shoe she liked, she bought thirty pairs, had the bill sent to Olympus, then returned the lot of them the next day.

Jackie experimented with ethnic looks. More often than not, she wore her hair pulled back in a ponytail with hoop earrings. Photos show her barefoot, in

sandals, dripping in jewels, wearing gypsy skirts or bikinis. Even her sunglasses got larger: look at me, stay away. Cool Jackie. Sexy Jackie.

She always dreamed of becoming more than just a housewife. And whatever the personal or psychic cost, she got what she wanted. Jackie turned to Vivian Crespi one day as they lay in the sun in their bikinis on a beach in Greece, drinking wine. "Do you realize how lucky we are, Vivi? To have gotten out of that world we came from. That narrow world of Newport. All that horrible anti-Semitism and bigotry? Going every day to that club with the same kinds of people. Don't you feel sorry for them?" The *Christina* bobbed in the harbor. With a word, Jackie could have anything, do anything she wanted, and she knew it. "You and I have taken such a big bite out of life."

In marrying Aristotle Onassis, Jackie turned her back on the expectations of the American people, too. *Watch me: I will do as I please.* Her will to survive was greater than her desire for acceptance. She moved on. Did they really expect her to live in the shadow of Dallas her entire life? "You know how it is," she said years later. "When you look back on your life, you hardly recognize the person you once were. Like a snake shedding skins." Benno Graziani, former editor of *Paris Match*, recognized Jackie's changeling instinct for self-preservation, too. "Jackie Bouvier has nothing to do with Jackie Kennedy," he says, "and Jackie Kennedy has nothing to do with Jackie Onassis. For those who knew her well, these were three different people."

Many of Jackie's friends feel she married Ari for the refuge he could offer her and for the security of her children whom she did not want dependent on the Kennedys. "She was very, very protective of her children," says Hélène Arpels. "They behaved beautifully and she really loved the children so much, her life was the children. And I think she married Onassis to ensure her children's security."

Jackie did everything she could to raise her children normally. Although America wanted to remember John as the toddler in a little blue coat saluting his father, he was now at Collegiate, a progressive private school in Manhattan, while Caroline studied at Convent at the Sacred Heart and the Brearley School before attending prep school at the Concord School in Concord, Massachusetts. Of course, once in a while something would happen to remind them they were not just like other children—like the time John punched a classmate in the nose and it made the national newspapers.

As Jackie hoped, Onassis's lifestyle shielded Caroline and John from the unending media interest they endured in America. Tommy Bruce, whose mother was a friend of Jackie's from Vassar, played with Caroline and John when his parents visited Greece. He knew Jackie worked hard to give her kids a normal upbringing. "Isn't it great we're lost?" John and Caroline said when they wandered away somewhere and couldn't be found. That was the word they always used: lost.

But in spite of the baubles, the island, and the airplanes, the price, for Jackie, was high. In addition to her battered reputation (which she may not have cared all that much about), many of her old friends said that they did not see much of her after she married Onassis, and that she popped back into their lives when she worked as a book editor in New York City after his death.

"I didn't see her too much when she was married to Ari. I don't know anything about that—I don't think she was very happy," says the outspoken C. Z. Guest. "I don't think she saw many people—she lived on a boat, what the hell could she do? She did the right thing for herself, though. She didn't have much money and it was never going to be the same again [after Jack's death], that's for sure."

After she married Onassis and left many of her friends behind, Jackie even looked different. Whether from yoga or from the 1960s styles of bell-bottoms and upswept Kenneth hairdo, she was thinner, more elongated. "You must remember that success and power can transform someone, even physically," says Graziani, who first met Jackie at a dinner in Paris given by Paul de Ganay. "The little brunet I remember—she was then about twenty—was shy, reserved, a little bit lost at this dinner, where there were many other women much prettier, more elegant than she. She hardly spoke!"

Craig Natiello, creative director of Halston, was barely out of Manhattanville College when he saw Jackie for the first time in the 1980s. "I was up on a mezzanine, six steps up, and this woman walked in. The party absolutely stopped — you had no idea who she was, and I was looking down on her, so all you saw was hair and the dress, which was Halston's velvet asymmetric dress, and I mean, *nobody* wore black velvet like Mrs. Onassis. But then she stood there and looked around in, almost, bewilderment. Not, look around and take my picture, almost bewilderment, like, 'Why are these people looking at me?' But Jackie had such a lightness of touch, that was the great part. She *owned* the moment, in an odd way."

Craig also noticed that Jackie transformed herself physically over the years. "Jackie's face changed dramatically, I don't know when I've ever seen that happen. I've seen ladies' faces change from twenty to sixty, where you don't even know if it's the same person. But I don't know if I've seen anyone's face change that dramatically, from fifteen when she was a rider, to first lady, to the Onassis years when all of a sudden she wanted people to look at her, but she didn't. The bone structure was still there, the glasses were genius — she could watch us watching her."

For Jackie, her jet-set years might also be called the Galella years. Ron Galella was not the only paparazzo to follow Jackie, but he was the most visible and, as such, came to symbolize the growing tension between the famous and the media, between the public's right to know and an individual's right to privacy. As often as they were linked on the cover of *Modern Screen*, Jackie was not Liz Taylor. Galella and Jackie collided at the start of celebrity culture, but there was tension between them — there had to be — because Jackie was not a Hollywood actress and did not depend on an adoring public for her livelihood. If anything, she would rather be left alone to raise her children in peace.

But the American public, and the world for that matter, was having none of it. They loved the late president and, by connection, his widow and children, too, and they wanted Jackie to know that. In one sense, their extreme interest in the Kennedys, and particularly Jackie, Caroline, and John, was a way of maintaining a connection with John F. Kennedy. As long as Jackie was roving around in the public consciousness and not ignored, then in their view, the president was not forgotten, either.

To further complicate matters, Jackie's attitude toward attention was complex. While she often wanted to hide and go unnoticed, at other times, she would do something guaranteed to grab headlines. Keith Irvine recalls visiting her on the Cape to discuss some decorating schemes right after the assassination. She drove him to the little airport in an open Cadillac convertible with her children and the Lawford kids hanging out the back, bringing along an American eagle on a chain that had been kept on the porch at Hyannisport. "So that was another aspect of Jackie — there were times when she *loved*

everyone looking at her. And, I mean, the commotion when she drove up to drop me off! It was the photo opportunity to end all opportunities."

In the beginning, when he first started covering Jackie, Ron worked mostly by himself. It was a lonely life, really — what girl would consider hanging out in front of Jackie's apartment a proper date? He was a single guy living in the Bronx. He shot Jackie mostly in the afternoon and at night. He got so he knew her hours, her routine. If she went to Kenneth's on Madison Avenue in the afternoon and got her hair done, then she was probably going out that night. If the town car pulled up in front of the apartment, that was another sign that she had plans for the evening — 7:30 meant the theater, 8:00 was the ballet.

Ron had all kinds of tricks. He never asked the doorman at 1040 about Jackie, because he would kick Ron off the sidewalk. The best thing was to ask the doorman next door — he wasn't getting a tip from Ari and Jackie at Christmas, right? And slip him a tenner, too. This often jogged his memory.

Sometimes Galella went too far, even he admits. He dated Jackie's maid to learn more about her. When Jackie came out and saw them speaking to one another, the maid was promptly fired. In 1970 he showed up at 1040 with a friend dressed in a Santa Claus outfit and tried to get a holiday picture with Jackie for the *National Enquirer*. (When it didn't work out he said, "She's fast and Santa was slow.") He even went to Greece, where Ari was surprised to see him.

"You travel around?" he asked Galella. He almost couldn't believe a grown man would do this for a living.

In 1970, worth close to two billion dollars, Onassis bent the world's will to his own. He built supertankers. Prime ministers and presidents were at his beck and call. He roamed the world on *Christina*, a 1,600-ton 325-foot ship with a crew of fifty. Before Jackie, there was Maria Callas, and before that, he had been married to Athina ("Tina") Livanos, the youngest daughter of Stavros Livanos, one of the most powerful of the Greek shipping magnates.

To Ari, Galella and in fact all paparazzi were inconsequential, part of the scenery. He couldn't see why Jackie got so upset over them. Onassis was a Greek, more philosophical. Let the public have their crumbs. "What's a few more raindrops when you're already wet?" he mused.

Before taking him to court, Jackie made her displeasure known. She foiled Galella by wearing black when she went out at night — a photographer's nightmare, since the picture ends up black on black. She had other tricks, too, like holding flowers in front of her face (a bouquet John had given her for Mother's Day 1969), never taking off those damn sunglasses (editors paid less when they couldn't see her eyes), or having the doorman of her building run interference when she walked to the car. But Ron admired her for being so

feisty. She was a challenge and he liked that. She didn't take anything from anybody.

Galella would have liked to have been an artist, too. A lot of people didn't know this, but he graduated from the Arts Center School of Design, one of the best art schools in L.A. Like Jackie, he loved to sketch. He had a dream of designing his own garden, with white statues and fountains and little brick pathways. He had it all in his head. It would have to be in Jersey, though, in the country. The city was getting too dangerous these days — you couldn't trust anybody with all these nutcases walking around. He could lay the brickwork himself.

New Jersey wasn't possible anytime soon, but maybe if this Jackie thing worked out — who knows? The sky's the limit for a guy who's not afraid to think big. That's how he saw it. The whole paparazzi thing was a challenge to him. "The best game in town," he called it.

Right now Ron lived in the Bronx. He wasn't rich enough to have a studio in the city like Dick Avedon and those artsy guys. But, hey, so what if he wasn't one of those lucky Harvard bastards with a rich father.

He always wore a jacket and tie when he went to Jackie's place to shoot (unless, of course, he was a stowaway at Skorpios; then he wore a pudgy sailor's uniform and fake mustache). When Caroline said he was bothering her tennis lesson in Central Park, what did he do? He left. But he knew that no matter how well he behaved, nice ladies like Jackie or Mrs. Mellon would never invite him to lunch. He was just a kid from the Bronx looking for a way out.

And Jackie was his way out.

As Galella says, "I started shooting Jackie in 1967. The first take was at the Wildenstein Gallery on Madison Avenue. When I followed her to the apartment that was, like, the gold mine — finding out where she lives!" Galella chuckles, not in a mean way. He was a kid looking to make a score.

"My first pictures of Jackie weren't very good. I wasn't really inspired at first. But gradually Jackie became more and more a part of my life. I became more and more fascinated with her. It was a challenge to photograph her. More editors started to ask for her pictures. Her name started to show up more and more often on the request lists that *Time* and *Newsweek* sent me every week. I began to realize that the media paid big money for good pictures of Jackie."

This was all well and good for Mr. Galella, but he was beginning to annoy the *heck* out of Jackie. Worse, he frightened her children. Even though the most pictures he ever took of her in one year was twenty, in 1970, he was turning into her little shadow, and she did not like it. She ordered her Secret Service agents to do whatever it took to keep him from her.

She finally lost her patience in 1969 when she and John were bicycling in Central Park and Galella leapt out of the shrubbery (she testified) "causing John to swerve violently." Jackie contends this was the end of the incident. But according to Galella, she ordered a Secret Service agent following on a bicycle to "smash his camera." No blows were struck, but Galella was arrested for harassment. Even though the charge was dismissed, the arrest prompted his suit against Mrs. Onassis.

In July 1972, Galella filed a $1.3 million lawsuit against Jackie, claiming that, as a public figure, she was keeping him from pursuing his livelihood. Jackie countersued, asking that he be ordered to stay away from her. Both sides provided more than forty-seven hundred pages of conflicting testimony, and federal judge Irving Ben Cooper (who had been appointed to the bench by President Kennedy) announced a decision that stopped just short of ordering Galella's camera smashed.

If friendship with the Kennedys was marked by bracing good times and a certain bonhomie, coupled with an almost Zen-like suppression of one's ego to their whims, then to be on the outs was to be dissed, big time. When he showed up in Capri in August 1970 trailing Jackie and her sister as they shopped, Jackie did not pay attention to him until she sat down at a sidewalk café, ordered an iced cappuccino, and told one of the waiters to "get rid of that man."

Judge Cooper decisively put an end to Galella's shenanigans, saying that Galella had "clearly perjured himself during the trial," and that "not a single event, episode, or incident was established in his favor." On top of that, the judge ruled that Galella must stay at least fifty yards away from Jackie, seventy-five yards away from the children, and a hundred yards away from the family's home and schools, nor must he communicate with them in any way.

They don't call her Jackie K.O. for nothing. On top of this, Galella was found guilty of contempt of court both before and during the trial and was fined on three separate accounts. But before you feel too sorry for Mr. Galella, consider this: Jackie made him famous — or infamous. Onassis, with his shrewd reading of human nature, was right about one thing, as Galella is the first to admit. During the trial he said, "Jackie put me on the map, no doubt about it. I got millions of dollars of free publicity from her."

Galella irritated Jackie, he frightened her, and, worst of all, he bothered her children; in doing so, he fiercely angered her. Paradoxically, he also took the most beautiful, casual pictures we have of her. And now, these pictures are some of the most visible reminders we have of Jackie's legacy.

In terms of Jackie's influence on fashion and style, one of Galella's shots is Craig Natiello's favorite image of Jackie. Showing the fashion industry's charming habit of not getting bogged down by moral semantics, Natiello

chooses (as many others have) the Galella photo of Jackie walking to Central Park. "I know he has a restraining order, but the Galella picture with the glasses up and she's turning — the little turtleneck — but everything is cut perfectly just to go walking in the park in the morning — *nothing* will ever top that, nothing!"

In spite of winning a judgment against Ron Galella, strange things began happening to Jackie. It was almost as if she had lost her bearing; she was unprotected from the extraordinary, almost perverse interest in her every move. In October 1969 she and Ari went to see the mildly titillating Swedish film *I Am Curious (Yellow)* at a theater on West Fifty-seventh Street. After they left, Jackie was accosted by a photographer whom she flipped over her knee, judo style. He ended up on the sidewalk as she continued walking, her head wrapped in an Hermès "Zodiac" scarf. At least this is Mel Finkelstein, the photographer's, version. Jackie's story is that Finkelstein was backpedaling in front of her, trying to get a shot of her and not watching where he was going. He tripped over his own feet as Jackie moved away. "It is really silly," said the quick-thinking Nancy Tuckerman, "to think Mrs. Onassis could flip a 168-pound man just like that."

In December 1972 a series of nude photographs of her on Skorpios appeared in the Italian skin magazine *Playmen*. Shot during the summer of 1971 by five or six photographers, some Italian, some Greek, they were bought by the Italian publication and put away for a rainy day. When the issue appeared, there were fourteen full-color shots of Jacqueline Kennedy Onassis. Nothing was left to the imagination, and within days no copies of *Playmen* were left on the newsstands.

"It was the women, above all, who were curious," observed Rome's *Il Messaggero*. "Not very sexy," purred one Italian matron, "and a little bit wooden." Milan's *Il Giorno* noted chivalrously, and accurately, that Jackie's figure, at age forty-three, was "still elegant, slim, and young." On Times Square a week later, scarce import copies of *Playmen* were selling for twice the normal U.S. price.

One rumor that quickly burst into circulation was that the whole thing was engineered by Onassis himself. (The thought does cross one's mind — how did anyone get that close to Jackie without being discovered by the Onassis security team?) Since the photos were taken around the time of the Galella trial, and Ari thought both the trial and dealing with Galella were a complete waste of his money, the story has it that Ari thought if these shots of Jackie were disseminated throughout the world, what else could she possibly expose? It's supply and demand: all the photographers' prices would fall and idiots like Galella would be out of business. For once, Onassis may have been too clever for his own good. He thought, naively it turns out, the photographers would finally leave her alone. He was wrong.

If Jackie was upset about her exposure, she never let on. One night at Le Côte Basque, Ari had just arrived from Europe and was raging about it—"I really don't like seeing pictures of my wife's behind in cheap Italian magazines!" Jackie jokingly replied, "They're saving yours for the Christmas issue, Ari."

To the world, Jackie had fallen far from the beloved slain president's widow; now she was the punch line to a joke. Just as Imelda Marcos came to be known for her shoe collection, the former first lady appeared to be a spoiled, money mad, "let them eat cake" Marie Antoinette. Jackie, who prided herself on her instinct to do the right thing, seemed perilously close to becoming a parody of herself. Even Onassis's wealth did not provide the safety wall of protection she felt she so desperately needed. If anything, she seemed lost. She was an enigma behind her black sunglasses; no one knew who she was. As Jackie O., she may not have known herself. Theodore Sorensen recalls her alluding to this years after the assassination: "She said to me once that a few of us should be forgiven for some of the things we did in the years immediately following the president's death. I think she was not only excusing me, but also excusing herself."

Jackie and Ari's lives were thrown into irrevocable turmoil when his beloved and only son, Alexander, was killed piloting a plane on January 22, 1973. Jackie swore to herself that her children would never learn to fly. Caroline, who had taken a few lessons while at the Concord School in Massachusetts, stopped immediately at her mother's command. "Until his son's death, Ari was one of the all-time greats," says Peter Beard. "He generated tremendous energy. He was obsessive, interested, obviously working on his own thing, but every now and then he would look you right in the eye and really talk to you. His talk was amazing — real genius-type stuff."

Onassis, who attacked the world with such relish, never recovered from his son's death. Grief is never rational and, in some way, Ari associated Jackie with Alexander's death; he even blamed her. Christina called her "the Black Widow." Hélène Arpels recalls, "The last time I saw Ari it was after his son's death. He was very, very touched by this, almost unhinged. He never got over it. It was a real tragedy."

Their relationship limped along. Ari was morose, superstitious. Jackie's habits that he once found so charming now enraged him. Where he once compared her to a misunderstood bird that must be given her freedom, now he wanted her at his side, not flitting about all over the world. While he once encouraged her shopping sprees — they amused him, after all; his income from shipping interests alone was fifty million dollars a year — now they sent him into a roaring fury. "What does she do with all those clothes? All I ever see her wearing is blue jeans!"

Jackie tried to console Ari. Eleanor Lambert remembers, "I was with her and Ari down at Loel and Gloria Guinness's in Acapulco the winter after Alexander Onassis was killed in the air crash. When it was midnight and the fireworks began, Ari started to sob. Jackie put her arms around him, just like the *Pietà*, and held him. She let him cling to her for what seemed like ten minutes. It was so touching because he was not kind to her. But she stuck by him in this awful time when he was mourning so terribly."

Jackie did the best she could for Onassis, ignoring his tirades, inviting friends to visit Skorpios to cheer him up, but they never recovered their early happiness. "They started with separate beds in the same bedroom," a colleague of Onassis said, "and ended with separate beds on separate continents."

The devastated Onassis sought comfort not from his wife but from opera diva Maria Callas, with whom he had resumed his lengthy affair. A year later, driven in part by his daughter Christina's hatred of Jackie, he consulted lawyer Roy Cohn about a divorce.

Death intervened, however, when Onassis succumbed to bronchial pneumonia at a hospital in Paris on March 15, 1975. Jackie had visited him the day before and was assured by his doctors that he was stable. So at the time of his death she was three thousand miles away in New York City watching a TV program Caroline had worked on. She raced back to Paris — what kind of a wife is not at her husband's side when he is dying? — but the damage was already done.

Surrounded by newsmen at Orly Airport in Paris, Jackie read a single paragraph. Her comments were as notable for their spare elegance as for what they did not say.

"Aristotle Onassis rescued me at a moment when my life was engulfed with shadows," she said. "He meant a lot to me. He brought me into a world where one could find both happiness and love. We lived through many beautiful experiences together which cannot be forgotten and for which I will be eternally grateful."

What would Jackie do now? It was unlikely that either Greece or Hyannisport would be her stomping grounds for the foreseeable future. From Manhattan, her sister, Lee, said, "I expect she'll come back here and carry on life as it was. After all, her children are settled here, she has her life here."

Once again, Jackie returned to Manhattan. Once again, the lesson she had to learn was the same: There is no one you can depend on but yourself.

"windblown jackie"

Are you *pleased* with yourself?

— JKO TO RON GALELLA

In New York, there are many things to do in a cab — call friends on your cell phone, fix your lipstick, kiss your date, wonder why the air-conditioning isn't working. But we should also remember St. Thomas More's dictum, "Chance favors the prepared mind," because one day Ron Galella — who never left the house without three fully loaded Nikons — rolled down his cab window and shot his most famous picture.

Sitting in his spacious home in New Jersey, which could properly be called the House That Jackie Built (with help from Liz, Marlon, Madonna, Brad, Gwyneth, and Winona), Galella remembers that October afternoon of thirty years ago as if it were yesterday. "It's funny," he says now. "It was a lucky take. It's all luck."

It was October 7, 1971, and he happened to be in Central Park, up by Jackie's place, shooting a model who needed pictures for her portfolio. He wasn't getting paid for it so he thought he might as well shoot her near Jackie's in case something came up.

It did.

He and the girl, whose name was Joy Smith, walked out of the park and Ron spotted Jackie leaving her apartment, heading toward Madison on Eighty-fifth Street.

"There's Jackie!" Ron exclaimed.

"That can't be Jackie," said Joy. "Dressed liked that?" Joy had just arrived from the University of Iowa Drama School and had come to New York to be an actress and model. Her mother would *never* believe this.

"Yeah, that's her," Galella said, trotting fast, his camera in his right hand ready to shoot. "Let's get her before she gets away!"

At Eighty-fifth Street, Jackie walked north on Madison and Ron had to make a decision. He couldn't run in front of her, because she'd see him, and once she did, she would put on those dark glasses and there goes the shot. So Ron and Joy jumped in a cab and, just like in the movies, Ron shouted at the cabbie, "Follow that woman!"

Traffic was lousy. They couldn't get past her. Jackie walked on ahead, beautiful, oblivious. She was alone, *bien dans ton peau*, happy in her own skin, as the French say. His eyes never leaving Jackie, Ron handed Joy a camera.

"Here — it's prefocused to fifteen feet. When we get out of the cab, take my picture! Get the two of us together —"

"Jackie in Jeans," he could see the headline now — man, this was *unbelievable!* This is why he loved being a paparazzo. The whole thing was a game for him, really. And what better quarry than Jackie O.? She was a great subject, he knew. The greatest subject he would ever have.

And right now, an amazingly spontaneous picture was unfolding right in front

of him, as the former first lady walked by herself in tie-dyed pants and Keds sneakers. He couldn't believe it! If he could get her, his editors would pay big bucks for it. But Ron was afraid of losing Jackie, of losing the moment.

At Ninety-first Street she headed toward the park, and Ron knew he'd have to make his move fast or it was over. They were alongside each other now; Jackie was in his sight line. He yelled at the cabbie to stop. With a gambler's instinct he rolled down the window and clicked. Jackie turned at the sound of the shutter with a half smile, not realizing who it was.

For once, her instincts were wrong. Instead of turning away, she looked right at Galella, and he got what he considers one of the most beautiful pictures taken of her. He had his shot. But they weren't done yet. As soon as Jackie saw them, she put on her glasses and strode away, her jaw set.

Ron and Joy scrambled out of the cab. They trailed Jackie like magpies down Ninety-first Street, snapping away. Jackie held her head up. She was furious. She was beyond furious. *Why can't these bastards— and it was always men—leave me alone?* The American Indian considers it bad luck to have his picture taken; believing that every time his image is reproduced for others to look at, another bit of his soul is stolen from him. Of course Jackie knew this.

For her, the afternoon was ruined.

She turned to Galella, the one behind all these ridiculous escapades. "Are you *pleased* with yourself?" she wanted to know, hoping to puncture what she assumed was his natural sense of decorum. She never addressed him by name, except later, in court, but she knew who he was.

Actually, yes, Ron was pleased with himself. Very. The light was fading and he knew he should hightail it out of there. It was one of his first rules of paparazzi journalism: Make like a ghost and disappear when people get ticked off at you. It doesn't make a good picture and could screw things up for you in the long run.

And that's what people didn't understand. He wanted to get pictures of Jackie looking good; he didn't want to embarrass her. If there was a bad picture of her, he destroyed the negative. Just like she did in the White House with Cecil Stoughton and Bob Knudsen. In that way, he was her best editor. As he put it, "Americans liked glamour, beauty, and success stories about famous people. They wanted to see Jackie walking in New York City on a lovely fall afternoon. And they wanted to see her as being even more beautiful than she already was."

This, as Ron saw it, was his job.

"Thank you," he said to Jackie, as he and Joy kept walking, cameras cradled carefully at their sides now, like rifles at the end of a hunt. He couldn't wait to get home to his darkroom and print the stuff. "Windblown Jackie," he would name his most famous picture. For him, it had been a very good day.

If you produce one book,
you will have done something
wonderful in your life.

— JKO TO NAVEEN PATNAIK,
ONE OF HER AUTHORS

working woman

IT BEGAN WITH AN IDEA, a conversation, the feeling that she had too much time on her hands. A widow again, Jackie was at loose ends. Caroline and John were away at school, involved in their own lives, and she was alone.

Twice widowed by the age of forty-five, Jackie swore that she would never marry again. "I have always lived through men," she confided to a friend after Onassis's death. "Now I realize I can't do that anymore." Jackie was casting about for what to do next. After all, she knew she could only spend so much time reading or devoting herself to the Kennedy Library.

The question was: what next?

Everyone (including her own mother) was pressing her to write her memoir, if only for history's sake. But the idea of writing an autobiography was unthinkable for Jackie. The way she survived was not by dwelling in the past, but by always moving forward — new books, new people, new thoughts were what interested her, not the past. She said, "Why sit indoors with a yellow pad writing a memoir when you could be outdoors?"

Still, Jackie had an urge to write something, even if it was not an entire book. She got the idea of writing a "Talk of the Town" piece (a "Talk" as it is known in the trade) for the front section of *The New Yorker*. The anonymity of "Talk" — they were unsigned in those days — was perfect for Jackie; it was one way to bring what she thought important to the forefront, without her celebrity, her *self*, getting in the way.

Lots of English majors dream of writing for *The New Yorker*, but only a select few achieve this lofty goal. As the most famous woman in the world, Jackie wasn't sitting around collecting rejection letters. One day in late 1974 she telephoned editor William Shawn and said she was interested in doing work for him, and they met for lunch at La Caravelle on West Fifty-fifth Street. Jackie and Shawn spoke eagerly about her writing for the magazine. After all, Jackie observed modestly, she knew about a lot of things, but she especially knew people, having met a lot of them from all walks of life.

Things went well, and a few weeks later Jackie — like so many famous writers before her — turned up at *The New Yorker* offices to hand in the "Talk" piece she had written about the International Center of Photography. She was ushered into Shawn's office, where she stayed a short while. He walked her out "precisely at a moment when an extraordinary number of writers and editors just happened to be milling around the watercooler and pacing the halls to stretch the legs a bit," recalled a staffer. Her appearance did not go unnoticed.

Jackie's piece about the International Center of Photography was published on January 13, 1975. After getting over *The New Yorker*'s use of the royal "we" ("Accompanied by Mr. Katz, we left the Metropolitan and walked up the Park side of Fifth Avenue in bright sunlight..."), it's clear how much fun Jackie must have had writing the piece.

Although Jackie's piece was unsigned, the New York publishing world is not known for its ability to keep secrets, and this was a biggie. Word quickly got out who the author was. Jackie never wrote for *The New Yorker* again.

JACKIE STYLE

200

Around this time, Jackie had lunch with her old confidante Tish Baldrige. Tish, who had worked her whole life, and knew the balm of it, told Jackie she ought to use that wonderful mind of hers. As Tish recalls, "I suggested publishing and her eyes lit up. I called Tom Guinzberg, head of Viking, that afternoon, and he and Jackie had a little chat. She began almost immediately."

It made sense that Jackie would work in publishing — ever since she was a little girl she had loved books. "She read *constantly* when she was in the White House," remembers Pat Suzuki. She once wrote a thank-you note to Bill Walton for an art book he had given her, stating, "All my books that I love are like cumbersome children — piled up all over the apartment — but I shall never love any as much as this."

After beginning at Viking in September 1975 and learning the ropes — "Like everybody else, I have to work my way up to an office with a window," she said — she worked on topics of personal interest to her: Abraham Lincoln's daguerreotypes; a novel about Sally Hemings, Jefferson's mistress; the court life of India. She got enormous intellectual stimulation from her work — stimulation she may have missed the past few years cruising the Aegean. As she herself later explained, "What I like about being an editor is that it expands your knowledge and heightens your discrimination. Each book takes you down another path. Hopefully, some of them move people and some of them do some good.... I think that people who work themselves have respect for the work of others."

In 1977, Jackie's well-ordered world was disrupted when she had lunch with Nancy Tuckerman and Lisa Drew, who were both working at Doubleday. Lisa had just turned down the Jeffrey Archer thriller *Shall We Tell the President*, the plot of which revolves around an attempted assassination of Ted Kennedy, and she had heard that Viking, Jackie's house, was going to publish it. Lisa was dumbfounded; she thought the book was totally tasteless and could not believe Viking had just bought it.

She asked Jackie about it.

"Who's Jeffrey Archer? I don't know anything about it," she responded. "What's it about?"

"It's a political thriller, and Ted Kennedy's a character, and I thought they would have mentioned it to you."

"I don't know anything about it," Jackie said. And Lisa thought. leave it alone.

Six months later, Viking published *Shall We Tell the President* to uniformly lukewarm reviews, including one by John Leonard in the *New York Times* that contained a hidden (or not so hidden) barb at Jackie: "Anyone associated with the publication of this book should be ashamed of herself."

With that, all hell broke loose. The book got even more attention and newspapers began calling Viking asking "How could she have done this!"

Jackie did not take any of the calls, but Tom Guinzberg said that Jackie was completely aware of the book from the beginning, and approved of it, and that Viking would not have bought the book if she had not. Lisa Drew says that Jackie learned of the book from her — after they had bought it.

One thing led to another. But the end result was that Jackie resigned from Viking and, a few months later, moved to Doubleday.

In February 1978, safely ensconced as an associate editor at Doubleday, Jackie was a dream editor. In some ways, she treated her authors the way she treated her Auchincloss stepbrothers. As Yusha recounts, "Her praise, when earned, would be lavish, and her admonishments, spoken or written, directed toward those fortunate few for whom she cared, could strike with severity and then serenely turn sympathetic. She would stamp her foot, clap her hands, point her finger, and then hug."

But mostly, she was solicitous toward her authors. John Loring, design director of Tiffany's, was a friend, and one of her favorites. Together they worked on six Tiffany lifestyle books that were oversized, beautifully designed, and very successful. (He was and is a charming man of prodigious energy; Eleanor Lambert once toasted him on his birthday: "John's not fifty — he's two twenty-five-year-olds pushed together.") One time, Loring was up late on a tight deadline for one of their books when the phone rang at 2:00 A.M. in his Fifth Avenue apartment. He picked it up. There was only one person it could be.

"Are you still writing?" wondered the familiar voice.

Yes, he was.

"I just wanted to encourage you and see how you were doing."

Publishing allowed Jackie to follow her innately curious turn of mind. "Although she didn't like them very much," says Loring, "she had the mind of a great reporter." One day she was lunching with her old friend George Plimpton, with whom she had gone to dances in her teens. The night before, there had been a fireworks display over the Metropolitan Museum, and Jackie had seen it from her living room at 1040.

"How about a book on fireworks?" she wondered, knowing they were a passion of Plimpton's.

Plimpton scoffed in his erudite way. "Come *on,* Jackie — no one's going to buy a book about fireworks!"

"Oh yes they will!" she assured him.

And it suddenly occurred to Plimpton that only one person in the world could walk into the director's office of Doubleday and say, "We are going to do a book on fireworks!" He imagined them groaning at the idea, bottom line and all that, but that was the beauty of having Jackie as your editor — once she saw a book's merit, anything was possible.

Next thing he knew, Plimpton was writing a book for Doubleday called *Fireworks: A Celebration and History.*

Once they began working together, what struck Plimpton was how careful Jackie was with his book and how perceptive she was with her editing. She brought to his book the same attention to detail that kept her awake in the White House, writing memos to J. B. West in the middle of the night. "All her messages were by handwritten notes," he recalls, "which was always surprising because you tend to get things by typewriter that some editor has dictated to a secretary. They were all handwritten notes in that famous handwriting of hers. Usually very astute editorial suggestions."

Like Louis Auchincloss, Carly Simon, Bill Moyers, and all her other authors, Plimpton kept his editor's notes. "She wrote me dozens and dozens of pages of suggestions. It's very, very rare. I have worked with many editors over the years. I don't think I've ever gotten one-tenth as many letters as I have from Jackie over the years about the books we've worked on."

George Plimpton also wrote the introduction for another book of Jackie's, a collection of photographs by the highly regarded American photographer Toni Frissell. Jackie and Toni had known each other growing up together in Newport and New York. After she died, her daughter Sidney Stafford wanted to get a book together and Jackie had written her a note — "When you do, please let me know, I would love to be part of it." Sidney called and tried to get in touch with Jackie but had a tough time getting past her two assistants, Scott Moyers and Bruce Tracy. They did not know who she was and would not let her speak with Jackie. Finally she said, "I have a letter from her." And they said, Well, show us the letter, and she did.

The next day, Sidney went to Doubleday to meet with her mother's old friend. Jackie walked out to the reception area to greet her. "Would you like a Tootsie Roll?" she asked, offering her some. Sidney took one, and they walked back to Jackie's office together.

In choosing the pictures for the book, Sidney did not want to push for including a wedding photo of Jackie and Jack, but Jackie said, "We're going to have to do it." Sidney asked Jackie to choose whichever photo she liked best. On the facing page is a portrait of Mike Todd, former husband of Elizabeth Taylor. Sidney had to get permission from Taylor to reproduce the image, but Liz did not like it. "It's going in — just forget about it!" Jackie laughed. And it did.

Robert Love, managing editor of *Rolling Stone*, has enviable memories of working with Jackie on a collection of essays entitled *Rolling Stone: 25 Years of Journalism on the Edge.* They were first brought together by Jann Wenner, founding editor and editor in chief of *Rolling Stone*, and a longtime friend of Jackie's. One day, he told Bob he had a surprise for him — they were going to have lunch with Jackie and the publisher of Doubleday at '21' to discuss book ideas. "So I wore my best Armani suit with a tie — it was a double-breasted blue Armani suit — and I walked in and Jann said, 'Jackie, this is Bob Love, he's Hunter Thompson's editor.' And Jackie looked at me and said in that whispery voice, 'You don't look like Hunter's editor.' It was pretty funny."

The four of them were seated at a corner table on the ground floor, back by the bar. "She proceeded to talk directly to me because we were side by side. It was very sweet and wonderful — everyone was table-hopping to say 'hi' to Jackie, but she gave me her full attention. That is the secret of the world-class ingenue: you think you're the only guy in the room when she's talking to you."

Bob found Jackie to be a real hands-on editor. First, there was a pile of Xeroxed magazine articles, hundreds of pages, that they had to wade through to decide what would make the cut. "She read all of it," says Bob Love. "She was totally there for the whole process."

The two editors communicated regularly, mostly through notes back and forth and telephone messages. "I called my mother because I had a message from Jackie Onassis on the phone and played it for her. 'Bob, this is Jacqueleen Onassis' — that's how she said it. . . . To me, her voice was whispery. It was very distinctive in that funny sort of Eastern Seaboard accent, a combination of New York and Boston. It's an interesting accent that you don't hear too much anymore — it's old New York that is fading out a bit."

As she had in the White House, Jackie quickly mastered the gamesmanship of publishing. Nancy Evans, then president and publisher of Doubleday, recalls that *The Power of Myth*, Bill Moyers's best-seller about Joseph Campbell, was Jackie's biggest claim to fame, but that at first nobody — including Moyers — was very excited about the book. Jackie had repeatedly raised the idea at editorial meetings and gotten a tepid response: no one had heard of Campbell or thought there was an audience for him. Fortunately for Jackie, Nancy Evans was hired. Jackie had known her socially and fairly skipped down the hall at her arrival. "Do *you* know who Joseph Campbell is?" she immediately asked Evans. Evans had studied Campbell at Columbia, sure she did.

Jackie's plan was back on track.

Together, the Smart Girls went after Moyers. A number of other publishing houses wanted him, but honestly, he had a hard time seeing the book. As Evans recalls, "We tried to explain to Moyers that we really wanted the book to be accessible and that we thought the formatting of the book was important to the accessibility, that it should not just be what we call a C-sized book of narrative. Bill, I must say, was not completely convinced when we first presented it, but somehow Jackie prevailed. We also decided we would make the bulk of the run in trade paperback. Jackie wanted it to have the feel of the *Whole Earth Catalog*, something that people would think of more as a handbook than a book that they buy and never read."

Jackie's book became a huge success, selling millions. Shortly thereafter, she would pitch books at editorial meetings that she knew might not become best-sellers, might not even make a profit, but that she felt were important. "With all the copies of *Power of Myth* that were sold," she asked, "don't I get a couple of books that I want to do?"

Joe Alsop, who had always lectured her about how to use power back in Georgetown, would have been proud.

After she had been working at Doubleday, friends noticed a change in Jackie. For once, she was not defined by the man at her side. For the first time since she was the "Inquiring Camera Girl" in Washington, D.C., in 1953, Jackie had a job of her own that depended solely on her own energy, skills, and initiative. "You have to do something you enjoy," she once said. "That is the definition of happiness: 'complete use of one's faculties along the lines leading to excellence in a life affording them scope.' We can't all reach it," she knew, "but can try to reach it to some degree." Through her work in publishing, Jackie was trying. This was an enormously happy and productive time for her.

To see how important work was to her, consider how she filled out a 1992 Alumnae Questionnaire from Vassar College. In red felt-pen ink, she struck the "Mrs." from her name, Jacqueline Kennedy Onassis. Under employment she filled in: "Doubleday, Senior Editor, 666 Fifth Avenue, NYC, NY," and that is it. Everything else on the four-page questionnaire—Additional Employment, Occupational Information, Spouse/Partner, Special Interests, Family, and (our personal favorite) Career Advisory Project—is left blank.

Like anything she attempted, Jackie took her editorial duties very seriously: carrying manuscripts in an Hermès book bag to Kenneth's when she had her hair done, interrogating her children about the latest celebrities, bombarding her authors with notes and ideas. It was almost as if she were back at school, walking to Thompson Library with Lucky Roosevelt.

As George Plimpton noticed, "Jackie really came into her own. When she was with Ari, she put aside parts of herself to pursue his interests. I sensed a change in her—once again, she was very much more like the girl I first knew, who had a great sense of fun and enthusiasm. It must have been an electrifying, extraordinary thing for her to be on her own—she was always somewhat diminished by the men around her."

But being Jackie Onassis, she ran into old friends from her past everywhere. One morning she was at Tiffany's to promote one of Loring's books. When she got into the elevator, alone, to leave, who should walk in but

Richard Nelson, the decorator who had helped her with her little Georgetown home so many years ago.

"Hello, Mrs. Onassis," he said, reintroducing himself — after all, it had been more than twenty years and he did not want to appear overly familiar. "I'm Richard Nelson."

"I know who *you* are!" she laughed mischievously, and they chatted as they walked across the main floor and out the revolving doors of Tiffany's. As they paused outside, Richard recalled bumping into her at the old Parke Bernet Auction House on Madison Avenue right after the assassination. She had just moved to New York. Curiously, his father had died the same day the president was killed. It was a terrible time.

Jackie wore a trim black suit. No longer the young newlywed thrilled to be doing up her first home, there was an air of heaviness about her. It was like watching someone underwater. She was still officially in mourning. Ignoring the passersby who were dumbstruck by her presence, she said softly, "Mr. Nelson, thank you so much for your letter. It meant the world to me. I understand we shared a tragedy on the same day." Richard was moved by her generosity and discretion, her sense, even then, of the right thing to say.

So many years ago. And here they were again, out on the sidewalk, only this time it was morning and the sun was out. "Well, I have to go to work now," Jackie said — the typical New York farewell, a bit proud of herself.

"So do I!" laughed Richard.

"Then walk me to work," she commanded happily, and they headed down Fifth Avenue together.

Around this time, in 1972, Halston came back into Jackie's life, having morphed from the affable midwesterner Roy Halston Frowich ("Fro"), to Halston, to simply "H." No longer just a talented young man producing *chapeaux* for society ladies at Bergdorf Goodman, Halston was now *the* American designer.

Halston had pretensions of grandeur when he worked as a young milliner at André Basil's hair salon at the Ambassador Hotel in Chicago and, later, at Bergdorf's. Now, with an office in Olympic Tower overlooking the spires of St. Patrick's Cathedral on Fifth Avenue, access to the company's workrooms to make his own wardrobe, a round-the-clock limousine, personal secretaries to oversee both his home and office activities, a continually refreshed supply of orchids, and a fabulous town house at 101 East Sixty-third Street, he was truly grand.

Halston's grandeur was no accident. His dream, he once said, was to be "the American Balenciaga." He succeeded, becoming the first American couturier whose creations could hold their own against anything the French produced. He combined the ease of American sportswear with modern luxury in ingenious ways, creating sensuous evening dresses in brilliant colors, cashmere knits that resembled nothing your grandmother wore, silk organza ruffled blouses, and modern pantsuits with sterling silver Elsa Peretti belts as accents.

For years, it seemed every woman on the Upper East Side, in Beverly Hills, and in Palm Beach — even Princess Grace of Monaco — owned his ultrasuede shirtdress. After Babe Paley wore one of his tie-dyed chiffons to a museum opening, a dozen ladies came in to buy what they had seen in a newspaper photo.

"You are only as good as the people you dress," Halston proclaimed. And he dressed them all. In addition to Jackie, who favored his softly draped evening wear, he created clothes for Lee Radziwill, Ethel Kennedy, Elizabeth Taylor, Marlo Thomas, Pamela Harriman, Babe Paley, Carrie Donovan, Barbara Walters, and a host of others.

It makes sense that Halston was the first real American designer Jackie frequented. For a woman used to the couture-level workmanship of Givenchy, Chanel, and Valentino, she appreciated Halston's artisanship. An enormously loyal person, she must have gotten a kick out of the fact that the polite young man who had designed and delivered her pillbox hats to the Carlyle was now such a big deal in the fashion world.

Of all people, Jackie appreciated Halston's attention to detail, which was as acute as her own. When invisible weights needed to be inserted into hems to anchor jackets that had no interfacing, he insisted on using jeweler's sterling silver chains, not silver-colored ones, for the samples and custom garments. All the made-to-order garments Jackie favored were completely handmade, which sometimes meant endless hours spent hand-rolling chiffon hems.

Halston revolutionized fashion with his ability to cut clothes on the bias. His sinuous evening wear *looked* simple, but his distinctive cut gave his gowns the sexy drape that made a Halston a Halston. "He liked the bias cut because it was so simple," recalls Yutaka Hasegawa, a Halston pattern maker from 1977 to 1982. "The bias tube skirt looks like nothing, it looks like a straight skirt. But if we made one mistake, a calculation slightly too small or big, we had to start all over again." The bias tube concept was used in caftans, dresses, skirts, and tops that would hang softly and sensually on the body. One of the most famous strapless evening styles that both Jackie and Lee owned closed only with self-fabric ends that were knotted on the bust.

But some of Halston's "simple" clothes caused rather funny incidents with clients who were not used to wearing such unconstructed garments. On one occasion, Ethel Kennedy insisted that she would not buy one of Halston's complex multilayered dresses to wear to a dinner honoring her late husband unless Sassy Johnson Connor, who catered to the made-to-order clients, agreed to go to the Waldorf-Astoria on the night of the event to help her get dressed. She did.

Jackie once called Sassy after wearing a Halston dress to complain that it had not been correctly fitted. It turned out she had it on backward. Another fitter recalls an incident when someone wore a dress with a deep décolleté neckline on the occasion of being presented to royalty. When she curtsied, her bosoms fell out. The client was going to sue Halston but calmed down long enough to bring the dress in. It turned out that she, too, had put on the dress backward.

Halston got the message and began sewing labels marking the front of his dresses.

When Halston opened his own boutique on Madison Avenue and Sixty-ninth Street (the second designer to do so, after Yves Saint Laurent), shopping there became an event. *Women's Wear Daily* dubbed it "the latest gathering ground for the Cat Pack." The ground-floor level had clothing for as little as $100, the second floor showed clothing at $100 to $400, and in his made-to-order salon upstairs, evening dresses could easily cost $10,000. Jackie was there fairly often, and because of her celebrity was often shown merchandise privately in the third-floor salon.

Fred Rottman, then a twenty-year-old design assistant, recalls, "Halston was doing some work for Martha Graham, and the workroom was full of costumes and great stuff—it was all so festive! And Jackie Onassis was there for a fitting. Halston was so proud of the costumes, and I think he wanted to show off Jackie. . . . He brought her from the fitting room to the workroom. She came in in her bare feet. And, of course, you could have heard a pin drop! Everyone's mouth dropped—Jackie Onassis is sort of strolling through the workroom."

Of course, Jackie liked a bargain as much as anyone and often nosed around the racks of Halston's more moderately priced items in the boutique, too. One Saturday, she inadvertently helped out on the selling floor when she spotted a customer trying on a green sweater set. She came up behind the woman and whispered to her, "You should take them, they go with your eyes." The customer immediately purchased the items—along with a Jackie anecdote to dine out on for some time.

"Is that all it takes to sell clothes?" she later asked Halston mischievously. "Just a tiny suggestion?"

Diana Vreeland—or "D. V.," as she signed her name—was also back in Jackie's life. It amused Diana to point out that D. V. also stood for *Deo volente*—God willing. "Popes sign that on their bulls, I believe, the way we write 'best wishes' on our letters."

Vreeland was a conjurer, a demon, unafraid of magic. In her twenty-seven years as a fashion editor at *Harper's Bazaar* and ten years as editor in chief of *Vogue*, she was extraordinary. As Jackie noted, "She sees infinitely more than the rest of us see, just crossing the street." Vreeland pointed people in the right direction and expected them to come up with the goods. As her friend photographer Richard Avedon (whom she inexplicably called "Aberdeen") noted, "She didn't report on fashion. Designers had to follow her. I once heard her say, in a moment of frustration, 'I know what *they're* going to wear before they even wear it! What they're going to *eat* before they eat it! I know where they're going before they're even *there.*'"

Diana and Jackie had been friends for nearly twenty years. Jackie had known her son, Frederick "Frecky" Vreeland, even longer. When she and Yusha traveled to the south of France together in the summer of 1950, they took a side trip to meet up with Frecky at Pamplona, where the two Yale classmates ran with the bulls.

When Jackie was in the White House, Diana, then at *Harper's Bazaar*, assisted her with her clothing selection. She advised her to carry a sable muff on Inauguration Day ("I thought she was going to freeze to death. But I also think muffs are romantic because they have to do with *history*."), and steered her in the direction of Gustave Tassell and others.

If you knew Diana and Jackie, it made sense they were friends. Although on the surface it might not appear obvious, in many ways they were very similar. Like Jackie, D. V. had discipline, guts, and a sense of showmanship (although Jackie's was, admittedly, subtler), and both shared a visceral, almost physical appreciation for beauty. Vreeland's sense of style was so acute she hypodermically injected perfume into the pillows in her red living room. ("I want this place to look like a garden, but a garden in hell," she famously commanded Billy Baldwin.) Like Jackie, she understood the power of illusion and discretion, and in maintaining a distance. "Keep your secret," she said. "That's your power over others."

But more important, both women used style as a way of perceiving the world. "Originality," Vreeland once said, "is the only reality." A friend of hers observed, "Diana Vreeland carried the aristocratic myth as far as it could go. And it was a perfect myth…because it was all done on air and her hard work. It was a life in style. Make the best of things, and make things look better than they really are." Jackie's ethos was similar. "You do the best you can, and then the hell with it," she believed, echoing what her husband Jack used to say.

Now it was time for Jackie to give something back to her old mentor. After getting booted out of *Vogue* in 1971, Diana was at loose ends. "They were not very good at letting people go," she recalled. "One of the great editors at *Vogue* was Margaret Chase. She threw herself out a window because she was eighty, she was out of work, she had no money—and she'd been dismissed in the most terrible way."

For Vreeland, and for *Vogue*, it was the end of an era. ("They wanted a New Deal there," she observed mildly. "And they got it.") Her beloved husband, Reed, had

died in 1966. The question was — what could she, a sixty-nine-year-old woman who had been at the top of her game in fashion, do next? She took four months off, traveled to Europe, visited Paris and the couturiers she loved. Then she returned to her apartment at 550 Park Avenue and pondered her next move.

One thing was for sure: she was not going to end up like poor Margaret Chase. Jackie made certain of that.

While Diana was in Europe, Jackie and a group of her friends — Jane Engelhard, Jayne Wrightsman, and Babe Paley, women Vreeland had advised on style matters in the past — came up with the brilliant idea of appointing her as a special consultant to the Costume Institute, the sleepy division of the Metropolitan Museum frequented mostly by fashion designers and scholars. Between them, Jackie & Co. had come up with Vreeland's salary for two years, as well, it is said, as paying for her maid, Yvonne.

They proposed their idea to Theodore Rousseau, chief curator, who ran it by museum director Thomas Hoving. "Coming out of a retail family," Hoving says, "I was high on the idea of the Costume Institute. But I thought, this is ridiculous. It will never work." Then Rousseau told him a group of Vreeland's supporters had raised the money for her salary for two years. "And I said, 'Oh yeah? Now I'm interested.' I didn't think Vreeland would last more than six months."

He was wrong. In her tenure at the Costume Institute, Vreeland became one of Hoving's top three curators. She mounted fourteen shows in as many years, and even brought them in, according to Hoving "on time and on budget." In 1977, Jackie wrote an essay about Vreeland and her work for the Costume Institute entitled "A Visit to the High Priestess of Vanity Fair." She described Vreeland as "whippet-boned, with black lacquered hair, looks like a high priestess, which in a way she is, and her temple is on the ground floor of the Metropolitan Museum of Art."

D. V. was back.

In the catalog for the Metropolitan's 1977 exhibit devoted to Diana Vreeland and her work, Valentino recalls an evening at her Park Avenue apartment when her worlds of fashion, style, and celebrity intermingled in one glamorous evening. "Once she called me, Come for dinner tonight, Jackie will be there. Who else would you like to meet?

"Oh, Diana," Valentino said. "Sophia Loren is in town, do you know her?"

Vreeland laughed, of *course* she knew her. "Eight o'clock sharp!"

Diana called about an hour later. Sophia could not make it, but she had a substitution, a surprise. At eight o'clock, Jackie, Valentino, and Giancarlo Giammetti were there. "Diana was not quite ready, as always... her maid,

Yvonne, scuttled back and forth from Diana's bedroom every five minutes, announcing that she'll be there soon, and giving us vodka.

"At 8:45 Diana arrived, all splendent in a red charmeuse pajama of mine. At 9:30 the guest arrived. She was Barbra Streisand. This was Diana," Valentino concludes, "she could have called anybody at the last minute — and everybody would run to see her!"

In spite of her own celebrity, in spite of her friendships with Diana Vreeland and Valentino, and in spite of the success of Moyers's book, Jackie — like every employee — occasionally had to work on a project she had little interest in. For her, that was Michael Jackson's autobiography, *Moonwalk*.

J. C. Suares, a freelance book designer who worked on many of Jackie's books, recalls, "The Tiffany books were the first ones we collaborated on, but the Michael Jackson was the big one — that was the one we traveled together for. And did we have some strange encounters with him!"

Suares knew Jackie had little interest in the project. "She had very rigid ideas about the kinds of books she wanted to do — that is why it was very distasteful to her to do this Michael Jackson book. She wanted to do books about classy things. She wanted good writing, and she wanted things to be lavish and sophisticated. She saw those books as an extension of her own lifestyle.

"Her library had a lot of big, gorgeous books in it. Old books! At a certain point she got bored and started classifying the books by color, so she had all the red books on one shelf. One time I asked her, 'What do you do — get bored and stay up all night and color code the books?'" Suares laughs at the memory. "She said, yeah . . ."

And as an editor, says Suares, "Jackie liked producing the kind of book that you'd keep for a hundred and fifty years. A lot of white space and such quality paper that it smelled good. She liked simple Italian typefaces."

With such a highly refined sense of aesthetics, Jackie's interaction with the King of Pop was bound to cause a collision. Suares says, "Michael Jackson was approached by some people in California to do a book, and he said 'fine.'" They went to Doubleday, and Doubleday offered a couple hundred thousand dollars for the book. But once Jackson found out that Jackie was an editor there, he didn't care about the money — only that Jackie had to be the editor.

Jackie said absolutely not! But Doubleday executives kept after her and finally she capitulated.

Jackie and her assistant, Shaye Areheart, started working with Michael on the manuscript. Of course he had a ghost writer, and when the first draft of the text came in, Jackie and J. C. went to California to get the pictures. Michael had his own staff photographer and photo editor. In one of the several buildings at his Encino compound was his office, and housed on the second floor was his photo file, with thousands of photos.

"So we started looking at pictures," recalls Suares. "We were there for *days* looking at pictures. Michael was out playing and Jackie and I were inside looking at pictures. We also shot a lot of pictures. We designed still lifes and things around the house. I shot his costumes, his gloves, his trophies.

"There was an incredible clash of cultures — because here was this gaudy house with no taste, with horrible faux Venetian chandeliers and portraits of weeping clowns on velvet, the whole thing. And Jackie had no use for him, no use for Encino, no use for any of it. The car would pick us up in the morning at the Beverly Hills Hotel and we'd dish on the way to Encino and at the end of every conversation, she would say, 'Do you think he likes girls?' I'd say, I don't know...I couldn't figure him out!"

So Jackie would say, "Well, has he ever been on a date?" Once the driver piped up, "I drove him and Brooke Shields!"

"Did they sit together?" asked Jackie.

"No, they were a few feet apart," the driver admitted.

"He probably likes very young girls," she said softly, so the driver wouldn't hear. "When he's thirty-five he'll marry a girl who's fifteen."

"I don't think that's legal in California," said J. C.

"It doesn't matter — that's probably what he'll do," Jackie decided.

Back in New York, the second draft of Michael's book arrived, and Jackie knew there was something wrong with it. She passed it around — Shaye read it, Bruce read it, Scott read it. J. C. recalls it was "drivel. It was like a giant useless silly press release." On their next trip to California, Jackie and J. C. decided to take off the gloves and tell their famous author the book was no good.

They got to Michael's house and sat at the dining room table with him. Jackie sat Michael down and gave him a very quiet speech, point by point, about how the book was terrible, there was nothing in it that anybody wanted to read, there was nothing new, and that we would all make fools of ourselves if it were published.

Michael agreed to rework the manuscript.

Maybe because they were so far away from home, funny things were always happening to Jackie and J. C. in California. For instance, there was the time Jackie and Martha Stewart had lunch, and the world *almost* had a line of Jackie O. Paints and Houseware Accessories to look forward to.

One day, Martha called J. C. about something and he said he was going to be in L.A. the next week. "So am I," said Martha. "Why don't we get together?" offered J. C. "I'll introduce you to Jackie." So they set a date for lunch, noon at Ma Maison.

The room was fairly empty when Jackie and J. C. arrived. Suzanne Pleshette was there. At one point Jackie turned to J. C. and said, "Do you think I should put my sunglasses on?" No, he didn't think so.

Jackie and J. C. waited from noon until ten to one for Martha. When she finally arrived, Martha offered neither an apology nor an excuse—not a good thing.

Jackie said nothing about the faux pas. She didn't care. It wasn't a big deal to her. In any case, Jackie could never get the point of Martha Stewart—she couldn't figure out what this woman did for a living. Wasn't it obvious that you should put cookies on a nice plate, or have cut flowers around the house?

She was too polite to take offense at her being late, but on the other hand, Jackie—who never forgot a thing—never could remember Martha Stewart's name after that lunch, referring to her thereafter as "you know, that pretty woman."

By contrast, Martha was immediately on the phone with J. C. pitching marketing schemes. J. C. knew better than to even suggest such a thing to Jackie. "Forget it, Martha — she's not going to do it."

So much for JKO at Kmart.

Now that she was a working woman, Jackie needed a working woman's wardrobe, and Valentino fit the bill. At Doubleday, she had a favorite uniform of pants and a silk blouse, with her Cartier tank watch and few accessories. She strove to fit in—getting her own coffee, waiting in line to use the Xerox machine, munching celery or chocolate in the afternoon when she got hungry, bumming matches for her cigarettes, and sitting in the stairwell during fire drills with everyone else.

Few people recall Jackie wearing dresses, which shows how far she had come from her Cassini-laden public life in the White House, except occasionally when she had to go out in the evening to dinner or a book party. J. C. Suares remembers well her customary wardrobe: "She wore mostly brown, purple, mauve, and a little bit of lavender, little bit of pink. Silk shirts and trousers, a skirt once in a while. That was her outfit ninety percent of the time. Sometimes she wore a dress, cocktail dresses to go out to dinner, and in California she wore sort of Katharine Hepburn trousers, but not that exaggerated."

And, says J. C., "She was very very jealous of her color combinations. She felt they were hers. So if you worked there and you wore a similar thing, she'd never talk to you again." He laughs. "You'd be dead! But nobody really had the money to buy six-hundred-dollar silk blouses in the 1980s — Doubleday's kind of a frumpy place."

Jackie had a few other style markers at Doubleday. Although she never wore much jewelry, she favored a pair of white enamel Schlumberger earrings.

"I can't believe she didn't lose her earrings, because she would always be walking around with one earring on, from talking on the phone," recalls Nancy Evans. Another time, she had on a glorious blue man's shirt. Where had she picked it up? At Brooks Brothers, from the men's department. She had her tailor insert shoulder pads for her.

Evans said that although Jackie typically wore pants to work, once when they were out somewhere together and she happened to be wearing a dress, Nancy noticed that Jackie's legs had a kind of sheen to them. "What *is* that?" she had to ask.

"Fogal," came the reply. Nancy, no slouch in the style department herself, had not yet seen these fine French stockings. Taking a tip from Jackie, she has been wearing them ever since.

But beyond fashion, beyond the raising of her children, beyond her success as an editor, or even the strains of coping with celebrity, Jackie's friends think one thing about her has been largely overlooked, and that is her secret subversive side. Nancy Evans thinks one of the things people miss about Jackie is "how hilariously funny she was. One time we were at the ballet at her box and we practically got kicked out! I can't even remember why we were laughing, we started laughing so hard! And then we got laughing even more, and people were looking! And then Maurice just said, 'You guys better just get out of here.' So we left the box, went out in the hallway, *really* convulsed, then got ourselves together and came back in.... And I mean it wasn't *me* making a fuss, it was Jackie," explains Evans hastily, with the tone of a girl who might be sent to the headmistress.

Jackie had a great sense of humor — how else would she get through the sometimes surreal experience it was to be her? One of her conceits was that everyone led a far, far more exciting life than she did. Lunching at the Four Seasons with her friend John Russell, art critic for the *New York Times*, she gazed at the dining room from the balcony table she favored. "Think of all the plots that are being hatched down there," she mused, her Schlumberger bracelet dangling over the edge, as the worlds of publishing, politics, and Wall Street congregated below. Russell recalls that "at lunchtime at Les Pléiades, the much-missed art-world restaurant, she would say, 'What do you think they're buying and selling over their cold sea bass?'"

In 1985 she was at a photo shoot for *Tiffany Taste*, the second of six Tiffany lifestyle books she and John Loring did together. (They had such a good time, "We'll be doing *Tiffany Mushrooms* when we're eighty," she joked.) Jackie was enchanted with the picture Billy Cunningham shot for the book of four silver Nepalese drinking beakers Loring had picked up for about forty dollars in the marketplace in Bhaktapur. The beakers were shot among bright

pink cubes of watermelon, and one of them was filled with a Nepalese drink of chilled watermelon juice.

Jackie went right over and picked one up. "Look how beautiful they are! If I had these, I'd give up iced tea in the summer and drink nothing but watermelon squash!"

This was unusual for Jackie, John knew, since she rarely expressed excitement about inanimate objects. Situations were what caught her attention.

Of course, John wrapped up the beakers and sent them to her office the next day because, after all, what's a guy to do? As a friend, he was pleased to be able to send Jackie something she truly liked as a souvenir of their books together. A few hours later, she called to thank him with a giggle in her voice — security had thought the package contained a bomb.

J. C. Suares agrees that although Jackie appeared proper, she had a rebellious side. Reflecting on the time they spent together, he says, "The best times we had were when we acted like two kids who had skipped school — who were running in the woods and up to no good. She was well versed in that kind of fooling around.

"She liked to escape. To play hooky. To drink too much, to eat too much, to dish too much . . . to play practical jokes. She liked us to show no respect for authority — that made her happy."

When they were together in Los Angeles, Jackie used to amuse herself by imagining all the madcap things she could do. "She wanted to make anonymous phone calls to the ASPCA in Los Angeles to welsh on Michael Jackson and his animals, because they were in miserable shape! He didn't know how to take care of them. He had a llama in this little pen — this llama just stood there all day long. And he had this dog in a playpen, in a room by himself. This dog is desperate for attention — it was horrible, really third-world mentality. And Jackie wanted to call the ASPCA anonymously and report it."

Did she do it?

"No," recalls Suares, "she was afraid she might be recognized somehow, but she loved the *idea* of doing it. And she felt very sorry for those animals."

the look

Jackie's most elegant and emulated look. Try these tips from celebrity makeup artist DARAC for Prescriptives, and you, too, will be a first lady.

lips

Lips are very structured: line first with lip liner and fill in with two layers of lipstick — a matte to anchor, then blot, followed by a crème. Finish off with a clear gloss to highlight.

cheeks

After foundation and powder, the face should be contoured, allowing your features to be more dimensional. Using a soft brown color, follow the perimeter of the face, blending up and away. Jackie would sweep contour along her jaw line to soften and make it more oval. Use a fat buffing blush and blend from light to dark for a seamless look.

eyes

The eyes are sophisticated, smoky, and elegant. Start with a soft muted pink tone over entire lid from lash to brow. Place a slate gray on the entire lid and blend up over the crease. With a black pencil, line the lid on top and bottom and smudge with a Q-tip. Apply a thick coat of black mascara; let dry. Add a deep granite shadow over the top liner and blend up toward the lid. Follow with a black liquid liner, then head out to your state dinner or an evening at the ballet with style and confidence.

According to DARAC, this look is modern and fresh with a European flair. Try these makeup tips and you will have the paparazzi buzzing after you in no time.

lips

Lips are plump and creamy. Using a warm soft sienna or redwood liner, blend the pencil with a Q-tip so the edges are seamless. Add a sunny coral and top with a golden gloss for color.

cheeks

For this "I spent last month on the *Christina*" look, DARAC prefers an all-over bronzer in a loose powder. Dip brush in the powder and apply all over face for a warm, sunny glow. Apply a rich coral blush on the apples of the cheeks, then continue the color softly over the bridge of the nose, brow bone, and chin.

eyes

Use a sheer crème gold shadow all over the lid, then layer a rich warm brown shadow on the lid using a touch of bronzer on your brush to blend color. Add a touch of blush directly under the brow to highlight. Line with a rich cocoa brown or black-green on the top lid only, smudging with a Q-tip. A thick coat of black mascara completes the look, taking you from India to the Greek isles.

editor in chief

This is Jackie's working look—empowered and confident, but always approachable. Follow DARAC's advice, and you will always put your best face forward.

lips

Lips are polished and defined. Follow with a pencil color close to your natural lip tone; fill in and blend with your finger. Follow with a russet or soft brick lip color, finishing with a touch of gloss.

cheeks

DARAC prefers crème blush for a seamless look. Blend warm honey beige from the apples of the cheek down and back toward the earlobe; add a hint on the bridge of nose, forehead, and chin. Finish with a touch of powder blush in a soft coral on the apples of the cheeks to make them pop.

eyes

The eyes should be soft but defined. Layer a pink sand beige shadow on the entire lid followed with a bone color under the brow. Define the brow with a pencil and brush up. Apply an espresso eyeliner on top of the lid, smudge and blend out, and follow with a dark brown mascara.

Jackie loved fresh air, friends, laughter, and cozy conversation. DARAC created this look for all the comfortable good times.

lips

Lips are moist but sheer. Use gloss or liquid lipstick with a hint of pink or warm mocha applied with pinky finger and gently blended. No lip liner is needed.

cheeks

Cheeks are very subtle but should have enough color for a healthy glow. Use a crème blush in soft pink applied with fingertips in a tapping motion on the apples of the cheek. Blend the edges with a damp sponge for the look after a brisk run in the park.

eyes

Try a soft silvery beige shadow applied to the entire lid, being sure to blend evenly, concentrating the color toward the lash line. With a small amount of darker brown shadow, sweep across the lash line to act as a subtle liner. Add a soft brown or a clear mascara for a natural look.

> Even if I have only five
> years left, so what?
> I've had a great run.
>
> — J K O

a glorious spring

ACKIE'S FORMER STYLE MENTOR, Diana Vreeland, died on August 22, 1989. As the *New York Times* reported, "She was believed to be in her eighties and had been in failing health for several years." Although D. V. was, on the outside, more flamboyant than Jackie, there were several similarities between the two women in addition to possessing great style: discipline, hard work, the ability to keep going in spite of whatever obstacles life presents you, as well as a belief in the power of the imagination.

In the fall, Vreeland's friends and family held a memorial service at the Metropolitan Museum. Lauren Bacall, Bill Blass, Kenneth Jay Lane, Richard Avedon, Oscar de la Renta, Paloma Picasso, and Peter Duchin were among those in attendance.

Shoe designer par excellence Manolo Blahnik has particularly fond memories of the evening. "They had put me at the end of the second row," he recalled, "and suddenly, they were about to begin the service, and this lady came up. I had my head in the prayer book, and I stood up to let this lady go in, and it was Mrs. Kennedy!"

Jackie sat beside Manolo and asked in a whispery voice, "Are you one of Diana's children?"

And Manolo said, "No — not really. I am here because Mrs. Vreeland is the architect of my doing what I do."

"And what is that?" Jackie asked.

He explained that he was Manolo Blahnik. She knew he was the man who made the shoes, since she had been wearing them for so many years, although they had never met.

"Oh, I *love* what you do," she said. They could not say much else, even in whispers, because the service was about to begin. For Manolo, meeting Jackie in that context was magical. "I was fixated on her, the wonderful aura around her, and the shock when I realized who she was — I was like, *oh!*" He laughs, recalling the sublime coincidence of it — wouldn't Diana have loved it!

Ever maternal, Jackie had wondered if Manolo Blahnik were one of Diana Vreeland's children. Although they were now full grown, her own children were, as always, very much on her mind. She was very proud of them and had good reason to be. After graduating from Harvard (where she lived in her father's dorm, Winthrop House) in 1980 with a fine arts degree, Caroline went to work at the Office of Film and Television at the Metropolitan Museum of Art. On July 19, 1986, she married her longtime boyfriend Edwin Schlossberg, thirteen years her senior, at Our Lady of Victory Church in Centerville, Massachusetts.

Unlike her own mother, who dictated what Jackie would wear when she married John F. Kennedy, Jackie kept a benign distance when Caroline chose her wedding dress. As Carolina Herrera recalls, "Unlike most mothers, Mrs. Onassis did not interfere with Caroline's dress design. In fact, she did not see the dress until it was finished. She said, 'I am not going to get involved because Caroline is the one who will wear it. I want her to be the happiest girl in the world.'"

Jackie was equally enthralled with her son, John. From the scamp who had raced up and down the White House halls, John had grown into a startlingly handsome and thoughtful young man. After graduating from Brown University in 1983 and flirting with the idea of becoming an actor (which his mother quickly nipped in the bud), John graduated from New York University Law School and — on the third try — passed the notoriously challenging New York bar exam. Although John was not the facile student Caroline was (after graduating from Columbia Law School, she passed the exam on her first try), he persisted, with Jackie's encouragement. She hosted his law school study group at her apartment and reassured him when his grades were not what he had hoped. "Don't worry, your father wasn't much of a speller, either."

Carl Sferrazza Anthony, who knew John and his mother, makes the observation, "I think John was a lot like her. They both had that funny, skewed take on the world." Jackie used to entertain White House guests with her impersonation of the French ambassador imitating de Gaulle. In 1974, when her maid Provi had the day off, Jackie would answer the phone in a fake Spanish accent, hoping callers would not recognize her voice. "I have to do that to get rid of people," she explained.

Like Jackie, John was an amazing mimic. As a teenager, his specialty was Mick Jagger. Peter Beard recalls, "One winter I took John and Caroline to the

Everglades, where photographers would follow us around, practically into the swamp. Early one morning, as we were leaving the hotel to go on a snake hunt, we passed this photographer who'd been on our trail for days without bagging a single picture — he'd finally fallen asleep in the lobby. John spontaneously started doing 'Jumpin' Jack Flash.' The reporter woke up to this amazing act, and while he was reaching for his camera John turned around and did his Mick Jagger walk-off. The poor guy never got the shot."

John wore his mantle as the heir to Camelot lightly. He knew, on some level, that because of who his parents were, people would always be interested in his life. But he took it in stride. He once joked to a friend: "The first time I went to therapy, I lay down on the couch and the doctor started telling *me* about my childhood."

For the most part, though, he was good-natured about it: this was the life he had been born into, and he dealt with it. Joseph Nye, dean of the Kennedy

School of Government, remembered asking him as they stood together in a White House receiving line: "Do you remember this place?" "Only vaguely," he answered. "Do you want to come back?" John smiled. "Only vaguely."

One time a friend wondered, "Sometimes it must be hard being you." John smiled and said, "Actually, I highly recommend it."

Of all her accomplishments, Jackie was proudest of the fact that she had raised her children to be good people, that they had sidestepped the minefield that seemed to trip up many of their less supervised Kennedy cousins. She was pleased, too, that Caroline and John were such good friends.

At the bridal dinner the night before Caroline's wedding, John gave a touching toast about how close they were. He said, "All of our lives there's just been the three of us." Now he welcomed a fourth. Later, biographer Doris Kearns Goodwin told Jackie how she hoped to have that kind of closeness for her own sons. Looking Doris right in the eye, Jackie said, "It's the best thing I've ever done."

"My mother has never had an agenda for me or my sister," John Kennedy Jr. explained to journalist William Norwich. "That's probably why we're all so close and have had a relatively normal life. Not being a Kennedy, she could recognize the perils and the positive aspects. One thing she has done is kept the memory of our father very vivid for us. She has not made us look to our father's life to worship at the expense of our own. Whatever Caroline or I chose to do, provided we were serious and committed about it, she would have supported."

In addition to her own children, Jackie took a decided interest in the younger people she worked with and came in contact with. At Doubleday, Bruce Tracy and Scott Moyers, who were her editorial assistants, became part of her little family. Scott recalls that Jackie was a "profoundly generous woman, a sort of mother figure to us all, with a lot of empathy."

If Scott rushed into work with wet hair in the middle of the winter, she would snap at him as she would have at John, "You're going to get a cold with your hair wet!" He ignored her until one day she brought him a blue wool hat to wear to work. Scott says Jackie "had her little pet theories that changed from month to month on how to cure a cold or flu. At one point she hit upon Thera-Flu. I remember being really sick and Jackie threw a bunch of TheraFlu on my desk and said, 'Take that TheraFlu!'"

Jackie was respectful of her coworkers' nonprofessional lives as well. Bruce Tracy recalls that in the summer of 1992, *The Last Czar*, a book about the Romanovs they had worked on, was about to be published, when suddenly he had an opportunity to go to London for a week for the cost of airfare. Bruce was in a quandary about what to do — he had worked with Jackie on the book, he wanted to go to the book party at the Russian Tea Room, he did not want her to think he was shirking his professional duties, but he had never been to Europe before, either.

He went to speak with her about it, saying, almost apologetically, "I just got this chance to go to Europe, and I've never been."

Jackie looked at him as if he had two heads. London versus the Russian Tea Room? "Of *course* you go — life comes first."

It was also during the late 1980s that many young designers, authors, and decorators who went on to greater success first met Jackie. Designer Shannon McLean met Jackie when she worked with private clients for the Italian fashion designer Giorgio Armani. Armani was not yet known in America, and Shannon's job was to familiarize the stylish women of New York with his clothing. When Shannon met Jackie, she was working at Doubleday and, Shannon thinks, at a different stage in her life. "I don't think that clothes were really so important to her."

Shannon says that "Mrs. Onassis was like a friend's mom. There really were no airs about her whatsoever." They discovered that they both rode horses. "It became a relationship that was really nice, we would talk about horses. And her son went to school with one of my best friends. So it ended up where it was really comfortable, and it wasn't as though she were viewing me as a salesgirl trying to sell her something."

A lot of the social women of New York would call the Armani corporate office and make a big deal that they were going to make an appearance at the showroom. Jackie called Shannon directly when she wanted to stop by and

look at a few things. Sometimes she would be out riding her bicycle and just park it out front and stop in. "She was very quiet in that way."

She also took an interest in Shannon personally. "Education was something that she always bothered me about. She asked me several times when I was going to finish school." And Shannon noticed that Jackie always wanted to know about new ideas, the latest trends. One of the last times Shannon saw her, she wanted to know what Emporio Armani, Giorgio's sportier line, was all about. She had heard about it and read about it in W. In those days, it was located on the third floor of the Armani boutique on Sixty-eighth Street and Madison. Jackie asked Shannon to take her there.

"We went upstairs, and there was some awful screaming music on the speakers — probably Devo or something. She gave me a little look and I asked one of the guys, 'Do you think you could turn it down?' And they did.

"It was interesting to me how curious she was and how interested in young people. She talked to everybody and not in a phony way. She was a very gentle person with a great mind."

Interior decorator Richard Keith Langham met Jackie when he was an associate designer at Keith Irvine's firm, Irvine and Fleming. They were located in the same building as Carolina Herrera, where Jackie used to come for fittings. Keith had a friend, Bill Hamilton, who worked for Herrera. Langham was so infatuated with Jackie that Bill would call and give him the heads up whenever she was scheduled to come in: "Mrs. O. at two o'clock, Mrs. O. at two o'clock." Langham would dash down to Fifty-seventh Street and wait until Jackie came around the corner, then he would quickly walk back into the building and send the elevator to the top floor so they'd have to wait for it to come down. He would be in the lobby, cooling his heels when Jackie entered, and then they would ride up in the elevator together.

This went on for months and months — if not years. Fortunately, Langham is a handsome southerner, so he got away with it without seeming like *too* much of a stalker. But one day Jackie came in to see his boss, Keith Irvine, who brought his young associate up front to meet Jackie.

She took one look at Langham, lifted her sunglasses, and said in that soft voice, "Oh, yes, my friend from the elevator." Langham wanted to *die* — busted by Jackie O.

Carl Sferrazza Anthony first met Jackie in 1976, as a sixteen-year-old at the RFK Tennis Tournament, held every year at Forest Hills. He was just a boy growing up in Bayside, Queens, but he had always had a fascination with first ladies, he didn't know why — he was enthralled by the White House, and he read everything he could get his hands on about it. This was his third year at the tournament and his third year watching Jackie. He saw

her sitting in a cordoned-off section; the seat next to her was empty and she wasn't really watching the game, so he worked up the nerve to go over and say hello.

Carl sat in the seat next to her and introduced himself. He began the conversation by telling her that someday he was going to write a book about the first ladies and their political power.

"Oh, are you *really?*" This was far more entertaining than tennis — who was this miniature Bill Moyers? "Why are you so interested in this subject?"

Carl started to tell her about his longtime interest in the presidents, and then Jackie started to talk about the great love of her life, JFK. Carl was hoping to get her autograph, so he mentioned, "I know President Kennedy collected autographs." And she said, "Oh, you knew that, did you?"

"Yes," he said. "I've got something like that — I've got all the presidents' wives except you and Mrs. McKinley." Jackie looked at him and said, "Well, you're going to have a hard time getting in touch with Mrs. McKinley, so I'll give you mine." She pulled an engraved envelope that said "1040 Fifth Avenue" out of her bag and signed it, Carl noticed, "Jacqueline Kennedy," not "Jacqueline Kennedy Onassis."

They talked some more. Jackie asked him about school — what his favorite subjects were and how his grades were — and then as he was leaving, she said, "Let me know when you get that book done." Nine years later, he was working on his book, *First Ladies,* and although he never reminded her that he was the dark-haired boy in a polo shirt she had met many years ago in Forest Hills, she took his manuscript down to Middleburg and added her insight to the sections that pertained to her.

And finally, there is a whole group of young designers Jackie influenced who were not even alive during Camelot (or are too young to remember it). Jackie inspired them in terms of style and design, of course, but more important, through her life's experiences. Jackie became a role model for young women and men who never even met her.

Cynthia Rowley recalls going through a phase early in her design career, from the mid-1980s to early 1990s, where "I hung on every word she said, every word written about her, every photo of her!

"I think her style was very optimistic, when you really felt that America could accomplish anything. Optimistic in a luxury sense — in the sense that she was living the life everyone wanted to live! So I think that definitely influenced me.

"What she taught me about design is that it doesn't have to be complicated. I remember seeing a picture of her walking in the park by her apartment in a sweater, really simple trousers, flats, and that sort of changed everything for me in a design sense. It made me realize that you can be really fashionable and really simple at the same time."

Designer Susan Dell, even though she never met Jackie, also cites her as an influence. "I am thirty-six now, so I wasn't even born when Mrs. Kennedy was in the White House. She began to influence me more when I was growing up, when I was in college and thinking What kind of a woman do I want to be? I looked at her as someone I wanted to be like. Not only in terms of what she wore, although that was clearly part of it. But she seemed so together, she seemed very sophisticated. She could stand with her husband and be totally her own person. She had her own true identity. And that's how I wanted to be."

Dell, who keeps a list of style mentors taped to her bathroom mirror (Jackie, Audrey, Coco Chanel, as well as her father) to inspire her each morning, believes that Jackie's appeal to a younger generation who did not grow up under Camelot goes beyond the clothing she wore. "In Jackie, I saw a woman who looked beautiful. I don't mean just aesthetically looking good; what I mean is, she radiated goodness. I liked that. And so here is somebody who really stood for — I want to do good, I want to be good, I want to look good."

Beyond fashion, Cynthia Rowley found herself thinking of Jackie, as she never imagined she would have had to, during a difficult time in her life after her husband died of cancer at an early age. "I never talk about this, but I became a widow at age thirty-five too. So, for me, being a young woman and dealing with that, I could really relate to what Jackie went through.

"I know she got a lot of grief for marrying Onassis, but to me, it made sense, because it's either you start over, or you don't make it. You have a choice — there's no way you can go back, and you don't want to go back because you know that world is over. You can't continue living that same life, whether it's consciously or subconsciously. I remember being a little, little kid when JFK was assassinated and watching it on the TV, and I kept thinking about that when my husband died."

Jackie's colleague from Doubleday Lisa Drew says, "Her life in the last fifteen years seemed to me to be the most satisfying. It seems her happiness in that period of time quadrupled." In addition to the success of her children and her career, Jackie had, for the last decade of her life, enjoyed a close relationship with diamond merchant Maurice Tempelsman, a Democratic supporter she had known since the mid-1950s. An erudite, teddy bearish man, Maurice was devoted to Jackie, and they were often seen together at the theater, ballet, and restaurants around town. Maurice was separated, but not divorced from his wife, Lily, and Jackie, for her part, had no desire to remarry. Theirs was a relationship of two mature adults, wherein Maurice gave her support and companionship.

In addition to devoting her time to her children, work, and Maurice, Jackie became more involved in yoga and meditation. Nehru had given her her first yoga lesson when she and Lee visited India in 1962, and in 1977, Jackie began to practice it seriously, when she took twice-weekly lessons with Tillie Weitzner, a tall Dutch yoga teacher. Tillie always went up to 1040 at 5:00 in the afternoon. Jackie dressed casually for her yoga class, sometimes wearing an old pair of black tights with holes in them. They practiced in Caroline's room, which had been left exactly the same as it was when she lived at home. Her marked-up schoolbooks still filled the shelves; the walls were decorated with black-and-white childhood photographs of Caroline and John.

Tillie would take her jacket off and begin leading Jackie through their initial stretching exercises. "Our yoga was quite intensive," Tillie said, "and Jackie was incredibly disciplined and eager to do well." After years of working together, Tillie was afraid that it might be getting boring for Jackie. "Oh, no," Jackie assured her, "it's never boring."

"The purpose of our yoga was to work out the spine and keep it flexible. Jackie was incredibly limber. She had youthful movements and was hardly ever sick. She was stoic, not a sissy. We did yoga at times when there was no

air-conditioning in that room and it was one hundred degrees and it was unbelievably uncomfortable. She was a real trooper.

"She was a horsewoman, which gave her strong legs. She'd had several falls over the years. They could have been deadly, but she was so limber she didn't hurt herself. We talked about old-ladyhood, and she said that the only thing she wanted to be able to do was ride."

Jackie also began the practice of meditating from 7:00 to 7:30 each evening. After Marly Russoff, associate publisher of Doubleday, introduced her to the work of Deepak Chopra, she read many of his books, wrote him a fan letter, and they became friends.

"We started a kind of a correspondence," Dr. Chopra recalls. "She was the only person that I know, in the last twenty years, who used to write letters in her own handwriting and actually mail them. So we had a long-term relationship and every time I went to New York I would call her. Often I would go to the apartment and we would meditate together.

"I remember once we went out to lunch at a restaurant in a hotel. A lot of people started staring at our table. I must have written only two or three books at that time. No one really knew who I was. A lot of people started gawking; two or three people started standing in the corner — it collected, you know? And she looked at me and she said, 'Gosh, Deepak, everybody seems to know who you are!'"

Dr. Chopra thinks many myths have grown up around Jackie that were created by people who did not know her and that few of them are true. "One thing that would truly surprise people to know about her is that she was unassuming, she was very spontaneous, she was — I don't know, the press has portrayed her as a recluse and somebody — you know, when somebody is a recluse, you think of them as being very egocentric. But she wasn't! She had no ego. She was very natural. She had a *great* sense of humor! She was a lot of *fun*, the way she joked and kidded around."

Perhaps through therapy and meditation and her conversations with Deepak Chopra, or perhaps through age and experience, in her fifties and sixties Jackie came to terms with her past and could even laugh at her own image. In 1977, when she and Diana Vreeland returned from a trip to the Orient, they had a layover in the San Francisco airport. It was Halloween and, unbelievably, they saw a man dressed as Jackie circa 1963 — the pink Dallas suit, the pillbox hat, the whole thing. Jackie went over to him (she could not help it; it had been a long flight and she and Diana were in the mood to blow off some steam) and said, "I know who you are!"

After David Heymann's biography *Jackie* came out in 1986, her friend Ros Gilpatric, a former Deputy Secretary of Defense in the Kennedy administration, asked Jackie what was so new about her life that the world did not already know? "I don't know, Ros," she replied with a smile. "Maybe something like — *Jackie: The Secret Vegas Years* — or *Jack and Bobby: A Love Story*."

Jackie devoted herself to a few select causes, but her number-one concern was the legacy of John F. Kennedy. To that end, she was the guiding force behind the John F. Kennedy Presidential Library and Museum in Boston, Massachusetts. Designed by I. M. Pei and opened in 1979, the library is a dramatic, curved building. Jackie's touches are everywhere — from the Boston clam chowder that is served daily in the café overlooking sweeping views of the Bay to the little floral centerpiece on each of the tables. At her suggestion, the landscaping includes dune grass because, as she put it, "I think the president was a wind man."

The Kennedy Library is first-rate — from the guards at the front door to the manner in which exhibits are displayed. Charles Daly, director of the JFKL Foundation, recalls that after the museum was refurbished in 1993, Jackie called to see if they could walk through it together. "You've got it just right," she said. According to Daly, "She was the perfect combination of being kind and tough."

Although Jackie no longer socialized with the frenetic pace of the Ari years, she still went out to boost her causes such as the American Ballet Theatre, which she had supported since she was in the White House, the Municipal Arts Society, and the New York Public Library.

And when she chose to, she still wowed the public. In addition to Valentino, she also wore the sleek designs of her friend Carolina Herrera (she once startled a group of buyers from Neiman Marcus who were visiting Carolina's showroom by modeling one of her suits she happened to have on). And in the late 1980s, she left her longtime hairstylist Kenneth for Thomas Morrissey after Morrissey opened his own small salon on Madison Avenue.

John Fairchild, editor of *Women's Wear Daily* and a fan, follower, and nemesis of Jackie for years, remembers running into Jackie at a small charity event, the annual Literary Lions dinner at the New York Public Library, in the winter of 1986. He says that when she entered the room, "even the most hardened members of society elbowed their way toward her to get a closer look or, best of all, to be recognized. She was still the Celebrity of Celebrities." Fairchild himself came face-to-face with her, and even though they had talked and corresponded before (in not very friendly terms during the White House years), Fairchild could only manage a "Hello, Jackie."

"Good evening, Mr. Fairchild," she responded, politely but coolly.

Well versed in the nuances of society, Fairchild knew he had been elegantly trounced, and regretted the rest of the night having called her "Jackie" instead of "Mrs. Onassis."

Jackie prepared for the American Ballet Theatre's Spring Gala on May 17, 1993, as carefully as she did any White House state dinner. New York makeup expert Pablo Manzoni, who did Jackie's makeup for the event, recalls that she insisted upon a "dress rehearsal" on May 6.

When Manzoni arrived at 1040 that evening Jackie was wearing a red robe because she was going out that night and would be wearing red. She wanted to make sure his colors were complementary. (For his next visit, on the seventeenth, she wore a white robe, because she was wearing a white Carolina Herrera gown to the ABT gala. It was the first time in his career of thirty years that a client had thought to coordinate such things.) "She had a very small waistline and this lovely walk," he remembers. "It was a voluptuous walk, very feline, but not affected."

Jackie and Manzoni went to her bedroom "with its large baldachino bed and millions of books," and from there, her old-fashioned bathroom, which he remembers as being "huge, with a porcelain sink on a pedestal and windows galore." He set up his brushes and equipment.

Jackie sat at a dressing table before the window, facing straight into the strong late-afternoon sun, a pitiless light that revealed the sun spots she professed being concerned about. Manzoni recalls that he did not think she looked well — her hair was rather sparse, and she was exceedingly thin.

"I'd like to watch everything, if I may," she said, and she proved observant to the point that he had to position himself quite gingerly to work. Finally they negotiated an agreement whereby she would hold her own mirror as she watched. "I would do a touch, she would check," he says. "I would do another stroke, she would watch. She would watch the adding up of the touches, one at a time." No detail escaped her attention: the soft makeup brush he used; the way he applied the eye pencil; but most of all, the way he successfully camouflaged her sun spots with Elizabeth Arden Flawless Finish foundation — a product she already used but in a shade that Manzoni thought was too light.

"She was a perfectionist who knew exactly who she was and what she wanted." Manzoni sensed that Jackie had a "good hand" at her own makeup, but, at sixty-four, she was still eager to learn.

On his second visit, the actual night of the ABT Gala, the process was repeated, and Jackie even went so far as to number and list each step on a long yellow legal pad. At one point Maurice Tempelsman came in and said, "Il ne faut pas faire une poupée." ("Don't make her look like a doll.")

Between Mr. Manzoni's ministrations and Herrera's stunning floor-length white satin sheath and white gloves (Jackie had asked her to shift the center button so that it would flow into the beaded detail at her waist), Jackie was ready. That night at the ABT gala, Jackie looked, according to one guest, "as if she were headed for the East Room of the White House for a state dinner. If Maurice Tempelsman hadn't been standing beside her instead of Jack Kennedy, I would have thought it was 1961 all over again."

After spending Christmas 1993 with her children and three grandchildren, Jackie and Maurice flew to the Caribbean, "for the sun," as she put it, and went on a cruise. After a few days, however, Jackie began to suffer extreme stomach pains. The previous fall, she had been thrown from her horse, Frank, in Middleburg, and had been knocked unconscious for about thirty minutes. Could that have something to do with it? With her exercise and the good care she took of herself, Jackie had rarely been sick — the worst illness she could recall before this was a sinus infection in 1962. Still, she knew something was wrong. After speaking with her doctors on the phone, she and Maurice cut their vacation short and returned to New York for a diagnosis.

Having reviewed the results of numerous tests, the doctors told Jackie what she could not have imagined. It was cancer, non-Hodgkin's lymphoma. But Jackie's chances were good — over 50 percent of people similarly diagnosed live more than five years — because there had been early detection.

Although she did not know it at the time, Jackie was dying. She called John and Caroline and asked them to come see her at 1040. With Maurice at her side, she told them the news. There was shock, tears. But Jackie had the best medical advice in the world; they vowed they would stick together, as they always had, and fight it. Jackie was philosophical. She had been through so much in her life. "Even if I have only five years left, so what? I've had a great run."

To her friends, Jackie continued to be cheery and upbeat. "I don't get it. I did everything right to take care of myself and look what happened — why did I do all those push-ups?" she mock-complained to Arthur Schlesinger. Her friends sent her letters of support so she would know she was in their thoughts. C. Z. Guest left her one of her gardening books and concluded her accompanying note by saying, "Let's go hunting together next year." Jackie sent back a handwritten note that said, "Wouldn't it be fun? Let's do it." To Kitty Hart, she wrote, "What a surprise, but I feel fine and we do have a lot of laughs."

Carl Anthony sent Jackie a letter saying that "all those people who had bothered you, all those millions of people who had followed every move you made, the good thing is that they are all praying for you. So think of all those years of hell you went through with all these strangers — now think of it as payback time: they are all rooting for you to get better."

Every time Valentino arrived in New York, his first telephone call was to Jackie and they would decide immediately, "We must see each other for tea, for lunch." Around the time of the diagnosis, he called her and she said, "No, Valentino, I'm very very sorry, I'm very busy. . . . We can speak on the phone, we can talk on the phone, call me please, call me." He knew something was wrong.

"From that moment on," Valentino recalls, "I never saw her any more. I knew that she had gone to the boutique because my people had told me she said, 'Please, if you speak to Mr. Valentino, give him a big hug from me, give him my love.' But for that last year I didn't see her. Maybe she didn't want me to see her . . . I was a very good friend of hers, but I was a designer. So maybe she didn't want me to see her not looking fantastic like she used to. I never felt this way, but maybe she did. Maybe it was hard for her."

Richard Keith Langham assisted Jackie in what was to be her last bit of decorating. As he recalls, "Her last refurbishings were done in the room where she was to die." Only months before she became ill, Langham replaced the bed hangings with the same Scalamandré glazed cotton she had used since 1963 in Georgetown called "Tuileries," a lavender and salmon pattern of undulating vines and small flowers. Says Langham, "It's almost as if she knew it was going to happen."

That winter in New York City was a season of blizzards. Jackie and her family drew even closer. John moved into the Stanhope Hotel just a few blocks from 1040 to be nearer his mother. When the weather made it impossible to go outside to the park, Caroline brought her children over every afternoon to play with "Grand Jackie" in her apartment. One of their favorite games was a pirate treasure hunt they conducted through all the rooms — ransacking closets, using blankets to make tents in the middle of the living room. Jackie crawled around on the floor with them and had a great time.

Jackie wrote final letters to Caroline and John, to be opened after her death. To Caroline, she wrote, "The children have been a wonderful gift to me and I'm thankful to have once again seen our world through their eyes. They restore my faith in the family's future. You and Ed have been so wonderful to share them with me so unselfishly." John, she knew, would carry a special burden as the son of John F. Kennedy. "I understand the pressures you'll forever have to endure as a Kennedy, even though we brought you into this world as an innocent. You, especially, have a place in history. No matter what course in life

you choose, all I can do is ask that you and Caroline continue to make me, the Kennedy family, and yourself proud." One afternoon, sitting in a comfortable chair by the fire in her library, Jackie reread the hundreds of personal letters she had received from friends and world leaders and tossed them into the flames.

While undergoing radiation, Jackie continued to work hard on behalf of her authors at Doubleday. Pamela Fiori, editor in chief of *Town & Country*, had a meeting with Jackie in April. As Pamela recalls, "Jackie was working on a book based on the photographs of Toni Frissell, who had photographed her wedding in 1953. She was very committed to the book. We received a phone call from Doubleday asking whether or not *Town & Country* would be interested in doing a feature on it, and we said yes. They then asked if we could come over to Doubleday and go over what material they had which might be up for subscription. They said this was Mrs. Onassis's very special project, that she really wanted to see a magazine like *Town & Country* do it.

"So I went over with a couple of people on my staff and that's when I met her, and she offered me a Tootsie Roll. What I noticed right away was that she had a bandage on her cheek and that she was wearing a wig. But beyond that, you never would have known a thing, because she was cheerful. They had a little buffet set up for breakfast — muffins, rolls — and she could not have been more gracious, offering to pour coffee for people, fill up plates with goodies, what somebody of very good breeding would do. And she then started talking about the book and what excited her so much about it and wanted me to see pictures that Frissell had done, photographs of children.

"She left the room and came back. I was sitting on a chair and she plopped down on the floor beneath me and started to very excitedly show me

Toni Frissell's work. It was a very warm, happy meeting. You never would have known that she was in the last weeks of her life."

When the end came, it came quickly. After a winter of almost weekly snowstorms, it was the most glorious spring many New Yorkers could remember. The forsythia and tulips up and down Park Avenue had been in bloom for weeks. Jackie noticed too. "Isn't it something?" she said to a friend. "One of the most glorious springs I can remember. And after such a terrible winter."

On Sunday, May 15, Jackie took a walk in Central Park with Maurice and her grandchildren, but she became weak and disoriented. The next day, she was taken to the hospital suffering from chills and incipient pneumonia. The cancer had invaded her liver. Nothing more could be done for her. On Wednesday, she discharged herself and went home to die.

Over the next few days, her family and close friends came to say good-bye. One of the few men permitted to see her in her bedroom was Yusha Auchincloss, who had been her loving friend since they first met in Washington in 1941. As he wrote,

> I finally kissed her au revoir, held her hand for a moment and whispered in her ear to keep up her courage and felt her sigh, "not to worry."...I should have felt sad, but she made me feel happy and proud to realize how privileged I was to have shared her friendship at the close. I knew that she knew when it was time to go on, and she wouldn't want to keep her maker waiting. She left without self-pity.

Jackie died at home surrounded by her children and those she loved, at 10:15 on the evening of Thursday, May 19, 1994. She was sixty-four years old.

The next day, John, wearing a dark suit, his eyes red from lack of sleep, went downstairs to say a few words to the hundreds of reporters, cameramen, well-wishers, and curious who had been thronging in front of 1040. Speaking slowly and without notes, he made a simple announcement of his mother's death.

> Last night, at around ten-fifteen, my mother passed on...surrounded by her friends and her family and her books and the people and the things that she loved. And she did it in her own way and in her own terms, and we all feel lucky for that, and now she's in God's hands.

Her funeral service was held the following Monday, May 23, a bright day, at the Church of St. Ignatius Loyola on Park Avenue, where she had been christened and confirmed. Surprisingly, Jackie had not left any instructions for her funeral. Although Ted Kennedy argued for a state funeral, Caroline, supported by John, Maurice, and her husband, Ed, planned a private ceremony to reflect her mother's taste. The service was not televised, although a single audio feed was allowed so that mourners and news media standing respectfully up and down Park Avenue could hear the proceedings.

New York City, particularly the Upper East Side, where Jackie had lived, was hushed that day, almost as if the entire metropolis itself was in mourning. In a poignant opening to the service, John stood up and explained how he and Caroline had struggled to find readings "that captured my mother's essence. Three things came to mind over and over again. . . . They were her love of words, the bonds of home and family, and her spirit of adventure."

Ted Kennedy eloquently described Jackie's grace, "No one else looked like her, spoke like her, wrote like her, or was so original in the way she did things. No one we knew had a better sense of self." Caroline read a poem, "Memory of Cape Cod," by Edna St. Vincent Millay, from a book Jackie had won as a prize while a student at Miss Porter's in 1946. The poem evoked Jackie's love of the sea and long-ago summers on the Cape, when Jack, Jackie, and their family had all been together.

> The wind in the ash-tree sounds like surf on the shore at Truro.
> I will shut my eyes . . . hush, be still with your silly bleating,
> sheep on Shillingstone Hill . . .
>
> *They said: Come along! They said: Leave your pebbles on the sand and come*
> *along, it's long after sunset!*
> *The mosquitoes will be thick in the pine-woods along by Long Nook, the wind's*
> *died down!*
> *They said: Leave your pebbles on the sand, and your shells, too, and come along,*
> *we'll find you another beach like the beach at Truro.*
>
> Let me listen to the wind in the ash . . . it sounds like surf on the
> shore.

Maurice read from one of Jackie's favorite poems, "Ithaka," by C. P. Cavafy, about the adventures of Ulysses. It symbolized, too, the journey of Jackie's life, her spirit of adventure, and the sense, too, that she had reached her journey's end here on earth. As a final coda, Tempelsman added his own stanza to the poem. Elegant in its brevity, heartbreaking in its context, it was the only public statement he would ever make about his relationship with Jackie.

And now the journey is over,
Too short, alas, too short.
It was filled with
Adventure and wisdom
Laughter and love
Gallantry and grace . . .

After the funeral service, as Jackie's coffin was carried down the front steps of St. Ignatius, hundreds of mourners stood silently, respectfully outside almost in disbelief that this woman who had been such a vital part of their lives, of their country's history, was no longer alive. The cortege proceeded through New York to Kennedy Airport. The casket was flown to Washington, D.C., and from there, to Arlington Cemetery, where she had lit the eternal flame for her husband's memory some thirty years before. There, Jacqueline Bouvier Kennedy Onassis was buried beside John F. Kennedy and their two children, Arabella and Patrick.

A few months after Jackie died, Maurice had dinner with mutual friends and wondered, "If Jackie is in heaven and they said she had to choose between her horses or her books, which do you think she would take?" Her books, everyone agreed — no, her horses! It would be a tough call.

Immediately after her death, Jackie-inspired fashions appeared up and down the runways. Although the sheath dress seems to roll around every spring,

Calvin Klein's to-the-knee A-line skirts and fitted jackets were unmistakably Jackie-esque. Prada introduced notch-collar coats like those she wore during the Onassis years, and Donna Karan ushered in hot pink. For once, though, fashion was not just cashing in on a celebrity—fall clothes were already in production when she died in May—but her death gave the trend more impetus. As Nicole Miller (who was planning her own Jackie-style dresses) told *Time* magazine, "Every magazine you pick up, she's in there, and she looks just great."

Almost two years later, the attraction of Jackie's style was undiminished when her odds and ends were auctioned at Sotheby's ("Jackie's Junque" the sale was immediately dubbed). Leafing through the Bible-thick sale catalog for the "Estate of Jacqueline Onassis," Tiffany's John Loring spied Lot 111 on page 105: "Four Indian Electroplate Tumblers, 20th Century—of tapering cylindrical form, variously engraved or flat-chased. 100–150." They were the simple beakers he had sent to her at Doubleday nine years ago.

As Loring recalls, "I knew I would pay dearly to do it, but I wanted them back as a remembrance of our fifteen years of collaboration. They were something I knew for certain we shared a liking for. And I did pay dearly. The beakers had originally cost $10 each in the marketplace of Bhaktapur. By the time they had followed their intriguing and somewhat illustrious path to Sotheby's in New York, they would cost me an additional $8,714.13. As a friend quipped, 'They went from Bhaktapur right back to rich.'"

Her old friends at Tiffany's were relieved to see that while all of her everyday costume jewelry and many of the big pieces Onassis bought her were sold, none of the Schlumberger jewelry came up for auction. The berry brooch that Kennedy gave her the first Christmas they spent in the White House is now on display at the JFK Library in Boston. And Caroline has been spotted around town wearing her mother's favorite white enamel and gold Schlumberger earrings.

The Sotheby's auction was not the only way Jackie's possessions were split up. The homes she had lived in passed on to new owners, too. Hammersmith Farm had been sold after Hugh D.'s death in 1976 to a group of investors who later opened it up for tours. The new owners called their corporation "Camelot Gardens," which Jackie, having always regarded it as an Auchincloss home, thought "tacky." Albert Hadley is now working with the people who bought her house in Peapack, New Jersey, where she used to hunt on the weekends. They have knocked it down and are building a new home on the property. On August 28, 1999, the Auchincloss's beloved Merrywood was bought by Steve Case, chairman of America Online. From Standard Oil to the Internet—surely Jackie would have loved that.

"What have we got in life?" wondered Diana Vreeland. "Love, friendship, work, guts, and all those delicious tiny fragments that can be the most attractive

things in the world!" And now that Jackie is no longer here, what can we learn from her life?

C. Z. Guest thinks that Jackie's legacy is "how she handled herself through life, the whole thing—through marriage, childbirth—living life is her legacy! You do it in the proper way, the way she did, as an example for her children."

Pamela Fiori believes that "keeping life in perspective" is one of the biggest lessons Jackie can teach us. "She always knew that her biggest concerns were her husband and raising those children. And she was really clear about that.

"And also, keeping her business to herself. If people wanted to pry and make up stories, I think her attitude was 'let them,' up to a certain point. But in most cases, she walked the streets of New York and Scorpios and Paris and London, and how she lived behind closed doors was her business and her business alone, which I think was really important for all of us."

Albert Hadley says, "When I think of her, I really think of that first day that I met her, when she came into the Family Quarters of the White House. She was wearing a pantsuit, which was rare for the time. . . . She was so radiant and so happy. So natural. That's the way that I sort of think of her, and that image has been constant through the years."

Jackie considered herself an aristocrat, but not "Queen of America" as some writers have tried to position her. (She didn't even want to be known as the first lady, she wanted to be known as Mrs. Kennedy.) Instead of tired bloodlines, she believed in the Jeffersonian ideal of a natural aristocracy made up of artists and poets, the talented and the brave—those who make the best of a situation and move ever forward, as she herself did.

In writing about the Danish author Isak Dinesen in the afterword of Peter Beard's book *Longing for Darkness,* Jackie might have just as well been describing herself when she said, "[Dinesen] felt that the noble spirit was the true aristocrat. She said aristocrats were not more virtuous than other people—'what they had above all was courage, and after that, taste and responsibility—and endurance.'"

In the final telling, Jackie had all of these things: taste, responsibility, endurance, and most especially courage. The courage to move beyond the tragedies that fate placed in front of her; the courage to raise her children simply and well; and the courage, finally, to live her life as *she* saw fit—intelligently, gracefully, even whimsically—putting society's and others' expectations of her aside. Through it all, she took her own measure and listened to her own inner reason.

There cannot ever be another Jackie—her singularity is what made her *sui generis,* unique. But this should not discourage us. Instead, we can study Jackie's life and the choices she made at each turn, as student, young mother, first lady, widow, and working woman, and work to make our own lives the best that they can be.

This, after all, is true Jackie Style.

grand jackie

She was someone special who inspired those near her to feel special.

— YUSHA AUCHINCLOSS

At the close of her life, Jackie was the matriarch to her children, grandchildren ("Grand Jackie," they called her), and the younger Kennedy cousins. But she also took an active interest in Lee's children, Anthony and Tina; Yusha Auchincloss's two children, Cecil and Maya; and — after she died of cancer at the age of thirty-nine — her half sister, Janet Auchincloss Rutherford's, children.

Jackie was close to her beloved Yusha's two children by his Russian wife from whom he was divorced. As Maya recalled, "Jackie was so good to her nieces and nephews. Little Janet [Janet Rutherford] stayed with Jackie and Alexandra [Janet's two-year-old daughter] was picking things up and throwing them out the window. Jackie would say, 'Oh, for God's sake, they're just things.' She loved children. She was the opposite of her

mother in that she didn't have things you couldn't touch. She just wanted you to be comfortable."

Jackie's maternal instincts were not limited to her blood relations. Helen Bartlett, whose parents had introduced Jack and Jackie, was Jack Kennedy's godchild. After Jack's death, Jackie took over as Helen's godmother. Helen recalls, "I was not Jackie's godchild, but she took over when the president died. She was my connection to Jack, and she kept up this guardianship. There was a letter for every birthday, every Christmas, every event of importance in my life. She was one of the most empathetic people ever. She could take in what you were saying and get it."

It is intriguing to realize that although society viewed Jackie as the most famous woman in the world, her actual priorities were closer to home. This was no accident. As Yusha knew, "Jackie was a dedicated person, to her children, her family, [and] her friends.... Whether as daughter, niece, mother, grandmother, wife, sister, cousin, aunt, or friend, the object of her caring knew they could depend on her and always knew where she stood."

Although Jackie famously said, "If you bungle raising your children, I don't think that whatever else you do well matters much," she meant this in a broader sense than just caring for her own children. As we see from her example, Jackie felt a compelling need to reach out to young people, as well as friends, who crossed her path — to encourage them in their own nascent abilities, to correct them when she thought it was necessary, to help them laugh at life's absurdities.

Perhaps in this moment, there is someone we can be a Grand Jackie to in our own lives — there must be. And as a legacy, wouldn't Jackie love it?

acknowledgments

Several people deserve special recognition for their contributions to this book. I would like to thank Caroline Kennedy for granting me permission to reproduce her mother's correspondence. I am especially grateful to Valentino for his heartfelt introduction, and also for sharing with me his private memories of Jacqueline Onassis. And thanks, of course, to Darac for his friendship, encouragement and creative guidance during the writing of this book — I look forward to future collaborations.

The family, friends, coworkers, and admirers of Jackie who graciously took the time to speak with me and share their memories and observations of her truly made this work memorable: Elizabeth Aiello, Carl Sferrazza Anthony, Hélène Arpels, James Lee Auchincloss, Hugh D. Auchincloss Jr., Peter Bacanovic, Letitia Baldrige, Manolo Blahnik, Kenneth Paul Block, Hamish Bowles, Tommy Bruce, Carmine Calenti, Catherine Callahan, Oleg Cassini, Dr. Deepak Chopra, Rose Citron, Bob Colacello, Vivian Stokes Crespi, John H. Davis, Tracy Budd Day, Susan Dell, Brian Doyle, Nancy Evans, Joe Eula, Doreen Fadino, Pamela Fiori, Kimberly Fortier, Ron Galella, Hubert de Givenchy, C. Z. Guest, Maureen Hornung, Renée and Suzette Guercia, Thomas E. Gorman, Albert Hadley, Campbell Hart, Solange Herter, Keith Irvine, Colton Johnson, Linda Kahn, Joan B. Kennedy, Richard Keith Langham, Eleanor Lambert, John Loring, Robert Love, Jacques Lowe, George Malkemus, Shannon McLean, Maggie McMahon, Beth Mendelson, Melody Miller, Craig Natiello, Richard Nelson, Carol Rawlings Miller, Pierce MacGuire, Mary Parson, George Plimpton, Robert Pounder, Lucky Roosevelt, Vincent Ropatte, Fred Rottman, Cynthia Rowley, D. D. Ryan, Hugh Sidey, Kate Spade, Sidney Stafford, Cecil Stoughton, J. C. Suares, Pat Suzuki, Gustave Tassell, Reid and Holly Walker, June Weir, Dennis Wong.

The oral histories at the John F. Kennedy Library were invaluable for putting the Kennedy presidency in perspective. These included: Larry Arata, Janet Lee Bouvier Auchincloss, Charles Bartlett, Bernard Boutin, Lord Harlech, Jacqueline Hirsch, Joseph Karitas, Laura Berquist Knebel, Peter Lisagor, Grace de Monaco, Jacqueline Kennedy Onassis, Maude Shaw, Dorothy Tubridy, Stanley Tretick, William Walton, Irwin Williams. The newly opened White House social files chronicling the hard work of Letitia Baldrige, J. B. West, Nancy Tuckerman, Pamela Turnure, and nameless others in carrying out the wishes of the first lady were also consulted.

In researching this book, I spent a great deal of time in libraries and would like to gratefully thank: everyone at the John F. Kennedy Library and Museum, particularly Allan Goodrich and Catja Burckhardt from the audio-visual department — they are divine (and patient) professionals. In the research library, I would like to thank June Payne and Michael Desmond, as well as Megan Desnoyers and Jim Wagner for their cheerful assistance. Major kudos to Frank Bonfiglio, who served New England chowder I still dream about. At Condé Nast, where one could spend years reading up on twentieth-century style, library director Cynthia Cathcart (once again), Anne Haggerty, Charles D. Scheips Jr., and Ena Szkoda were enormously — and graciously — helpful. At the Fashion Institute of Technology Library, Dorothy Globus, Jane Duda, and particularly Bret Fowler of the Halston Archives were a great resource. Mark Piel and the staff at the New York Society Library made it a welcoming place to work. At the Metropolitan Museum Costume Institute I would like to especially acknowledge Stephané Houy-Towner, who runs the library with a finesse Diana Vreeland would appreciate, Monique van Dorp, and Harold Koda, curator in charge of the Costume Institute. At Vassar College, the dean of students, Colton Johnson, saved me as an undergraduate by allowing me to drop freshman biology, sensing, quite rightly, that I had no future in the sciences. Terri O'Shea of the AAVC, Maryann Bruno, Nancy McKechnie, and Elizabeth Daniels, the college historian, were most helpful.

Jacqueline Onassis was the most photographed woman in the world, and I would like to recognize the photographers who shared their memories and opened their photo files in my continued quest for images that have not been seen a million times before. Linda Buckley and Carlton Davis (Tiffany & Co.), Deanna Cross (Metropolitan Museum of Art), Hannah Edwards (Corbis), Deborah Evans (Library of Congress), Ron Galella, Ann Garside (The Peabody Institute), Tom Gilbert (AP), Suzanne Goldstein (Photo Researchers), Allan Goodrich (JFKL), Kathy Lavelle and Eric Rachlis (Archive), Jacques Lowe, Natasha O'Connor (Magnum), Dean Rogers (Vassar College), Michael Stier (Condé Nast), Cecil Stoughton, and Joshua Waller (FIT).

I would like to acknowledge Steven Gaines for definitively solving the "who designed the pillbox hat" mystery by letting me in on his taped interview with JKO in which she said "Halston."

I am indebted to Deirdre Keogh-Anderson and Peter Saisselin, once again, for their invaluable ability to translate Hubert de Givenchy's elegant French.

At HarperCollins an enormous thank you to Jane Friedman, president and CEO, and Cathy Hemming, president, for publishing my second book; my brilliant new editor, Marjorie Braman, for seeing the project through to its completion, and Leslie Engel and Christine Walsh for their editorial assistance; as well as design director Roberto de Vicq de Cumptich. I would also like to gratefully acknowledge HC's crack marketing team headed by Christopher McKerrow, Christine Caruso, and Dawn DiCenso. Thank you for working so creatively on my behalf.

A resounding thank you to Laura Lindgren and Celia Fuller, who worked under formidable time constraints to bring this book to light. They made it fun and I think Jackie, a book editor herself, would be pleased with the result.

I would like to acknowledge Joëlle Delbourgo and Joseph Montebello, who took a flier on my first book, *Audrey Style*. Their advice and encouragement during the writing of this one has been invaluable, and they have remained a wise sounding board.

I would also like to thank my literary agents Joanna Pulcini and Linda Chester of the Linda Chester Agency, as well as Gary Jaffe and Kelly Smith — they are a joy to work with.

A huge, huge thank you to John Masker for his invaluable help whenever I have a computer meltdown. And for their friendship, bonhomie, and unerring fashion sense (to say nothing of those watches!), a nod to my fellow readers in the Greening Cottage Book Club of Locust Valley, New York — they have true Jackie Style.

I feel enormous gratitude to my parents and brothers and sisters, Patricia, Peter, Deirdre, and Scott for their friendship, laughter, and support. And finally, knowing how much Jackie loved her own children and grandchildren, I would like to offer this book to my nieces and nephew — Julia Catherine Anderson, Fitzwilliam Anderson, Maura Grace Keogh, and Georgia Austin Keogh, with the trust that their own dreams will take them far.

illustration credits

2: "Portrait in a Yellow Dress," JBK in Hyannisport, Massachusetts, summer 1960. This was JFK's favorite picture of his wife. Photograph © Jacques Lowe

6: Newlywed Jackie in Georgetown, 1954. All Peabody images were shot on spec May 4–9, 1954, by Orlando Suero for the 3 Lions Picture Agency, NYC. These images have never been published before. Orlando Suero/Lowenherz Collection of Kennedy photographs at the Peabody Institute of the Johns Hopkins University, Baltimore

8: Jackie in Valentino at Metropolitan Museum of Art, opening of the Costume Institute's *Hapsburg Era* exhibit December 3, 1979. Ron Galella

11: The first lady at the Piedmont Hunt Point-to-Point races in Upperville, Virginia, March 25, 1961. AP/Wide World Photos

12: Jackie and Caroline, playing in Nantucket Sound, Hyannisport, Massachusetts, fall 1960. The Mark Shaw Collection/Photo Researchers, Inc.

15: The first lady meeting other congressional wives. John F. Kennedy Library, Boston

16: Incognito Jackie, 1970s. © Corbis/SYGMA

21: The morning after election day, JBK on the beach at Hyannisport, Massachusetts, November 9, 1960. © Corbis/SYGMA

24: The clan, Hyannisport, Massachusetts, November 9, 1960. © Corbis/SYGMA

29: JBK's dressing room, the White House. If you look closely, you can see many famous framed family pictures, as well as inaugural shots thumbtacked to the bulletin board on the left. Robert Knudsen/White House, John F. Kennedy Library, Boston

32: JBK's thank-you note to Cecil Stoughton. Courtesy of Caroline Kennedy Schlossberg and the estate of Jacqueline Kennedy Onassis

33: "La vie en rose," Dior runway fashion sketch by Joe Eula, Paris, circa 1958. Courtesy of Metropolitan Museum of Art, The Irene Lewisohn Costume Reference Library, Gift of the Artist

37: *Look* magazine photo, John F. Kennedy Library, Boston

39: JBK getting tossed off "Bit Of Irish" at the Mellon estate in Virginia. She was annoyed when this picture appeared in the newspapers, but her husband reminded her, "When the first lady falls on her ass, that's news." John F. Kennedy Library, Boston

40: Sailing on Narragansett Bay, Newport, Rhode Island. From left, seated, Hugh D. Auchincloss (partially obscured by) Janet Auchincloss, JBK, JFK. Note JBK's Jack Rogers sandals. Robert Knudsen/White House, John F. Kennedy Library, Boston

41: Due to JFK's driving habits, racing golf carts on the Compound was a favorite, if risky, activity. August 1961. John F. Kennedy Library, Boston

42: Evening reception for the president of Tunisia and Mrs. Bourguiba; JBK wears a yellow one-shouldered "Nefertiti" gown designed by Oleg Cassini, 1961. Robert Knudsen, John F. Kennedy Library, Boston

45–47: Fall 1959 through the late 1960s. All sketches are Halston originals from FIT and have never been published before. The Halston Collection, Courtesy of the Fashion Institute of Technology Library (Special Collections)

49: Young Jackie. John F. Kennedy Library, Boston

50: Jackie and her parents at the Southampton Riding and Hunt Club, Southampton, New York, 1934. Archive Photos/Richard & Bert Morgan Collection

54: Lee, Jackie, and their mother attending a wedding in East Hampton, New York, July 26, 1941. Archive Photos/Richard & Bert Morgan Collection

57: The debonaire Jack Bouvier holding hands with Miss Virginia Kernochan at a Tuxedo Park horse show, 1934, as his wife sits beside her. The day after this photo appeared in the New York *Daily News*, all hell broke loose and the Bouviers were soon divorced. Bettman/CORBIS

60: JBK riding "Danseuse" at the Piping Rock Horse Show, Locust Valley, New York, September 30, 1938. Archive Photos/Richard & Bert Morgan Collection

65: JBK seated on fence at the Smithtown Horse Show, Smithtown, Long Island, August 28, 1937. Archive Photos/Richard & Bert Morgan Collection

68: JBK and Elizabeth Fly (the future Mrs. Felix Rohaytn) at a fashion show at the Maidstone Club, East Hampton, New York, July 1949. Archive Photos/Richard & Bert Morgan Collection

70: Debutantes Lee and Jackie appear in March 1, 1951, *Vogue*. Cecil Beaton/ © Vogue, Condé Nast Publications, Inc.

73: Lee and JBK with Anthony Radziwill and Caroline, Hyannisport, Massachusetts, summer 1961. Photograph © Jacques Lowe

75: JBK's *Vogue* portrait, 1951. All of the winners of the Prix de Paris contest attended one of the Seven Sisters and wore little white gloves. © Condé Nast, John F. Kennedy Library, Boston

76: Main Building, Vassar College, circa 1950s. JBK's room was on the third floor of the left wing, facing away from the circle. Courtesy Special Collections, Vassar College Libraries

81: JBK going AWOL from VC. John F. Kennedy Library, Boston

86: The new Mr. and Mrs. John F. Kennedy on their honey-moon, somewhere in Mexico, 1953. John F. Kennedy Library, Boston

89: This was Jackie's favorite shot of her wedding, September 12, 1953, Newport, Rhode Island; she chose it to appear in a Doubleday book she edited of photographer Toni Frissell's work. Toni Frissell, courtesy of the Library of Congress

90: Honeymoon, Acapulco, Mexico, September 1953. John F. Kennedy Library, Boston

92: Jackie with "Gaullie" (her dog) channeling Audrey in Georgetown, May 1954. Orlando Suero/Lowenherz Collection of Kennedy photographs at the Peabody Institute of the Johns Hopkins University, Baltimore

95: May 1954: JFK and JBK looking at wedding photos. Orlando Suero/Lowenherz Collection of Kennedy photographs at the Peabody Institute of the Johns Hopkins University, Baltimore

96: JBK preparing for a Georgetown dinner party, May 1954. Note that she is wearing the same diamond brooch she wore for her wedding. Orlando Suero/Lowenherz Collection of Kennedy photographs at the Peabody Institute of the Johns Hopkins University, Baltimore

98: JBK, pregnant with JFK Jr., campaigns on Wall Street at the close of the 1960 election with JFK. Stanley Tretick © Corbis/SYGMA

101: Late night on N Street. Note the abundance of French limoges bowls used as ashtrays. JFK is in foreground. The Mark Shaw Collection/Photo Researchers, Inc.

102: Luck be a lady tonight: Frank Sinatra escorting JBK at the inaugural gala, Washington, D.C., January 1961. © Bettman/Corbis

105–106: Spring 1951 editorial comments (never before published) from various *Vogue* staffers re JBK's Prix de Paris application. Some liked her, some did not. © Condé Nast, courtesy John F. Kennedy Library, Boston

109: JBK, reading Jack Kerouac's *On the Road*, taking a break from campaigning aboard the *Caroline*, fall 1959. Photograph © Jacques Lowe

110: JBK on her first official state visit to Canada, wearing Pierre Cardin, May 1961. The Royal Canadian Mounted Police, John F. Kennedy Library, Boston

113: JBK in Paris, May 1961. *Paris Match*, John F. Kennedy Library, Boston

To continue the work of
Jacqueline Kennedy Onassis,
please visit
The John F. Kennedy Library and Museum,
and consider supporting the
John F. Kennedy Library Foundation
Columbia Point
Boston, MA 02125

1-877-616-4599
www.jfklibrary.org